Halfway to Paradise

Also by David & Caroline Stafford

Cupid Stunts: The Life and Radio Times of Kenny Everett
Big Time: The Life of Adam Faith
Fings Ain't Wot They Used T' Be: The Lionel Bart Story
Maybe I'm Doing it Wrong: The Life & Times of Randy Newman

THE LIFE OF
BILLY FURY

BY DAVID & CAROLINE STAFFORD

OMNIBUS PRESS
London / New York / Paris / Sydney / Copenhagen / Berlin / Madrid / Tokyo

Exclusive Distributors
Music Sales Limited
14/15 Berners Street
London
W1T 3LJ
UK

Music Sales Pty. Limited
(Australia and New Zealand)
Level 4, 30–32 Carrington Street
Sydney
NSW 2000
Australia

Printed in Malta.

A catalogue record for this book is available from the British Library.
Visit Omnibus Press on the web at www.omnibuspress.com

To Gilly Schuster, in loving memory.

CONTENTS

INTRODUCTION

Malcolm McLaren, co-founder with Vivienne Westwood of a clothes shop called Sex and later manager of the Sex Pistols, was a big Billy Fury fan. In the late sixties, when he was at art college, McLaren wrote to Billy. He wanted to make a film of him. As far as we know, Billy never replied, and the film never got made.

The Smiths' 1987 single, 'Last Night I Dreamt Somebody Loved Me', features on its sleeve a picture of smiling Billy. "Billy's singles are totally treasurable," said Morrissey. "I get quite passionate about the vocal melodies and the orchestration always sweeps me away. He always had such profound passion." When Billy died, Morrissey admits he cried, "Persistently. Loudly."

In 1977, the singer/songwriter/artist/genius Ian Dury wrote a song called 'England's Glory', which lists some of the "jewels in the crown of England's Glory". Alongside Winston Churchill, spotted dick, Woodbines and Cilla, he name-checks, "Billy Bunter, Jane Austen, Reg Hampton, George Formby, Billy Fury, Little Titch, Uncle Mac, Mr Pastry".

Billy Fury was always more than just a pop star. He was *the* pop star: an archetype, combining the ingredients of beauty, sex, innocence, talent, passion, charisma and heartbreaking vulnerability in an exact mix.

Almost incidentally, he also recorded and wrote every track on *The Sound Of Fury*, the album described by Keith Richards as "one of the greatest rock'n'roll albums of its era, and one I swear by" and by John Peel as "the only authentic British rock'n'roll album around at that time". Its 10 short tracks still shiver with sex, tragedy, death and anarchy, the same timeless forces that drove punk, that drove the jazzers in the twenties, drove the apprentice boys of Elizabethan England, drove the kids that Socrates complained about in ancient Greece who had "bad manners, contempt for authority" and showed "disrespect for elders".

If he'd merely stood like a statue on stage he would have flooded theatres with hormonal longings, but he was incapable of standing still. He pulsed. He writhed. He invalidated the manufacturer's guarantee on microphone stands. He provoked shock and awe. He got banned in Ireland, and even the British music papers, usually quite chipper about that sort of thing, suggested that a line had to be drawn somewhere.

Offstage, he was shy, introspective, needy, a worrier. He had been a sickly child. Long periods in hospital left him an outsider. He missed a lot of school and learned to enjoy his own company, going off on long walks, birdwatching – a passion that stayed with him for the rest of his life.

"One thing about me," he said, towards the end of his life, "is that I'm a terrible loner. I think I was born with three brick walls around me. No – four brick walls. I knocked the back one out. It's only in the past few years that I've been able to break the rest of those walls down at all.

"This has all to do with shyness and paranoia and being vague. And being super critical of myself. But all the shyness I had I could throw away when I was on stage with 30 minutes of exhibitionism. It was a way of letting the cap off. People sometimes would think I was a moody sod. But I was just shy."

This is, of course, the raw material from which all the best legends are made: the hero's triumphs in the wider world balanced by doubt and raging inner torment.

And in all the best legends, the hero is always attended by the spectre of his own death.

In the early sixties, the rumour went around that Billy was dying. He had something wrong with his kidneys, his lungs, his heart. The tragedy, of course, was that the rumours were true. He was a sick man. The defective heart valves left by his childhood rheumatic fever would eventually lead to his premature death.

Beauty, sex, innocence, talent, passion, charisma and heartbreaking vulnerability. Any religion that hasn't already made him a god is theologically defective.

"There's only ever been two English rock'n'roll singers," Ian Dury said, "Johnny Rotten and Billy Fury."

And nobody's too sure about Johnny Rotten anymore.

CHAPTER ONE

"...A BIT POSH FOR ROUND HERE AT THE TIME."

1940 was a vintage year for pop stars: it was then that Gene Pitney, Smokey Robinson, Tom Jones, Nancy Sinatra, Adam Faith, Cliff Richard, two Beatles (three if you include Stuart Sutcliffe) and a Mother of Invention all made their first appearances, mewling and puking.

These 1940 babies reached puberty at around the same time as Elvis slunk into Sun Studio, the first Gaggia arrived in Soho and the *Daily Express* coined the term "Teddy Boy". By the time they reached their late teens, they were prepped to take the great banner of progress from the hands of Bill Haley, Ray Charles, Lonnie Donegan, Little Richard and the other pioneers, and go on to rule the world. Something like that, anyway.

Ronald Wycherley, the boy who would be Billy Fury, came into the world on April 17 at the Smithdown Road Infirmary, Sefton, Liverpool, weighing in at a healthy seven pounds. His parents thought about calling him Kenneth, but his mum had twin brothers called Ronald and William so they went with Ronald.

Little Ronald was a beautiful baby. It was in the genes. His mother, Sarah Jane Homer, known universally as Jean, was a beauty, blessed with the sculpted cheeks, the brooding eyes and the heartstopping smile she

3

passed on to her son. She was just 17 when Albert, a cobbler, met her. He put an engagement ring on her finger within the month. They were married a year later and moved into a place on Sefton Square, Liverpool 8, a street the bulldozers demolished 50-odd years ago.

Albert and Jean both had vague showbiz connections. Jean had an uncle who'd worked with a minstrel show. Albert had a cousin who, reputedly, at some time or other, accompanied Gracie Fields on a piano accordion.

At the outbreak of war, the previous September, there had been talk of gas attacks, invasion and bombing raids. None of which had happened.

Billy's arrival seemed to get things going.

By the end of May, Hitler had taken France, Belgium, Luxembourg and the Netherlands and the British army had lost 68,000 men.

In August, the Luftwaffe started dropping bombs on mainland Britain. London, Liverpool, Birmingham, Hull, Coventry – all the major ports and centres of industry got hammered. And the heroes of pop who lived in those places grew up in a world of Anderson shelters, patched-up houses and blacked-out alleys; an often fatherless anarchy of aunties and grannies and cuddles, punctuated by bouts of inexplicable terror, thumps and screams.

Merseyside, where the Atlantic convoys docked, was an obvious target. One hundred and sixty bombers came on August 28. They came again on the 29th and the 30th and then came back regularly until May the following year. A direct hit on an air raid shelter at the Ernest Brown Junior Instructional Centre in Durning Road, Edge Hill, killed 166.

The Wycherleys in Sefton Square, less than a mile away from Brunswick Docks, were in the firing line. "We were under the stairs and in and out of shelters," Jean said, "and I think that told on Billy."

Ricky Tomlinson, the actor, was living nearby with his brother Albert. "The sirens would sound and Albert would make his way down the stairs in the pitch black, while mam held tightly on to my hand. She came down on her bum one step at a time. If the bombers were already ahead she bundled us under the stairs lying on top of us. Some nights mam was too exhausted to care. She gathered us into bed, wrapping us in her arms saying, 'If we go, we'll all go together.' We lay under the blankets listening to the explosions and the bells of the fire engines. I was too young to realise the dangers we were in or to understand death and war."

Eventually, Albert Wycherley's papers came through and he was sent to the Woolwich Arsenal in London to service anti-aircraft guns with the Royal Artillery. In 1942, Jean and Ronnie went to be with him for a bit, staying in digs. The bombing had stopped by then, but still the family suffered its only wartime injury when Ronnie was bitten on the cheek by their landlady's dog. He bore the scar for the rest of his life.

The Government Evacuation Scheme gave assistance for children, the elderly and pregnant women to move out of major cities into the comparative safety of the countryside. In 1943, in the later stages of her second pregnancy, Jean moved out to Prestatyn on the coast of North Wales, where she gave birth to another son, named after his dad, Albie. But the sea air didn't seem to suit her. As soon as Albie was out she scurried back home to Liverpool.

Ronnie had developed an inquisitive nature.

"First thing I can remember in my whole life," he said, "was this time my dad came home on leave from the war and bought presents for me and my little brother – two little Dinky cars. An army lorry and a Riley car. I remember exactly.

"I took the army lorry and my brother took the Riley. We started playing with them on the kitchen floor. Then my mum and dad went out to the pictures and I suddenly got the idea of finding out what was inside. So, I took an axe and smashed it open. There was nothing inside. So, I took the axe and smashed up my brother's Riley."

Why mum and dad went out leaving two toddlers home alone with an axe remains a mystery. But it was wartime. Things were different.

By the end of the war, the Wycherleys were living up the road from Sefton Square at 34 Haliburton Street – now swallowed up by the big Tesco Extra on Park Road. It was an area known as "the Holy Land" because on the other side of Park Road was Isaac Street, Jacob Street and David Street. Dad had his own shoe repair shop just around the corner, named 'Jean's' after the missus.

The Wycherleys' was a decent terraced house – parlour, back parlour and kitchen downstairs, and three bedrooms upstairs. The outside lav and coal house were in the entry at the back.

"My dad had his own shop, so that meant we had more money than other folks," said Ronnie's brother Albie. "We could afford to spend a bit more on a nice and tidy house. Black and white tiled step. Only one in the street, probably. It was a bit posh for round here at the time."

Post-war Liverpool, like most of the big towns, was a mess, physically and psychologically.

Everybody spoke of time in terms of "before the war", "during the war", "after the war". Everybody knew somebody who'd been killed, been maimed, been bombed out, been buried in an air-raid shelter or still woke up screaming in the night. They'd all come to terms with mayhem. And they had, like good Boy Scouts, done their best to smile and whistle under all circumstances.

In the 21st century, people get counselling for post-traumatic stress syndrome, but how do you counsel whole countries, whole continents? You don't. "Britain can take it," the newsreels at the pictures said. And so it did. Most of it did anyway, and most of the rest pretended. When the war was over, the need to get back to some half-remembered state called "normal" was urgent and the new National Health Service, the 1944 Education Act and the lovely new houses with inside lavs promised it would be "normal" with knobs on. Kids played on the rubble that had buried their aunties and uncles and neighbours and had a terrific time.

"Cratered and pocked with bomb sites," was how author Lorna Sage remembered Liverpool. "I saw in reality the cityscape of the newsreels – the remains of the tenements, wallpaper, fire grates and private plumbing exposed, clinging to the walls which were buttressed with wooden props while they waited for demolition."

"We used to play on what we called the Diamond Dump," says Pat from Birmingham, later a Billy Fury fan. "There'd been a jeweller's shop there and it had been bombed out. We used to dig down and sometimes you'd find bits of metal and shiny stuff we pretended was gold and diamonds."

"Opposite our school was a huge bombsite we called the Tip," says Marion from Hull, another fan. "It was all grown over with weeds and we used to catch butterflies and put them in jam jars. All different kinds of butterflies, half of them kinds you don't see any more at all."

They were skinny kids, the post-war lot. Sweets and sugar were rationed until 1953. Meat until '54. "Mum used to mix a bit of the sugar ration with some cocoa and we'd dip our fingers in it and suck them. That was the nearest we ever got to sweets," says Pat.

Lorna Sage remembers her first sighting of a bag of crisps. "I couldn't at first understand my mother's delight in these crumpled fossils with chewy grey bits (they must have used frost-bitten potatoes back in the beginning as a concession to austerity) although I saw the point of the blue twist of salt from the first moment. It was a matter of luxury, having portable food you could play with."

Scarcity left the pop stars of the future blessed with the drainpipe-legs, the needle-cheeks and the damaged adenoids with which they captured the hearts, minds and money of their fans.

Ronnie started school at St Silas' C of E Primary on High Park. He never took to it.

"I suppose I was a dreamer," he said, much later. "I remember sitting all by myself in the playground in school, in a corner away from the other kids and dreaming about this island I was going to have. About half a mile square it was, and about half a mile off shore, with a big white crescent-shaped house in the middle with a swimming pool. When you think of the place that I come from – the Dingle district of Liverpool, you'd think all this dreamy stuff would be knocked out of me. I just didn't like going around with the other kids. I suppose there's something about a kid that's always drifting off by himself that makes him a kind of natural target for other kids. They think it's weird that one kid could do without company."

By the age of six, he was taking himself off on expeditions to collect bird's eggs – a hobby that was banned in 1954 but was once deemed an almost respectable occupation for the budding ornithologist. When he was a bit older, he'd take a bus to West Kirby on the Dee Estuary to see oystercatchers, redshanks, plovers and, if he was really lucky, a godwit or two; or nearer to home, he'd hang around Sefton Park or Prince's Park, and wait for something to show up on the boating lake.

"I had this big book at home and I used to write down all the details I could remember about every bird I saw. I even had the idea I would write a book about birds. This kind of thing must have made everybody at school think I was weird. So, whenever anything went wrong they picked on me – the teachers too."

The idea of writing the book about birds never left him. He was in discussion with a publisher at the time of his death.

The misfortune that was to blight the rest of Ronnie's life came when he was just six and-a-half. Up until then, he'd been a bouncing baby and a healthy toddler, full of beans.

These were the days before comprehensive inoculation programmes, before effective antibiotics, when diphtheria, scarlet fever, whooping cough and even a nasty cut could kill you. If you survived, convalescence could run into months. In the poorest areas of the big cities infant mortality was twice or three times the national average.

Billy and his schoolmate Ritchie Starkey – the boy who became Ringo Starr – both did a lot of hospital time. Ritchie had troubles, first with his appendix then his lungs, that put him away for years. Ronnie came down with rheumatic fever, a disease almost unknown in 21st-century Britain but still "very common in poorer parts of the world… where there's over-crowding, poor sanitation and limited access to medical treatment." In 1946, Alder Hey Children's Hospital in Liverpool admitted 300 children who were suffering with the disease.

According to the actress Amanda Barrie, later to become one of Billy's leading ladies and his girlfriend, Billy was convinced that it was the birdwatching that did for him. "I remember him telling me a story about how he got rheumatic fever," she says. "He'd been playing out and got wet and when he got home he was punished for it. So, next time, he stayed outside until the clothes dried on his back before he dared go home."

Another similar story tells of a time he made himself a raft and wondered if it would float. It didn't.

Rheumatic fever usually starts with something simple like a strep throat – these days a condition treated with oral antibiotics and a few days off school. Without the help of antibiotics, the body's immune system can kick into overdrive and, in some cases, as well as attacking the bacteria causing the infection it begins to affect other parts of the body, most damagingly the joints and the heart valves.

Alder Hey Children's Hospital in West Derby was five or six miles and an awkward bus journey from Haliburton Street. Visiting hours were short. The treatment was long and difficult. The first stage required Ronnie to lie motionless on his back for two months.

He'd been through a war, separated from his dad, uprooted to London, then Prestatyn, then back again, then he had to lie absolutely still on his back for two months with only the occasional visit from his mum and a few kind nurses for comfort. None of this can have helped his sense of isolation as a child. All the same, given the circumstances, it is a miracle that for the rest of his life he remained relatively stable while so many of his contemporary pop stars, even those with less troubled childhoods, ended up shouting at windows in Venusian or dead from an overdose at 27.

Ronnie failed his 11-plus, the exam that decided whether you'd go to a grammar school or a secondary modern. Grammar school kids did Latin and were in with a chance of an office job or even university. At secondary moderns the teachers were paid less, the students were "shielded from the stultifying effects" of O-levels or A-levels, and the curriculum offered a basic grounding in the usual subjects heavily supplemented by 'practical subjects', like metalwork and gardening, according to *The New Secondary Education*, Ministry of Education, 1947. Girls got an even rawer deal: while the boys did their English and maths, they were often sent away for extra cookery and needlework.

In both type of school, most lessons were slammed home by liberal use of the cane, the tawse, the slipper and the ruler. Corporal punishment was widely regarded as an indispensable element in a fully rounded education.

They were harsh times. In 1956, the *Liverpool Echo* published a series of letters about the lack of discipline in schools. Many blamed it on working mothers ("the pivot is removed and the family, as such, just disintegrates"). Some correspondents advocated the introduction of the cat-o-nine-tails, which had served so gloriously in Nelson's navy, while others favoured whippy twigs: "Why not bring back the birch, like the Isle of Man?" (The Isle of Man's strangely independent judiciary still allowed birching for young offenders.)

Billy went to Wellington Road Secondary Modern. He'd barely got used to the punishment rituals before he fell ill again and was sent back to hospital.

This time, after the hospital had finished with him he was sent to a convalescent home in Wales.

He hated the place – especially the food. At mealtimes, the kids would sing: "Far away, far away/Far away, far away/Eggs and bacon we don't see/We get beetles in our tea/That's why we are gradual-lee/Fa-ding away/Far, far away..."

After two weeks he could stand it no longer, and he climbed down a drainpipe from the second floor.

"I didn't get very far. They came after me in a car and took me back to the home and stuck me alone in what they called 'the small room'. I would have run away again the first chance I got but they must have got in touch with my mother. She came and took me home."

Home meant back to school where, once again, he was Billy no-mates, the boy who'd fallen behind with his studies. He called the time he spent at Wellington Road the "dunce years". The only subjects that interested him were art and woodwork.

He was often in trouble: once for indulging his interest in art by drawing a dirty picture on the blackboard and once for starting a fire in the cloakroom.

"One day I was late and knew I would get whacked. I'd heard somewhere that if you put soap on your hands the cane just slides off. I covered them with soap but Mr Thomas made me touch my toes instead."

Eventually Ronnie was assimilated. He started hanging around with other kids, and learned to smoke, play out with the lads and generally do boys' things.

He and Albie joined up with a bunch of kids who went to the Catholic church at the end of the road. Sometimes they even went to church with them, for the company. The Wycherleys were Protestants. A neighbour spotted the lads and shopped them to Mum.

"Then we got the knock on the door," said Brian Johnson, one of the Catholic lads, in the BBC *Omnibus* documentary *Halfway To Paradise*. "'You're not going to convert my sons to Catholicism.' So, we were banned from speaking to 'em."

"If you went in their house, you weren't welcome," said Harry, another neighbourhood friend.

"It was his mum protecting him," said another.

"If we were going to the park to play football or down to town to do a bit of shoplifting or whatever, we'd say we were going to the park and they'd follow us later on."

As Chris Eley, founder member of the *Sound Of Fury* fan club and editor of the club's magazine, put it, Jean Wycherley "was lovely, but she was steely. She was tough."

Playing out, as Ricky Tomlinson remembered, "meant action, danger and imagination".

"By far the most terrifying game was played along the entries, which ran between the houses. The passages were about three feet wide flanked by high brick walls slick with moss. It was a test of bravery to balance on the wall and then hurl yourself across the gap, hopefully landing on the other side on your stomach. We called this belly banding.

"Bigger kids could jump from wall to wall in one long stride and would have races leaping from one side to the other. One slip could mean a broken neck."

Ronnie and his friends liked to do the "chicken run", down the railway track towards an oncoming train, jumping out of the way at the last minute. One of the friends was eventually killed doing this, which must have upped its value as a test of courage no end.

"There was this factory," said Ronnie, "and they used to shoot peanuts from one factory building to another along an outside chute. We used to climb on the chute, wait for a load of peanuts to come down, grab as much as we could and beat it. Then there was a sugar warehouse where they stored what we called 'jago', brown sugar with big chewy lumps in it like candy. We used to wait for the lorries to come out of the factory gates, jump on the back, rip open a sack and knock off big handfuls of the stuff."

Later, Billy occasionally spoke of being bullied at school, but it's doubtful whether, despite the birdwatching and illness, his suffering was exceptional. Casual violence, big kids kicking little kids, was taken for granted.

Once, when he came home yet again with a black eye, his dad took him out and bought him a pair of boxing gloves, as if their very existence would magically transform a shy lad of uncertain health into a professional street fighter, feared by all.

"Though I was always close to my mother, I never had much communication with my father," Billy told the *Daily Express* in 1979. "Although I now realise that I loved him very much, when I was young we did not understand each other."

"We tried to give the boys what we could," said Jean. "They did get a bit more than others [in the neighbourhood]. Billy went to piano lessons when he was about 11 because he was so interested in music."

The piano lessons didn't take. Ronnie never practised. Later he realised he'd got off lightly when brother Albie was presented with a piano accordion.

The Wycherleys never had a record player, but Gran, round the corner, had a radiogram and a decent collection of 78s that Ronnie played until the grooves ran smooth. The music bug had got him.

"Before rock'n'roll, I'd been into country and western music, because I couldn't get anything out of the popular music of the time. Actually, in Liverpool, everybody used to play country and western – Hank Williams or whatever. Anything with some real lyrics about a bit of trouble or a bit of heartbreak."

"I heard country and western before I heard rock'n'roll," said John Lennon. "The people there [in Liverpool] – the Irish in Ireland are the same – they take their music very seriously. There were established folk, blues and country and western clubs in Liverpool before rock'n'roll."

Similarly, Ringo learned Gene Autry's 'South Of The Border' at around the same time as he learned to walk. He grew up with country music. "A lot of it was around from guys in the navy. I'd go to parties and they'd be putting on Hank Williams, Hank Snow and all those country acts."

Country and western music, cowboy music, hillbilly music (few people were as discriminating in their musical definitions as they are now) featured infrequently in the charts – which until 1952 were based on sheet music sales rather than records – and was almost completely ignored by the BBC. However, it had a passionate following in the UK, primarily in working-class communities, and had been adored since the early thirties when the singing cowboys – Hopalong Cassidy, Tex Ritter, Gene Autry, Roy Rogers and the rest – first appeared at the pictures.

Never underestimate the importance of the cowboy in post Second World War British history. Men born between 1940 and 1955 anywhere west of Berlin are fundamentally darn-tootin'. You can call them baby-boomers, pensioners, fat, old bastards, anything you like, but they know their real names are Slim, Pecos, Wild Bill, Bucky and Sundance. If you scratch them they bleed cowboy blood. Their hands are shaped like six-guns. When they ride their mobility scooters, they ride tall in the saddle. When they succeed in business or win the lottery, the home they build near Epsom, Surrey is inevitably "ranch style". And all of them, when the cowboy on the poster invited them to "come to Marlboro country", went.

As soon as they were able, these men abandoned suits, jackets and ties and went into Levis and check shirts, or something more elaborate. With practically his first wage packet, Ronnie Wycherley bought himself a "two-tone Texas" jacket – like a western shirt, but more substantial. Early publicity stills show him wearing just such a jacket, although whether it's the original or one of many acquired down the years is impossible to say.

In other publicity stills he wears the full Monty – satin western shirt with neckerchief.

Robert Zimmerman has often denied that he chose the name Bob Dylan in honour of the Welsh poet Dylan Thomas, insisting instead that it was in homage to Marshal Matt Dillon, hero of the TV western series *Gunsmoke*. David Jones stole the name 'Bowie' from Jim Bowie, the frontiersman who died at the Alamo with Davy Crockett.

"Whenever I make a date with a girl," Billy told *Mirabelle* in 1960, "I always hope she likes cowboy pictures because to me no date is complete unless we go see one. Not that I would meet my date at the cinema. I like to get to know a girl before we go in. I usually take my girl to an espresso bar first where we can have a cup of coffee and talk."

In March 1954, a month before Ronnie Wycherley's 14th birthday, Roy Rogers, the singing cowboy, his wife and partner in harmony Dale Evans, and his horse Trigger came to Liverpool. Roy and Dale had both come down with the flu, and though they bravely struggled through the show at the Empire Theatre, afterwards they were confined to bed in the Adelphi Hotel. Trigger brought them flowers.

"For an hour, the horse wandered upstairs and downstairs like Goosey Gander," said the *Liverpool Evening Express*, "and finally into his lady's and master's chamber.

"Some 4,000 of their young subjects, some of them loyal enough to have taken their places early in the afternoon, crowded the pavements of Lime Street and kept up a continual chant, 'We want Roy Rogers.' But the cowboy was not well enough to oblige them.

"And so, his horse, Trigger, did his best to fill the breach. He reared high on his hind legs, took a bow or two outside the Adelphi Hotel and later – the first horse to set a hoof inside – he took more bows from a first-floor window as hundreds of watchful boys and girls caught sight of him.

"Before that he had made his mark at the registration desk with a pencil clutched between his teeth.

"Then he went at a couple of bounds into the residents' lounge followed by an entourage of intrigued guests, young excited admirers and reporters attending their oddest press reception."

Hank Williams was from Alabama, Hank Snow from Canada, but both wore stetsons and western jackets, so passed muster. Frankie Laine had recorded the theme song from *High Noon*, 'Mule Train' and 'The Call Of The Wild Goose' and later did the theme songs for *Rawhide*, *Gunfight At*

The O.K. Corral and *Champion The Wonder Horse*. Tennessee Ernie Ford, one of Ronnie's personal favourites, had done 'Shotgun Boogie' and a 'Rootin' Tootin' Santa Claus'. They were all honorary cowboys.

Singing cowboys played guitars, an instrument which, along with the stetson, the buckskin fringing and the Colt 45, became a must-have for cowboy fans long before Lonnie Donegan, Tommy Steele, The Shadows and The Beatles made it into the universal fetish object it later became.

Ronnie got one for his 14th birthday, bought new from Frank Hessys' Music Centre on Stanley Street. Oddly it wasn't his best present ever: that came eight months later.

"When I was 14," he told *Valentine* in 1961 in a 'Pop Stars Best Present Ever' feature, "I came down to breakfast on Christmas morning and my dad said, 'Son, put these milk bottles outside the front door' – and when I did I saw this fabulous bike parked outside and it had a label on the handlebars with my name on it! It was a really slick racing job. So, I've had motor bikes since then and cars and I've been up to 120 miles an hour. But, man, there's never been quite the excitement I had with that bike: I reckon I got well over thirty out of it at times."

Nevertheless, the guitar must have come a close second, or maybe third. He never became a virtuoso, but on the various self-accompanied demos he made throughout his life, you can hear he was a useful strummer, able to offer a convincing indication of a song's feel.

He started playing with a friend, Billy Hatton, who later sang and played bass with The Fourmost – stablemates of The Beatles under Brian Epstein's management. "Owning a guitar in the early fifties was uncommon," says Billy Hatton, "and there were very few people to teach you, so most budding guitar players were usually self-taught. You can imagine the sort of sounds that we wrenched from the strangled strings. It was bad enough for the artisans who fashioned the tools of our dreams to wish that they had never put chisel to wood. Add to this the howling that came from our untutored tonsils and the meaning of post-war depression takes on another aspect."

Billy Hatton lived a 10-minute walk from Ronnie's house. "We were very close," he says, "because of the bond that music gives you and we spent many nights in the front rooms (the posh ones) of our homes playing and singing to the guitar and working on that rare gift that Ronnie had of songwriting. This was so unusual at that time because being a songwriter was something that people did in films or on the radio. It was a fantasy that did not visit young working-class lads in a poverty-stricken area of a city. It did not happen in a little terraced house in Dingle. But it blossomed in our houses, with Ronnie coming up with the ideas and me slotting in the chords that he wasn't sure of."

Ronnie himself had a more down to earth explanation for his interest in composition. "I could only play three or four chords," he said. "So instead of trying to play songs that needed chords I didn't know, I started writing my own songs using the chords I did know."

Something had begun.

CHAPTER TWO

"HEY RONNIE, YOU LOOK A BIT LIKE EDDIE COCHRAN."

In 1955, Ronnie left school.

"There were about five minutes to go before the final bell," he said. "I couldn't stand it. I put my feet up on the desk and lit a cigarette. The teacher told me to put it out and said school wasn't over yet. I just laughed and said, 'Go on, teach, make me.' With only a minute to go before the end of school, he thrashed me six times on my hand. With each stroke, I laughed louder and the bell rang as he brought the cane down for the sixth time.

"I hated school," said Billy. "It was like being in jail. Now I was being released, a free man. I went wild, running out of school shouting 'I'm free, I'm free, I'm free!' They told me at school you'll achieve nothing, you'll come to a bad end. So, when I'd made it, I went back there in my car just to show them. They seemed different somehow – more human than I thought, but I still showed them the car."

As always, the elation of leaving was quickly squashed by the need to get a job. His dad wanted him to go into the family business. "But I thought shoe repairing was a load of cobblers," Billy – or maybe a waggish press officer with a bad taste for puns – said later. "I only stuck at it for a week."

So, Dad sorted him out a job at Ellison's Engineering. Initially, he was a tea boy, but was quickly promoted to heating rivets for the welders on £2 18s (£2.90) a week. "My second pay day I bought myself a sharp two-tone Texas jacket and my first pair of real slim pants."

After about a year, Ronnie and a friend, bored, decided to weld together a couple of random bits of metal. The foreman, who took a dim view of unauthorised welding, started bawling Ronnie out in front of his workmates, so Ronnie took a swing at him with the welding gun. The electrode – the sharp bit at the end – jabbed into the foreman's arm. The police were kept out of it but Ronnie's career in engineering, such as it had been, was over.

His health was never good enough for a job at sea in the merchant navy, but his dad asked around and found him the next best thing – pootling up and down the river as a deckhand on the tugboat *Formby* with the Alexandra Shipping Company. Jean still thought the work was too taxing for her delicate son, but it paid £7.00 a week, more than twice what he'd been getting at Ellison's.

"I had loads of money. I was living with my parents. All I had to do with it was buy clothes and records and go to dances on Saturday night. Maybe I'd buy a few bottles of Harveys Bristol Cream on a Saturday."

This, one hopes, is a euphemism of sorts. Harveys Bristol Cream is a brand of sherry, once popular with clergymen and the elderly. A single glass can be cloying. A "few bottles" doesn't bear thinking about.

"We made a point of not going to places like the Locarno ballrooms because they had these terrible 40-piece bands on with people doing waltzes and foxtrots."

Ricky Tomlinson knew that scene well. "The Grafton, a famous local ballroom, had a Saturday afternoon tea dance. For a shilling, you got a cup of tea, two biscuits and the chance to hold a girl close during the slow numbers.

"Girls would stand on one side of the dance floor and boys on the other. The no man's land lay in between. The walk back seemed twice as long if a girl refused to dance with you."

Ronnie Wycherley rarely, possibly never, knew that walk of shame. Speak to anybody who knew Ronnie Wycherley and there's one thing they need to impress on you early in the conversation. Yes, he was good looking, you can see that from photographs, but more than that he had what can only be described as an aura. Dressed up, hair combed, face washed, he was devastating. He didn't have to say or do anything, just look at you out of the corner of his eye, shy and distant.

"He was a sexy sod, wasn't he?" says Billy Hatton. "He would walk into a party and all the girls would turn into blobs of oil. I was lucky to be with him."

More and more of Ronnie's pay packet went on clothes. "I got all my trousers taken in to 13-inch drains [drainpipe trouser, or ankle huggers]. I used to wear a lot of bomber jackets at first. Then I thought I'd really like a nice drape jacket. But there was no one selling them off the peg. So I got a little tailor figured out who could do anything.

"We'd just go round and tell him what we wanted. Finger-tip length. Or just under finger-tip. The lapels had got to be only so wide. Did I want slant pocket? And then suddenly I had loads of jackets hanging up!"

"His dad used to go mad," said Jean. "With him having the shop, people used to go to him and say, 'Oh, those Teddy Boys!' And him being in business. Well."

"Teddy Boys", with their drape jackets and drainpipe trousers, were big news. According to the papers they were responsible for most of the trouble in the world, especially when it came to smashing up cinemas and fighting with chains and flick-knives.

Ever since the ancient Greeks and possibly before, there has been a tribe on which the average citizens could hang their terror of uncontrollable youth. Shakespeare's generation lived in permanent fear of "Apprentices"; since then there's been mashers, wide boys, peaky blinders, mods, rockers, skins and a thousand others, all bent on shredding common decency.

Albert had read the papers and didn't want his son turning bad. He made the rules – "No drapes, no drains."

"I got into a lot of trouble with my dear father," said Billy. Wearing Ted gear "meant a clip round the ear hole."

So, he'd hide the fancy stuff in the outside lav and "what I used to do was dash up the entry, change into my tight trousers, over the wall and I was out on the town."

George Harrison, by all accounts, did the same thing. Outside lavs all over the country must have been stuffed with contraband clobber.

And, just as Dad had feared, he began to mix it with the bad guys.

He might have, anyway.

It's difficult, in retrospect, to get a proper handle on Ronnie Wycherley's reputation as a tearaway. Larry Parnes – his eventual manager, who also looked after Tommy Steele, Marty Wilde, Vince Eager, Joe Brown and a handful of others – had a tendency to big up his clients' street cred. The myth of the tearaway is potent. Neither James Dean nor Marlon Brando made their names playing trainee solicitors' clerks.

Sorting out from interviews, press releases and news reports what might have been fact and what was the product of Larry Parnes' motormouth is next to impossible. One of the early Billy Fury press releases, faithfully reproduced in the *Record Mirror*, described him as a 16-year-old (he was 18) who'd been working in a shoe shop but was "fired for spending too much time singing to the girls".

And this, from *The People* in 1961, may have some core of fact in it somewhere, but it's hard to see it through the fog of casual racism and lurid journalese.

"After the pictures," Billy, or Larry Parnes, or somebody said, "I was walking home humming 'That Old Black Magic' when I turned into Upper Parliament Street. A bunch of coloured boys were hanging round the corner. One fella with long sideburns moved right in front of me on the pavement. 'You looking for me, lad?' he said. I said, 'No', and made to move on. He grabbed me and shoved his fist – wham – into my face."

Billy, said *The People*, hit back. This led to a general rumble with fists, belt buckles and coshes. "They grabbed me by my hair and started jabbing their fags into my cheeks. The pain was so terrible that it must have made me mad. I kicked and lunged with my whole body. Next thing I remember I was staggering along my own street, Haliburton Street. A couple of fellas I knew grabbed hold of me and said, 'You're a right mess, skin. Who done you up?' 'A team of kinkies over in Upper Park,' I said. 'Round up all the fellas you can and we'll go get them – wherever they are.' We tracked them down to a Chinese on Mill Street. But the proprietor saw us coming and locked up."

In the end, one of Billy's mates smashed the door down. The fight continued. Billy was knocked out and came to in a bombed-out house – and so on.

For readers unacquainted with the jargon of delinquency, *The People* appended a helpful glossary.

"Pad – flat or rooms
Rumble – gang fight
Skin – chum or pal

Kinky – unbalanced
Chick – girl
Hola – bomb site or waste ground
Team – gang
Scuffers – policemen."

After the fight, the police cracked down on the whole district.

"The word got round that there would be a £5.00 fine for anyone caught wearing a studded belt. It looked like team fighting was over for good. I'm not chicken but I was really relieved. If the scuffers hadn't cracked down, I don't know where it would have ended."

There are darker stories of brushes with organised crime.

Billy Hatton doesn't believe a word of it, but there was a rumour, used as the basis of the play written by Alan Bower about Billy, called *Like I've Never Been Gone*, that Billy lost his virginity to the girlfriend of Beechy Keatley, a local bouncer, driver and friend to the groups.

Much later, in 1974, Beechy went to prison but was widely regarded as a hero for killing Eddie Palmer, leader of 'the Stanley Boys', named after the craft knife, their weapon of choice.

Basically, Eddie deliberately ran Beechy over in a car. So, after a long recuperation, Beechy stabbed Eddie. It's said that when the police heard that Eddie Palmer was dead, they ordered a case of champagne.

At the trial, the prosecution described Eddie Palmer as "the most feared man in Liverpool". The jury found for manslaughter, but not murder, and the judge sent Beechy down for three years, wishing him "good luck" as he left the dock.

The idea that Ronnie Wycherley, a shy boy with a weak chest, would have run with gangsters seems improbable. To Billy Hatton, even the idea that he would have cuckolded Beechy Keatley is preposterous.

"We both knew Beechy Keatley," Billy Hatton said, "but I don't think Ronnie would be as reckless as that. There would have been ructions to put it mildly if Beechy had found out."

"We just hated authority," Ronnie said, the 'we' being him and his mates.

"If there was nowhere to go and we stood on a street corner, a copper would come up and tell us to move on. So, you'd go down the road and then come back to the corner. And then he'd probably come back again, and give you a whack with his stick. It was pretty rough. If a few Teds got together at a dance, the police would have to stick their nose in –

they'd never seen these kinds of gatherings before, unless it was for some kind of gang fight.

"I know I just wasn't happy with my lot. Whatever I wanted to do, someone would always seem to get in the way, particularly people in uniforms. It had started with teachers in the classrooms and carried on from there. We thought we'd be free after school but you had to find a job and then you had a boss. And it was authority again."

Skiffle was what the cowboy generation did in 1957.

It wasn't so much a style of music as an attitude, a virus that affected pretty much every young man, and many young women, from the quads and dorms of the great public schools to the slummiest of inner-city slums.

It had been building up a head of steam for years. In 1951, at the Festival of Britain, the heir to the throne, Princess Elizabeth, and her husband Prince Philip attended a jazz concert. There, George Melly sang 'Rock Island Line' – a train blues track that John Lomax, the American folk-song collector, had recorded at the Arkansas State Prison. It tells the not very stirring tale of a goods train driver who evades a toll by misrepresenting his cargo.

Three years later, during a recording session by the Chris Barber Jazz Band at Decca Studios, while the rest of the band took a break, banjo and guitar player Lonnie Donegan, accompanied by Chris Barber on bass and Beryl Bryden on washboard, recorded a couple of numbers that had been going down well in their live shows. One of them was that same 'Rock Island Line'.

The track mouldered in Decca's vaults and wasn't released as a single until January 1956, a full 18 months after the session, by which time, on the basis of live performances and album tracks, a grassroots enthusiasm for 'skiffle' – the name given to Donegan's style of music – had already seized the country.

Like the punk revolution 20 years later, skiffle was essentially "this is a chord, this is another, this is a third, now form a band" music, with the added advantage that it was much cheaper: no amps, no drum kit, just an acoustic guitar or banjo, a washboard (still a common household appliance back then, at least at your gran's house), a broomstick-and-string 'bass' and a check shirt.

Before long there was an uncountable number – sometimes it must have felt like trillions – of skiffle groups up and down the country singing a repertoire of country and western standards, slave plaints, railroad shuffles, murder ballads and prison moans, all songs with sentiments as comprehensible to the average 16-year-old in Acton, Erdington, Ipswich or Taunton as the Latin Bible or Logical Positivism. And even though, in the cack-hands of amateurs, the white-hot passion that characterised Donegan's delivery was usually replaced by a generalised boy-scout bonhomie, the music had drive. It had energy. For grammar school lads from 'nice' families, skiffle, even in its most cheerless form, was a release from the stifling Lord's Day Observance Society, sports jacket and grey flannels, Perry Como and Eddie Calvert, post-war pusillanimity of the fifties. Beneath the whiff of lavender water and meat-and-two-veg was a distinct smell of teen spirit.

Skiffle was where the stars of tomorrow learned their trade: Tommy Steele and Lionel Bart were in The Cavemen; Mick Jagger was in the Bucktown Skiffle Group; Cliff Richard was in the Dick Teague Skiffle Group; John Lennon and Paul McCartney were in The Quarrymen; Roger Daltrey was in the Sulgrave Rebels.

The James Page Skiffle Group appeared on the kids' TV show *All Your Own*. "What do you want to do when you leave school? Take up skiffle?" asks the show's presenter Huw Weldon, with a patronising smile.

"No," says a freshly scrubbed 13-year-old Jimmy Page, "I want to take up biological research." As good a euphemism as any for Led Zeppelin's subsequent career.

Ricky Tomlinson played banjo with The Guitanios. "The motivation for the band had nothing to do with dreams of stardom or wealth. We wanted to pull birds and in my experience there were two surefire ways of doing this – being a good dancer or playing in a band. Even my mate Brian Craig, who had a glass eye (the legacy of childhood measles) and was going bald at 16, pulled the most amazing looking girls when they heard him sing and play guitar."

Ron, the skipper of Ronnie Wycherley's tugboat, played the ukulele; Jack, the ship's foreman, played guitar; the chief engineer could get a tune out of a mouth organ and the first mate played crazy spoons. Ronnie took the vocals and played the broomstick bass. They called themselves, indicating that they weren't committing to the skiffle ideal quite as earnestly as others, 'the Formby Sniffle Gloop' and started getting gigs at a local caff and a working men's club in Aintree.

Ronnie described the scene in 1961 to *The People*. "My first public performance was to swing out 'Singing The Blues' [a 1957 hit for both

Guy Mitchell and Tommy Steele] to the crew of a Mersey tugboat, wearing stoker's overalls and slapping at a gazoon. A gazoon? It's a thing I invented on this crazy tugboat. I got an old tin and filled it with dried peas, then stuck a broomstick in it. I stripped a piece of electric flex and stretched the wire along the broomstick to the tin. Then I cut notches on a wooden stick. I played the wire with the stick and boy it sounded just like a jazz drummer when he's really making with the brushes. Crazy!"

But things did not turn out well. The band broke up and Ronnie moved to another boat, where the skipper was not the ukulele playing type. "Brother, was he twisted. I don't think I ever saw him smile. He ran that tug like one of those kinky pirates in those films about old sailing ships. He started picking on me. One morning I was just finishing off (cleaning the deck) when he walked into the cabin and he yelled, 'SCRUB MY CABIN OUT'."

He scrubbed it out four times before he walked.

Ronnie's next job was at Joshua Harris, a department store. "I was the labourer there," he said. "I made the tea and carried all the stuff to the top floor."

At around the same time, or not long after, Paul McCartney would have been working in Lewis's department store on Church Street and George Harrison at Blacklers on Great Charlotte Street.

Yvonne Irving had a Saturday job at Joshua Harris when she was 14. "That was where I first met Ronnie. All the girls were absolutely head over heels about him – he was absolutely gorgeous! He used to have an old guitar that he carried around the shop with him and in the breaks he'd be in there strumming."

The songs he wrote were inspired by his affairs of the heart, which had become a troubling preoccupation and a challenge to his multi-tasking abilities.

"There was one he was going out with, one he was trying to go out with and one who was trying to go out with him," said his friend Brian Johnson.

In 1961, Ronnie (he was Billy by then) told Donald Zec of the *Daily Mirror* about his heartbreak inspiration. Donald Zec, it must be noted, was a fine journalist who took great delight in quietly taking the piss out of his subjects.

"'Yeah, I'm difficult I suppose. I get these moods and the girls can't take it. So the love affairs get all washed up you know. Then I get depressed.'

"'And that makes you write the songs?'

"'There was a girl called Frances. Pretty in a funny sort of way she was. We were getting along fine. And then she left me.'

"'So you got depressed?'

"'That's right. And straight away I wrote 'That's Love'.'

"'And after Frances?'

"'Margo.' Billy blushed. 'She's five years older than me. I'm very attracted to older women. I don't know exactly why. Anyway, she said I wasn't mature enough so she broke it off. I got depressed again.'

"'And that gave birth to...?'

"''Margo', 'Don't Knock On My Door' and (a bit hopeful) 'Maybe Tomorrow'.'

"'That was pretty good value – three songs from one girl?'

"'Yeah. When she stood me up, I got so mad I punched my hand through a window. Here's the scar.'

"'You could have written a song, 'Margo, I Bleed For You',' I suggested.

"'Yeah, I never thought of that.'"

Margo King was a real person. She worked on the counters at Joshua Harris. Even towards the end of his life, Billy was still talking about Margo.

"I thought she was really beautiful but she turned me down and to get over the frustration and stuff, I wrote this thing called 'Margo, Don't Go'. But she went."

"Margo, don't go
I need you so
Oh, please be mine
most all the time."

The song eventually became his second single.

By this time skiffle had been abandoned. It had always been a bit too grammar school and youth club for Ronnie, anyway. He was more secondary modern and Teddy Boy. Teds didn't do youth clubs.

"It was fantastic being a Ted, it was a new identity. We had our own music. Definitely we'd been waiting for something to happen, though I don't think we realised what we wanted, because there wasn't anything else."

But something had happened. Bubbling up at the same time as skiffle, but so much more glamorous, so much more dangerous, was rock'n'roll.

In his book *Margrave Of The Marshes*, John Peel describes the effect that Presley's 'Heartbreak Hotel' had on him when he first heard it on the BBC's *Two-Way Family Favourites* as that of, "a naked extra-terrestrial walking through the door and announcing that he/she was going to live with me for the rest of my life. There was something frightening, something lewd, something seriously out of control about 'Heartbreak Hotel' and alarmed though I was by Elvis, I knew I wanted more."

It was the same for John Lennon. "It was nothing but Elvis Presley, Elvis Presley, Elvis Presley," said John's Aunt Mimi. "In the end I said, 'Elvis Presley's all very well, John, but I don't want him for breakfast, dinner and tea.'"

Lorna Sage merged all of her teenage crushes into a composite bad boy: "He was mostly Elvis: his knees buckled with lust when you let go his strings and he clung to the mike or his guitar for dear life, keening, 'Jus' take a walk down lonely street, jus' put a chain around my neck and lead me anywhere, don't be cruel.'

"Elvis' sort were shiftless, driven not by ambition but glands."

In the summer of 1957, *The Girl Can't Help It*, a rock'n'roll film starring Jayne Mansfield and Tom Ewell, arrived in the UK. There had been and would be other rock'n'roll films. From the previous year, *Rock Around The Clock* had featured The Platters, Freddie Bell & The Bellboys and the relatively middle-aged Bill Haley & His Comets. *Rock, Rock, Rock* gave us Dion & The Belmonts, Frankie Lymon & The Teenagers and a brief glimpse of Chuck Berry.

Neither of them, nor any other attempt to put rock on film, did it quite like *The Girl Can't Help It*. Gene Vincent sang 'Be-Bop-A-Lula', Eddie Cochran sang 'Twenty Flight Rock', Fats Domino sang 'Blue Monday', Little Richard sang the title track and 'Ready Teddy'. That first sighting of Little Richard, a black man of uncertain sexuality spitting lyrics with a laser beam precision, was, for many, a Damascene moment.

The Girl Can't Help It was a message from the gods, a call to arms, an inspiration that brought a deep sense of shame to skifflers all over the country. Their broomstick basses, their check shirts, their tiny half-inch Brylcreemed pompadours suddenly seemed footling. At home, they put pick-ups on their guitars and turned the family radio into an amp. Then they got proper guitars and proper amps. Then they got bigger amps.

Grown-ups and youth-club leaders, the ones who smiled indulgently at skiffle, hated rock'n'roll. When Princess Margaret went to see *The Girl Can't Help It*, Anthony Heap, royal reporter for the *Daily Telegraph*, didn't even try to conceal his disapproval.

"Last night she went to see the latest trashy 'rock'n'roll' film at the Carlton – she never goes to an intelligent play or film – and, taking off her shoes, put her feet up on the rail round the front of the circle and waved them in time with 'the hot rhythm'.

"When is Princess Margaret going to act her age and behave like a member of the Royal Family instead of a half-baked jazz-mad Teddy Girl?"

The princess was 26.

"Some of the guys in this gang I was with said, 'Hey Ronnie, you look a bit like Eddie Cochran'. And I was chuffed, you know."

He began to style his hair just like Eddie and practised the shaky legs and the hunched shoulders. He never abandoned the hunched shoulders.

He had a go at a couple of talent contests, without success. At one in Bootle, he wasn't even placed. Undaunted, he applied to Carroll Levis.

Carroll Levis, "Mr Starmaker", was a Canadian who'd been living in the UK since the thirties. He ran talent contests around the country – "the focus for every ocarina player, razor-blade eater and bird song imitator in England".

Word that the show might *come to your town* kept many young hopefuls singing, conjuring or fiercely tap-dancing in back parlours on the off chance that the great man would walk up their entry. The best acts were showcased on his BBC radio show which, over the years, appeared with various names around the theme of 'Carroll Levis And His Discoveries'.

In the mid-fifties the show transferred to television. ATV's *The Carroll Levis Show* sometimes knocked *Sunday Night At The London Palladium* off the top of the ratings. Nicholas Parsons – still, at the time of writing, hosting the BBC Radio 4 panel game *Just A Minute* – came to fame thanks to Carroll Levis. So did ventriloquist Terry Hall and his dummy, Lenny the Lion.

Exact details about who auditioned for Carroll Levis when he came to Lancashire are hard to come by. As we'll see in the next chapter, memories get garbled, dates confused.

For instance, in his autobiography *Wild Tales: A Life In Rock And Roll*, Graham Nash reckons that on November 19, 1958, The Beatles, under the name of Johnny & The Moondogs, appeared along with Ron Wycherley, while Graham Nash and Allan Clarke, both later of The Hollies, auditioned as Ricky and Dane. Other accounts give October 18, 1959 as the date of the Johnny & The Moondogs appearance, although they'd also auditioned in 1957 as The Quarrymen. And anyway, by November 19, 1958, Ron Wycherley had given up his amateur status, had his name changed to Billy Fury, appeared on TV and was signed to Decca Records. So, maybe the Graham Nash account is a conflation of various auditions, designed to give a flavour of the times, for which reason it's worth quoting.

"I recognised Johnny Peters, the front man for The Rockets, whose coolness quotient was way off the charts," Graham wrote. "Ronnie Wycherley, who later morphed into Billy Fury, was slumped in a chair backstage, as was Freddie Garrity, a short guy with glasses who was to have hits in the sixties with Freddie & The Dreamers. Most of the preshow buzz was around a group from Liverpool called Johnny & The Moondogs, who did a Buddy Holly number, 'Think It Over'. I think they were pretty good, which confirms my taste, considering it was John Lennon, George Harrison and Paul McCartney, with Johnny Hutchinson sitting in on drums. Allan and I decided to stick with 'It's Only Make Believe' [a later hit for Billy] because we could wring every last ounce of emotion out of the lyric."

According to various jumbled accounts, Johnny & The Moondogs had to leave early to catch their last train back to Liverpool. Ronnie Wycherley did well, but not as well as The Harmonica Rascals, a group that subsequently featured on many TV variety shows, played light classics on mouth-organs and included a person of restricted growth playing bass harmonica, who got knocked over by the bigger boys as they gyrated in time with the music to semi-comic effect.

"When Levis dragged us all onstage at the end it was anyone's guess who would take first place," wrote Graham Nash. "He lined up each act in a single row, then walked behind us and held a hand out over our heads. If the crowd went crazy, you knew your chances were good."

The glamorous compere, according to Nash, was Jackie Collins, the novelist, then better known as the younger sister of starlet Joan Collins. A hush fell over the acts and the audience as she announced, "The winner is…" hold the pause until somebody leaks, "…Ricky and Dane."

Graham and Allan went on to the finals in Morecambe. The Harmonica Rascals reckoned they was robbed. Johnny & The Moondogs vented their frustrations with a little light vandalism on the train home. Ronnie Wycherley's thoughts weren't recorded. And none of it might have happened at all.

In 1925, when many Liverpool homes still hadn't been connected to the electricity, Percy Philips opened a "Battery Recharging Depot" at 38 Kensington. By the fifties, he'd branched out into electrical appliances and gramophone records, and was known for keeping a stock of American jazz and country and western releases. Then, just as his namesake Sam Phillips had done in Memphis, Tennessee, Percy opened a recording studio and disc-cutting service. The studio was a downstairs room (the shop was converted from a terraced house) with a piano and blankets on the window and door for soundproofing.

The studio was kept busy. Endless streams of children were shepherded in to do their party pieces. After a terrible argument with his wife, a man recorded an apology. People would bring their pets to Percy's studio and walk away proud owners of a 78 rpm acetate disc of, perhaps, Rover's special bark, or Brian the Budgie singing 'Rule Britannia'. The sleeves were stamped "Phillips Sound Recording Service, Personal Discs cut in studio or from customer's tapes, 38 Kensington, Liverpool 7".

Ken Dodd, Freddie Starr, Willie Russell, Liverpool FC Supporters' Club and countless others all made records at Percy's, but the Blue Plaque outside the building celebrates the day, in 1958, when John Lennon, Paul McCartney, George Harrison, John Lowe and Colin Hanton, The Quarrymen, identified in the studio log as "Skiffle Group", recorded two sides: Buddy Holly's 'That'll Be The Day' and McCartney and Harrison's 'In Spite Of All The Danger'.

An entry in the studio logbook for April 18, 1958 – three months before The Quarrymen showed up – states: "Youth with guitar. One 10-inch double sided disc". The session cost, according to the invoice, £1 18s (£1.90). The "youth" was – possibly, it's hard to be certain – Ronnie Wycherley. It was the day after his 18th birthday. A "10-inch double sided disc" would have been an exciting present to himself.

The result of the session still exists; six tracks, all truncated so as to leave a total running time of seven minutes, just Ronnie and his guitar. It's clear that by this time the Eddie Cochran influence had largely been supplanted by Elvis. Four of the songs – 'I'm Left, You're Right, She's

Gone', 'Paralyzed', 'Playing For Keeps' and 'Have I Told You Lately That I Love You?' – are Presley covers. The other two, 'Love's A-Callin'' and 'Baby', are Ronnie's own compositions.

It would be stretching a point to suggest that any of the tracks give much evidence of a star in the making, either as singer or songwriter. The Quarrymen in the same studio sound rough and in dire need of arrangement and production but their commitment is unmistakeable. Ronnie sounds like a shy kid who can do a passable Elvis impersonation, just like a couple of thousand other kids around the country.

And a shy kid doing a passable Elvis impersonation he might have remained, were it not for one fateful night at the Essoldo Cinema, Birkenhead.

CHAPTER THREE

"I SING, PLAY THE GUITAR AND WRITE SOME OF MY OWN SONGS."

If you ask six eyewitnesses to describe an incident they all claim vividly to remember, no two accounts will agree. Nobody's lying or even embroidering. It's just the way memory works. Cops know it, lawyers know it and biographers know it.

The variation in accounts, theories and hypotheses surrounding Ron Wycherley's visit to the Essoldo Cinema, Birkenhead and the signing of his contract with Larry Parnes, the country's top pop manager, make "who shot J. F. Kennedy?" look like an open and shut case. Even Billy contradicts himself.

In some early interviews, he said he sent off the tapes he'd made at Percy Philips' recording studio to Larry Parnes, along with a photograph he'd had taken at Star Studios in Bold Street, but received no reply. So, hearing that Marty Wilde – whose 'Endless Sleep' was riding high in the Top 20 – was appearing at the Essoldo in a *Larry Parnes Extravaganza* along with Vince Eager, another of Larry's signings, and The John Barry Seven, Ronnie went along, possibly in the hope of being granted an interview or audition with Mr Parnes, or at least of meeting Marty Wilde or Vince Eager.

This hypothesis is borne out by the evidence of Patrick Doncaster of the *Daily Mirror* who, in his *Doncaster's Discs* column of August 31, 1961, says: "I have the letter written by a then tug-deckhand in Liverpool. 'I sing,' it said, 'play the guitar and write some of my own songs. I enclose a tape recording and photographs of myself.' The signature: R. Wycherley." The letter was addressed to Larry Parnes.

But in a September 1981 interview, Billy said that rather than sending the tapes to Larry, he sent them to Dick Rowe, the A&R man at Decca who later turned down The Beatles (but subsequently redeemed himself magnificently by signing, among others, The Rolling Stones, Them, The Moody Blues, John Mayall's Bluesbreakers, Tom Jones and the Small Faces.)

"He said, 'Come down and do a recording test', which was what you did in those days," Billy said. "So I did. And I was offered a deal by Decca."

But before anything was signed, Rowe got in touch with Billy again to tell him that the *Larry Parnes Extravaganza* was coming to town and he should check it out.

Then again, Ronnie's mum, Jean, told Spencer Leigh a slightly different story. She said that, on the strength of Ronnie's success in the Carroll Levis show, she wrote to Larry Parnes – "to see whether he wanted Ronnie or not as somebody else was interested. Larry asked Billy to go to the Essoldo, Birkenhead for an audition when Marty Wilde's tour was there in October 1958."

Billy Hatton's account goes: "Ronnie arrived at our front door and said that he had received an invitation to go to the Essoldo Theatre in Birkenhead to meet none other than Larry Parnes, who was the top manager of the hour. I had to be up for work at five o'clock the next morning so I couldn't go with him, but I loaned him my guitar case because he didn't have one and I thought that he needed to arrive with some sort of style. Off he went to meet his fate."

Marty Wilde remembers it thus: "I think he couldn't have come to the theatre without having made an appointment with Larry. I don't think he would have just turned up with a guitar in the hope that he would have got backstage and played some songs. So I think a bit of organisation had gone on there."

If Ronnie did borrow Billy Hatton's guitar case, it was left at home. Brian Bennett, the drummer then playing with Marty Wilde's Wildcats, remembered that "Ronnie had his guitar in a plastic bag."

And, to muddy the water still further, Ronnie's brother, Albie, told Spencer Leigh, "Billy couldn't afford a guitar case at the time. He used to put his guitar in a bolster case, one of those long pillowcases that went along the bed."

Billy Hatton mentions that, like the "second gunman on the grassy knoll" Kennedy assassination theory, the tapes (or discs) that Ronnie sent to Larry Parnes (and/or Dick Rowe) were possibly not the ones recorded at Percy Phillips' studio. Rather they may have been a second set of tapes, now lost, that Ronnie, Billy Hatton and an unnamed percussionist, playing with brushes on a tin tray, had recorded on a friend's tape recorder in the stairwell of a block of flats (for the echo).

Larry Parnes, of course, has an entirely different story. According to him, it was neither Ronnie nor Jean who'd got in touch but, perplexingly, the object of Ronnie's affection and cause of his heartache, Margo. "I discovered Billy Fury and Jimmy Tarbuck [the comedian] at the Essoldo, Birkenhead," he told Bob Azurdia of Radio Merseyside. "It was the second Sunday in July 1958."

The Essoldo show was actually on Wednesday October 1, 1958. In July of that year, Marty Wilde was touring with a variety show featuring Jackie German the Amazing Unicyclist, and Gillian and June "Taps In Tempo".

"Billy's girlfriend Margo," Larry continued, "had written to me several times, sending me his photograph and a tape and lyrics and poetry that he had written. She was very persistent and the photos kept getting bigger and I finally wrote back and said, 'Well, if ever you see a show of mine near to a place where you live or where Ronnie Wycherley lives, tell him to come backstage and ask for me, and if I am there, I will see him and audition him on the spot.' That is exactly what happened."

One can only be grateful that nobody was murdered that night because undoubtedly the wrong man would have been hanged.

Compared to the murk surrounding the events leading up to the Essoldo audition, what happened on the night itself is relatively clear.

The *Larry Parnes Extravaganza* was billed to do two shows, one at 6.30 and another at 8.15, definitely on October 1, 1958 – which was also definitely a Wednesday. Billy took the train to Birkenhead with two of his mates, Brian Johnson and Les Tennant. They got to the theatre early, around one o'clock, because they didn't know what time the acts would start rehearsing. No one was around so they went to another cinema, then on to a café to kill some time.

Vince Eager took up the story in a 1988 interview for Radio Trent. "When we'd completed the sound check at the Birkenhead Essoldo, John Barry's drummer, Dougie White, and I decided to have a Wimpy hamburger.

"As we stepped out into the dampness of a very overcast Merseyside afternoon, a slightly built young man wearing a gabardine overcoat with the collar turned up and looking very much like a cross between Elvis and James Dean walked towards us and asked whether Mr Parnes was inside the theatre.

"We told him that he was and the young man went on to say that he had recorded some self-penned songs onto a tape and sent them to Larry, [*aha!*] but as he hadn't had a reply, he wanted to know whether he liked them.

"I went back into the theatre and Larry was in the dressing room, which Marty and I were sharing. I explained the situation to Larry and he asked me to fetch him in.

"On seeing the young man enter the dressing room Larry's face just lit up. He was immediately in awe of what he was looking at. Larry introduced himself and asked the guy his name. 'Ronald Wycherley', he replied.

"Larry told him that he didn't remember receiving any tape from him, but asked whether he could perform any of his songs on the spot if he found him a guitar."

Vince remembered that although Billy had brought a guitar with him, he actually borrowed another guitar – a Hofner Committee or possibly a Hofner President – from Marty Wilde's guitarist, Kenny Packman. "He [Ronnie] was very, very good looking. Very sensual. Obviously photogenic."

Ronnie checked the guitar's tuning, tried a few experimental chords, then kicked into his first number, 'Maybe Tomorrow'. "And the thing was in those days," continued Vince, "very few people, artistwise, wrote their own material. About 90% of it came from America, no British star who had written and recorded a record had had a hit."

After 'Maybe Tomorrow', he did 'Margo'. "Those of us inside were astounded by what we were hearing and seeing, and after a brief moment of disbelief we all broke into a round of applause."

Larry Parnes remembered it quite vividly but, once again, slightly differently. This is normal. Rock writer Pete Frame describes Larry as, "an accidental revisionist. He had no sense of chronology and little recollection of the way things actually happened."

"They had no stage door at the Essoldo," Larry said. "It was just a fire door with a tinny sound if you knocked it or rattled it. I happened to be walking through to the dressing room that Marty was in and I heard this door rattling. I said, 'Who is it?' and someone said in a Liverpool accent, 'We have come to see Larry Parnes. We have got Ronnie Wycherley with us.' I opened the door and this very shy, quiet young man came forward with an open-necked shirt, black trousers and an old guitar and I said, 'You lot can wait outside and you, Mr Wycherley, can come in.' I took him into Marty's dressing room and said, 'Come on, give us a song.'

"He played us a beautiful song that he had written, which became his first hit, 'Maybe Tomorrow', and 'Margo (Don't Go)' and another song that he hadn't written called 'Just Because'. We were on the ground floor and when he finished, the hundreds of girls outside of Marty's dressing room window started to scream and applaud."

"I just remember I was in my dressing room," says Marty Wilde, "and in came Larry with Billy (he wasn't called Billy then, he was Ronald Wycherley) and Larry said: 'This is Ronnie Wycherley – he's got some songs he wanted to play to you.' And so I said OK. He played the songs and my comment to Larry at that time was, 'I think they're great. I think there's certainly potentially a couple of hits there but he should record them himself because they're his songs and there's no point in me doing them.' I was quite protective of songwriters because I was a songwriter myself and I didn't want to see Billy cheated."

Then, in Larry's version of the story, Larry turned to Billy and said, "Have you got guts?"

"He said, 'Yes.' I said, 'How would you like to do a couple of songs for the opening of the second half of the show tonight?'

"I was getting ready and doing my own thing," said Marty, "but I think Larry pushed him on stage. Billy went down well obviously because otherwise Larry wouldn't have been interested. He went down really well with the audience."

In the 1933 film *42nd Street*, set in the glamorous and gritty backstage world of Broadway theatre, a leading lady sprains her ankle on the opening night of a big new musical show. Luckily a young chorus girl, Peggy Sawyer, played by Ruby Keeler, knows all the songs and dances after five weeks of rehearsal. The show's director decides she's the only chance he's got, takes her to one side and, in one of the most inspirational speeches in showbiz history, says, "You've got to go on, and you've got to give and give and give. They've got to like you. Got to. Do you understand? You can't fall down. You can't because your future's in it, my future and everything all of us have is staked on you. All right, now I'm through, but you keep your feet on the ground and your head on those shoulders of yours and go out, and Sawyer, you're going out a youngster but you've *got* to come back a star!"

It's pretty much exactly what happened to Billy – except without the inspirational speech. Or the five weeks of rehearsal.

Larry Parnes was up for a few experiments that night. He'd also agreed to try out another youngster, 18-year-old Jimmy Tarbuck, as compere. After a quick briefing about the change in the programme, Jimmy went out and made the announcement.

"Larry Parnes has given breaks to young people in his time and tonight he has invited a young local boy to entertain you."

"Billy was standing in the wings waiting to go on," said Jimmy, remembering the occasion years later. "The band struck up and played a few bars. But I could see Billy was about to change his mind – he always was a very nervous boy. But I was standing right behind him, and I knew there was only one thing to do. So I gave Billy a big push in the small of the back and that was it – he was on stage. And that was the start of Billy's stage career."

Ronnie, with his borrowed guitar, his knees trembling like the leaves on the trees, sang the three songs he'd auditioned – 'Maybe Tomorrow', 'Margo' and 'Just Because', a number from Elvis' first LP.

"Everyone must have thought who's this guy with the shaking knees," he said.

The *Liverpool Weekly News* splashed the story: "Two thousand screaming teenagers held up the programme at *Larry Parnes' Extravaganza* – which featured rock'n'roll idol Marty Wilde – last Wednesday when an 18-year-old Dingle boy, Ronnie Wycherley, of 35 Haliburton Street, completed a three-minute spot in the star-studded programme.

Ex-tugman Ronnie, with a little apprehension, took the stage at the Essoldo Theatre wearing a two-tone Texan jacket and a guitar slung over his shoulder. Ronnie nervously walked on to the stage, and swung straight into the first number with an Elvis Presley inspired style.

"His three minutes were constantly punctuated by screams and shouts from hundreds of teenage girls, which were intensified at the least move of his body.

"Larry Parnes – manager of Marty Wilde, Tommy Steele and other top-line entertainers – came from the theatre dressing rooms and sat on the end of the eighth row smiling broadly as he chewed his cigar, weighing up the possibilities.

"Afterwards in the dressing room, Ronnie sat on the corner in an armchair and told the *Weekly News*: 'I was nervous, but it's only natural.' He composes his own music and has written 25 rock'n'roll tunes within two years."

Later that evening, Larry pressed a five-pound note into Ronnie's hand and asked him to join the tour the following morning. Dazed, Ronnie got the train home to Haliburton Street.

His mother wasn't keen. What mother has ever wanted to see their boy sail away to a life of rock'n'roll. Dad, however, was more amenable to persuasion. "He was pleased to get rid of me," Ronnie said. "I'd been making a lot of noise around the house."

The arrangement was for Ronnie to rendezvous with the others at 10.00 the next morning outside the Lord Nelson Hotel in Liverpool, where the band bus would be waiting. Ronnie showed up early. There was no sign of the bus, or of Larry Parnes, Marty Wilde, Vince Eager or any of The John Barry Seven. He decided that the whole thing had been an elaborate and particularly cruel joke, and began the walk of shame back to Haliburton Street. Then – whaddya know – he discovered the bus waiting around the corner.

"And that was it," said Billy. "It was all so quick it almost wasn't true."

Jean said, "I never forgot that morning when Albert carried his suitcase down the stairs and we said goodbye to Ronnie Wycherley. Two months later Billy Fury walked through my door."

CHAPTER FOUR

"AND I SUDDENLY SAID, 'FURY!'"

Larry Parnes was the most influential man in British pop. He set the pattern that to some extent still endures for how a pop manager should speak, behave, dress and steal from his clients. Twenty-five years later he was the role model for the Sex Pistols' manager Malcolm McLaren, who even planned to put together a stable of punk acts, like Larry's stable of rock'n'roll stars.

"I don't know Larry Parnes," McLaren said, "but I must respect him... for sure! Very clever, what he did. In fact, he was British rock'n'roll for the first six or seven years."

Since Larry's job was to generate a mist of glamorous legend around his clients and around himself, few of the 'facts' about Larry's life, and particularly his early life, stand up to prolonged scrutiny, but the usual story goes something like...

...left school when he was 16, and went into the rag trade. By the time he was 18, he was running three ladies' dress shops in Romford, Essex. One of them, allegedly, even turned a profit.

His primary interest, though, was not ladies' frocks, but theatre. One night – the legend says – he got uncharacteristically drunk, in which state he was induced to invest £500 in a touring play called *House Of Shame*.

The play was not doing well. But its fortunes changed when either Larry or the show's publicist, a journalist named John Kennedy, changed its title to *Women Of The Streets* and hired a couple of young women to stand outside the theatre dressed as prostitutes.

When the play closed, Larry was delighted to have turned a 15s (75p) profit on his investment.

Sometime later, John Kennedy, the publicist, was hired to take pictures of a young singer named Tommy Hicks, who was appearing at the 2i's coffee bar in Old Compton Street. He observed that the singer's charm and energy, and the music he was playing, had a profound effect on the audience. Afterwards he accosted Tommy in the street outside and offered to manage him. After a brief exchange – Tommy: "What do you know about show business?" Kennedy: "Nothing, what do you know about singing?" – a deal was struck.

Kennedy changed Tommy Hicks' name to Tommy Steele, and set about turning him into a star, recruiting Larry Parnes, dress-shop owner and small-time theatrical impresario, to help with the money side of things. (Kennedy soon learned that asking Larry Parnes to 'help with the money side of things' was like asking Jerry the mouse to keep an eye on your cheese.)

Tommy Steele's first record, 'Rock With The Caveman', written by Tommy with Mike Pratt and Lionel Bart, who later wrote the musical *Oliver!*, went Top 10. His third record, 'Singing The Blues', a country song originally recorded by Marty Robbins, went to number one.

It was clear that the new(ish) rock'n'roll music engendered thrills like no other, and Larry, having established with Tommy that there was gold in them thar thrills, eased John Kennedy out of the picture and began to cast around for another promising youngster.

Lionel Bart, a Soho boho who slipped with suede-shod grace between the coffee bars, clip joints, spielers and ritzy niteries, spotted a chap called Reg Paterson singing in the Condor Club on Wardour Street. The youth had undoubted talent and dimples to die for, and was clearly infected with rock'n'roll fever. Lionel reported his findings to Larry who, by this time, had learned to trust Lionel's judgement. The following morning, a Sunday, Larry drove his pink and grey Vauxhall Cresta out to Greenwich, where, he had established from the Condor's management, Reg Paterson lived with his parents.

Reg was out. At church.

"It was one of the most incredible things," Reg says. "I used to go to church. Mostly it was a social thing. I was never religious at all, but it was a great way of meeting girls. So, I came home on the bus and came in the door and my father said, 'There's been a man. He knocked at the door and he wants to sign you up.' And I said, 'Who's that?' and he said 'Well, he said he's a man called Larry Parnes.' I said 'Larry Parnes came to our house?' I knew he was Tommy Steele's manager. He was famous. 'He said somebody had seen you at the Condor Club and he's come round with a contract.' I said, 'You're joking!' And he came back again that evening with the contract. One day in your life – a total change."

The name was the first thing to change. Tommy Hicks had hit the Top 10 as Tommy Steele, so, argued Larry, it was clear that a name change was an essential part of turning a nobody into a somebody. All of Larry Parnes' subsequent 'stable' of rock stars, on joining up, were first stripped of their civilian identities and then issued with a new name. Usually this consisted of an out-of-the-ordinary, maybe American-sounding first name and a second name that indicated some dubious personality trait or other: Vince Eager, Duffy Power, Dickie Pride. Only one stablemate put up so much resistance to the re-christening process that, rather than adopting Larry's suggested Elmer Twitch, he was allowed to remain plain Joe Brown.

Reg had already changed his name from Reg Smith to Reg Paterson for the sake of his art and saw no reason to take the process any further. However…

"Larry said, 'I want to call you Marty. I've just seen a film called Marty and it's a very popular film and the character in it reminds me of you. He's quite shy at times.' And I thought it was a horrible American name, so I said, 'I want to keep Reg,' so he said, 'We'll toss a coin.' Fair enough, 'cos he was a gambler and I was a gambler to a certain extent, but he was a big gambler. So he said, 'All right, toss a coin.' And he won. So then he said, 'Now for the surname. I see you as someone wild. You've got a bit of a wild nature. A wild streak in you.' I said, 'Oh no, Marty's bad enough, but not 'Wild'.' And he said, 'Yes, I can see it. Toss a coin again.' I lost. And it wasn't until about three weeks later when I actually saw my name in print I thought, 'Wow, he actually got something right.'"

Marty Wilde got on the telly, too, and between July 1958 and December 1959 scored five Top 10 hits and was never out of the Top 40.

After the Essoldo, Birkenhead, the next stop for the *Larry Parnes'*
Extravaganza, now featuring the newly discovered Ron Wycherley, was
the Essoldo, Stretford. Ron ran through his songs and proved the screams
weren't just a lucky one-off.

The next day they travelled to London. For some reason, and
uncharacteristically profligate for Larry Parnes, they flew. It was Ron's
first time in an aeroplane. He was sick all the way.

Most of the rest of Larry's stable were from London or thereabouts. If
the gig was within shouting distance, or if they were needed in London
for recording or TV, they stayed at home, usually with their parents. The
two out-of-towners, Vince Eager and Ron, were expected to lodge with
Larry, at his flat on the Gloucester Road in South Kensington, just
around the corner from the Albert Hall and Kensington Palace Gardens.
Ron was given the bedroom next to Larry's. Vince's room was at the end
of the corridor.

The flat was a far, far cry from Haliburton Street. The lounge – not
'parlour' – had classical pillars, gilt chairs covered in silk and a massive
marble-topped table. The master bedroom was a riot of fluffy pink, with
lambskin rugs, lacy lampshades and a kidney-shaped dressing table.

On the dressing table was a gilt-framed photo of the crooner Johnny
Ray, "the nabob of sob", whose sexuality, like that of Liberace and Noël
Coward – and Larry Parnes – though an open book to the showbiz and
gay communities, was still a closely guarded secret for publicity and legal
purposes. Homosexuality wasn't decriminalised until 1967.

Larry was making a career out of finding good looking young men,
dressing them, posing them and 'grooming' them – the word was used
then without the present-day connotations – for stardom. In other words,
he lived in the sweet shop. To have expected restraint would have been
like telling Hugh Hefner of the Playboy Mansion that he could look but
never touch.

Muriel Walker, Larry's secretary, took responsibility for the day-to-day
running of the Parnes empire and the well-being of the lads.

"There was always a troupe of boys in and out of Larry's flat, of
course, but not the singers, not the acts. He always separated business
from pleasure – road managers, perhaps, hangers on and helpers, but not
the acts."

Vince Eager remembers it differently. "He fancied all of us plus loads
of matelots and marine boys down Piccadilly every night."

Most of the lads, in those days, had but a sketchy knowledge of human sexuality in all its rich and nuanced diversity. Not long after Vince Eager had joined the stable, Kenny Packwood, Marty's guitarist, took him to one side and brought him up to speed on one or two things he should understand about Larry.

In the BBC *Omnibus* programme, *Halfway To Paradise*, Brian Gregg, the bass player (The Beat Boys, Johnny Kidd & The Pirates, The Tornados), told of how he gave Billy a similar word to the wise. "First time I saw Billy, he was standing with Larry Parnes in the 2i's, where rock'n'roll started in this country. And I said, 'Where are you staying?' And he said, 'Well, I'm staying with Larry.' So, I suggested he didn't because he'd get himself a bad name. He said, 'But I've only just moved here.' So, I said, 'Well, you can stay at my place.' And he gave *me* a funny look then. 'With my girlfriend,' I said."

In those days of cramped housing and Abbot & Costello, it was not considered unusual or compromising for two grown men to share a bed, so Larry's showing Vince, when he first arrived, the pink master bedroom and indicating which side of the bed was his could not in itself have been considered particularly significant. All the same, Vince was suspicious.

"I spent an hour and a half in the en suite bathroom," Vince told Sue McGregor in BBC Radio 4's *The Reunion*, "and after brushing my teeth I got into the bed and what I did was very crafty for one so young. I actually got in between the top sheet and the duvet as opposed to getting in between the two sheets and I was lying there and I was scared stiff. I was shaking. And I felt this hand come across and of course it couldn't get any further because of the two sheets. And he said, 'Oh you've got the... er...' And I said, 'No, I always sleep like this.' And I grabbed one of these lacy pink bedside table lamps and I just put my hand on it. I just went like this so that he could see it. And he turned over and went to sleep. I didn't sleep all night but he did. And why he called me 'Eager' I don't know 'cos I certainly wasn't that night."

Not long into his membership of Larry's team, young Ron Wycherley gleaned closer insight into the boss's lifestyle when he observed the behaviour of his stablemates as they checked into the Midland Hotel, Manchester. The other lads had seen the way Larry looked at Ronnie and began to wonder.

"Marty and I were sharing a room," Vince Eager told the crew of the documentary *His Wondrous Story*. "Larry was either on his own or sharing with a 'friend' and there was Chris Reynolds, the PR guy, with us as well.

"So we went to bed [...] and we decided because of our experiences with Larry to have a bit of fun. So, Marty made out he was Billy and I made out I was Larry and I chased him round the bedroom. And we were bouncing from bed to bed, and I picked up a bedside table light, because that's what I'd used to defend myself against Larry about six months earlier, and threw it down and we had this great fun chasing round the bedroom.

"Then we just crashed out and went to bed and that was it."

At breakfast the following morning, Larry was livid.

"I overheard you and Marty belittling me and pulling me to pieces and I object to that. So, for that reason I'm selling Marty's contract because I've been offered £80,000 for it. And as for you, you are finished in the business. What do you say to that?"

Parnes later relented. Marty wasn't sold and Vince Eager stayed with the stable for another couple of years.

Ron's name, of course, like all the others, had to go.

In Liverpool, Ronnie had toyed with and sometimes used the name "Stean Wade".

"That came from the days when I liked country and western music," Ronnie said. "Anyway, I had an interview with the *Daily Mirror*. So, before going to see them, Larry was going to give me a little chat on what to expect, what kinds of questions they'd ask – which really did help. Then he said, 'What do you think about having a stage name?' And I said 'Well, I'd feel fine about it – I'd like to change it, anyway.' And he said, 'What do you think about Billy Fury?'"

Larry's thinking went like this: "He was a very shy, modest person – always was, right through his career. He loved animals... would do anything for animals... loved the country life... didn't like nightclubbing or anything like that. He was very modest... a lovely person. And I said to him, 'You've got to have an ordinary, friendly name – look at Billy Cotton, and his 'Wakey Wakey' show... what a friendly man!"

Billy Cotton was the portly leader of a dance band, then in his late fifties. His show, *The Billy Cotton Band Show*, appeared on radio and eventually television for nearly 20 years, usually on a Sunday. Its unrelenting uptempo gaiety, its novelty songs ('I've Got A Lovely Bunch Of Coconuts' and 'What A Referee!', 'Cos His Little Wooden Whistle Wouldn't Whistle' were popular choices) and Cotton's opening "Wakey Waaaaa-khay", cited by Mr Parnes, had brought many to the edge of despair.

"'Billy', 'Billy', that's it, 'Billy'," Parnes said. "And now, you're going to be a symbol, one day, you're going to be really tops in this country, no question about it. We want a name that drives everything home, to everybody, before they even get to see you.' And I suddenly said, 'Fury!'"

Ronnie had nothing against 'Billy' – he had an Uncle Billy, the twin of his Uncle Ronnie, so it was only fair to give both a crack of the whip – but he wasn't comfortable with 'Fury'. On balance he preferred to stick with 'Stean Wade'.

"So, we tossed a coin on it. I actually won the toss and I thought that the next day there was going to be a picture of me in the *Daily Mirror* and it was going to say 'Stean Wade'. The next day, there was a bang-bang-bang on the door, and I opened it, and one of my friends was there with a copy of the *Daily Mirror*, and there they had 'Billy Fury'."

The press had taken to calling Larry "Mr Parnes, Shillings and Pence". The cap fitted. He offered his artistes a choice of contract: they could either take a straight percentage, 60% to them, 40% to Mr Parnes – his management fee – or they could take a wage. Billy took the wage, probably around £25 a week, which to a teenager earning less than half that working in a shop or factory probably must have felt like winning the pools. At the time, a clerical officer in the Civil Service was only on £15 a week.

Marty Wilde, a smarter cookie, took a percentage. "I think if Larry had offered me wages, I wouldn't have taken that. But some of the other artists accepted a different format with Larry and were on wages. There is no way I would do that. I wasn't overconfident, but I knew my worth."

Vince Eager realised early on that when it came to finances Larry Parnes did not play with a straight bat. In 1959, he vented his spleen to the press, saying he wanted to tear up his contract. "I am fed up with being bled white. Sometimes, if I do a concert for which the fee is £50, I count myself lucky if I collect a couple of quid from it. The simple fact is I don't see 49% of my salary. It goes to Larry Parnes. And on top of that I have to pay my own travelling expenses and pay the group that supports me." He said he ended up with about £40 a week.

Larry fired back: "This boy is uncooperative and ungrateful. Before he signed with me he was making £1 10s a night with a singing group. During the last 14 weeks his earnings have been £48 a week. Is that daylight robbery? I ask you? The boy's ingratitude appalls me. I have figures showing that he earned a gross total of £1,194 6s 6d between March and July. Out of that he got £828 19s 6d – so I didn't even take the 40% I'm entitled to. He hasn't a chance of getting out of his contract with me, anyway. It has three and a half years to run – and it's rock solid."

Keeping Billy on the £25 a week meant that Larry Parnes' share of the take was a good bit more than 40%. It's hard to estimate how much more but as a guide it's worth mentioning that by the end of 1960, Adam Faith, a rival star, with different management and clearly a better deal, was estimated to be taking home about £1,000 a week.

Vince Eager reckons that the deal sometimes left him and Billy too skint to eat. A local Italian restaurant would now and then take pity on them and let them have a free plate of spaghetti.

Otherwise they just stole from the boss.

"I took it in turns with Billy to crawl into Larry's bedroom at night. He'd be in bed with some matelot or whatever and we'd sneak in on the carpet with the sheepskin rug and we'd take pound notes 'cos we wanted to go out and we didn't have any money. It was bad enough taking the money but we also took his car keys and the trouble with it was the gear change was on the steering wheel and I couldn't find reverse, so everywhere we went we had to make sure we parked so we didn't have to reverse out."

Over the years Larry made a sizeable fortune out of Billy and Billy sneaked a few quid out of Larry's trouser pockets, but, to the end, there was never a falling out between them. Even when historic tax issues – all the fault of Mr Parnes – drove Billy to bankruptcy in the seventies, there was no real resentment. Billy remained grateful to his mentor until his dying day.

"Larry Parnes was an excellent manager for the time," Billy said, looking back in 1981. "As for money, I got everything I should have got. I paid a big percentage, but I knew what I was getting. He was very, very capable. He really did work hard."

The "excellent manager" got to work straight away. Less than a month after the contracts had been signed, he'd secured Billy his first appearance on telly, not in a pop show, but a play.

John Moxey, a director working for ATV, phoned Larry looking for a wild-looking youth. Ted Willis – the official *Guinness Book Of Records* 'Most Prolific TV Writer In The World Ever' – had written a play for the *Television Playhouse* slot, called *Strictly For The Sparrows*, a gritty piece about Teddy Boys loitering in coffee bars looking for kicks and extra froth. Moxey wanted a wild and crazy youth to sit in the back of shot strumming a guitar. Larry said he knew just the chap.

Moxey was so impressed with Billy that he promoted him from 'youth sitting at the back strumming' to 'youth sitting in the front strumming and singing'. Billy sang his own composition, 'Maybe Tomorrow'. The play went out – live – at 9 p.m. on Friday October 31, 1958, straight after top-rated sitcom *The Army Game* and with only the *Nine O'clock News* for competition on the BBC.

He had the name, he'd done a telly, now he needed a record.

Larry approached Philips, Marty Wilde's label, to try and stitch up a deal. Billy, by his own account, "failed the recording test", so they ended up with Dick Rowe, with whom previous contact may or may not have been made, at Decca.

In November 1958, Billy went into Decca Studios at Broadhurst Gardens in West Hampstead, London and made his first proper record. Larry persuaded Frank Lee, the distinguished artists' manager at Decca, to let Billy record his own compositions. Harry Robinson was hired as musical supervisor.

Harry was the leader of Lord Rockingham's XI, the house band on TV's top rock'n'roll show *Oh Boy!* with a line-up consisting mostly of jazz musicians slumming it to pay the rent. Benny Green, as well as playing baritone sax with the band, was turning in a regular *New Musical Express* column, sometimes taking the piss out of the very rock'n'rollers who come Saturday he'd be backing, albeit heavily disguised in dark glasses.

Lord Rockingham's XI's first record, 'Hoots Mon!', was a novelty instrumental based on the 19th-century Scottish song 'A Hundred Pipers', with a tag line, hollered in a broad Scots brogue, "Hoots Mon, there's a moose, loose, aboot this hoose".

For a month or so, the holler could be heard in every playground and works canteen in the country. Later, the band was commanded by Her Majesty to appear at the 1959 Royal Variety Show, so it's likely that, for a time, "Hoots Mon, there's a moose, loose, aboot this hoose" became the customary greeting used by Prince Philip in the corridors of Windsor Castle when he encountered the Queen.

For Billy's session, Harry assembled a stripped down version of the XI, as well as The Vernons Girls, the posse of singers recruited – it's a long story – from the offices of Vernon's Football Pools, to do backing vocals. Perhaps as a rather belated attempt to cash in on Billy's *Strictly For The Sparrows* appearance, the song chosen was 'Maybe Tomorrow'.

Like most early British rock'n'roll, the record, and Billy's performance, is drenched in Elvis. The song itself is a triplets piano smoocher, and the performance is pretty much channelling the young Elvis as he stood there on his first day at Sun Studio in Memphis whining 'My Happiness' for his mamma.

Musically, it's four-chord minimalist.

"'Maybe Tomorrow' is C major, A minor, F major and G major," Billy said, "and that's all there is to it."

The lyric bemoans how the singer rises in the morning to discover that his true love is nowhere to be found, even after a thorough search, and is up to if not above… . the standard required in an age when Paul Anka's 'Diana' (the first line of which – "I'm so young and you're so old" – would surely have brought the relationship to an acrimonious ending) had spent nine weeks at number one.

Eric Ford, the guitarist on the session, said he nicked the arpeggio figure that he used for the verse from 'Looking Back', a hit for Nat 'King' Cole earlier in the year, but it could have come from a dozen other sources. The guitar is teamed with piano, bass and subtle brushes on snare drum. A soprano sax player, most likely Benny Green, who usually played baritone with the band but had learned first on the smaller instrument, adds some very un-rock'n'roll but apt melodic phrases, and The Vernons Girls call in their harmonies from distant mountains. It's a little bit disturbed, but delightfully so. And it proved conclusively, to anyone who cared to listen, that the new boy was as authoritative on record as he was on stage.

The B-side was another of Billy's compositions (although in the event the credit was shared with Harry), 'Gonna Type A Letter', a floor-filler. They didn't quite nail the song at the first session, so they all came back the following month for another go. This time Harry added a real typewriter to the instrumentation and beefed up the sound with a sax section, giving them licence to indulge in rock'n'roll stutters as insistent as asylum laughter. It's not perhaps the authentic rock'n'roll that Billy wanted to make, but neither is it some throwaway piece of cynical junk to catch a market trend. Harry cared.

Afterwards, Billy sent his parents a telegram – they didn't have a phone: "HAVE PASSED RECORDING TEST. DECCA. HAVE FIVE YEAR CONTRACT. BILLY."

"Who's Billy?"

"He's your eldest son."

"I thought his name was Ronnie."

"Try to keep up, Albert."

CHAPTER FIVE

"THERE WAS A THEATRE IN EVERY TOWN. WE USED TO PLAY THEM ALL."

The single was released on January 19, 1959. The publicity stills show Billy dressed as a singing cowboy – satin western shirt with bandana.

It was a slow starter, not hitting the singles chart until the end of February. It yo-yoed up and down the Top 40 for a few weeks, finally peaking at a healthy number 18, one place above Lonnie Donegan's 'Does Your Chewing Gum Lose Its Flavour (On The Bedpost Overnight?)', and three places below Pearl Carr & Teddy Johnson's 'Sing, Little Birdie' (semi-finalist in that year's Eurovision Song Contest). Marty Wilde was at number 10 and Buddy Holly at number three. Number one was 'Side Saddle', a jaunty pub-piano solo by Russ Conway, who regularly guested on the *Billy Cotton Band Show*. They were strange times.

Larry tried to drum up airplay by sending a copy of the record to Bill Worsley, a BBC Radio Light Entertainment producer, with an accompanying letter saying that Billy had, "commenced his professional career only at the beginning of this year, but already this first record is appearing in the 'Best Sellers' and he has appeared several times on television. Next month, he commences his first concert tour of the country.

"This song, 'Maybe Tomorrow', was composed by himself and he will also be composing the theme music for Marty Wilde's film, *Jet Stream*. I should be interested to learn your views on this artist."

The reply, if there was one, doesn't seem to have survived.

The Marty Wilde film Larry referred to, eventually retitled *Jet Storm*, was released later in 1959. It starred, along with Marty, Richard Attenborough, Stanley Baker and Hermione Baddeley. The theme music was composed not by Billy but by Thomas Rajna.

In the same month that Billy's single entered the Top 40, Larry was featured in an episode of the BBC documentary series *Panorama*, made, it appears, in response to a generalised moral panic about teenage hi-jinks. Billy sits on a sofa between Johnny Gentle and Vince Eager. Duffy Power sits behind them. There's a framed photograph of Tommy Steele on the window ledge.

The interviewer was Christopher Chataway. Five years earlier, Chataway had acted as a pacemaker to Roger Banister when Banister ran the first sub-four-minute mile. Later in the same year, Chataway broke the world 5,000 metres record. Later still he became a Conservative MP, a front bench minister in the Heath government and did immense and important work for the charity ActionAid: a paragon of good-chappishness.

"Do you feel that the teenagers that you entertain," he asks Duffy Power, "do you have a good effect on them or a bad effect?"

"It all depends on the teenager," says the eminently sensible Duffy.

"But when they get hysterical and shout and scream and so on, what do you think about that?"

"I love it."

"Don't you ever feel," Chataway asks the assembled lads, convinced there's something fishy going on here and he's not leaving until he's got to the bottom of it, "that you are being manipulated just like a puppet sometimes?"

"No, I think it's up to you," Billy says. "The performance you do, it's all your own... it's all your own work what you do on the stage."

"It all amounts to having faith in your manipulators," says Vince.

But here Chataway clearly finds himself dealing with an elemental mismatch of understanding. He was nine years older than Billy and speaks to him, speaks to all the stablemates, like a disappointed probation officer. His attitude is that of decent folk everywhere, much bruited in the press: a knee-jerk, non-specific disapproval of these young, ill-educated, working-class lads, and a suspicion that their Svengali, the mastermind Larry Parnes, had taught them some sort of diabolical trickery, a form of hypnosis (voodoo rhythm probably had something to do with it) that made young women – some of them by all accounts perfectly decent girls; not quite the sort you'd meet at the tennis club, but certainly not prostitutes – simulate, or perhaps even experience, a sort of sexual ecstasy.

And if the 'voodoo' hypothesis didn't hold water, then the only other explanation for what was going on with this 'music' these 'young men' and these 'young women' were thrilled by was that the whole world was going to hell in a handcart.

It was a view widely shared.

The list of complaints usually started with general thoughts about juvenile delinquency, then went on to mention the pop stars' abject lack of skill, training or talent, never forgetting to mention that some of them were rumoured to earn more than the prime minister.

The juvenile delinquency charge was understandable. As we've seen in the Billy vs the Scuffers piece published in the *People*, Mr Parnes wasn't averse to putting it about that his lads had had a tearaway past. It was good for the image. A tearaway present, though, was a slightly different matter.

Earlier that year, Terry Dene, with three Top 20 hits under his belt, had been arrested for smashing a shop window and vandalising a phone box in a drunken frenzy exacerbated by woman trouble. The press had a high old time, the subtext of their headlines being that, "Rock'n'Roll Leads To This Sort Of Thing".

"The case of Terry Dene puts a question over the whole of this rowdy world of new music," said the *Daily Express*, "and over these new 'stars' who within weeks can take over the dressing rooms of the top variety stars."

"It's not the fault of kids like Terry Dene," said old Etonian jazz trumpeter Humphrey Lyttelton. "Someone gets hold of them and exploits them, they boost a hysterical following and the kids they plug haven't the faintest idea what's hit them.

"A kid under 20 with no training and no background can't take it. There is a very unhealthy streak in show business at the moment and one can't just pin it on unscrupulous agents. I think the record companies have been very much at fault. Ever since Presley came up in the States they have scrambled without worrying about talent to find British kids to sing his songs."

"Sheer amateurism is bringing the entire music business down to rock bottom level," said bandleader Cyril Stapleton. "The record makers turn round in the pub and say, 'We've just made a ruddy awful record, but it'll make a fortune.' It seems a fearful standard to set. But the cash comes rolling in."

Mr Parnes worked his acts hard.

"There was a theatre in every town in those days, let alone in every city," Billy said. "We used to play them all."

This was long before the days of luxury tour buses, private jets, celebrity chefs and colour-coordinated M&Ms in the dressing rooms.

There were no motorways. Hospitality, now considered a noble profession, was then an imposition. There were odd spots of sunshine, but for every landlady who, on hearing that the lads were hungry after a seven-hour drive through snow, would rustle up something warming, there were a thousand who only went into the business for the pleasure of watching young people starve, who put up signs saying, "Patrons are requested to disinfect the porcelain fittings after usage" and who would hurl you out into a stormy night for having the gall to turn on your transistor radio.

Cafés closed at six. Pretty much anywhere outside the more chichi neighbourhoods of London spaghetti outside a tin was a novelty item, olive oil was best obtained from the chemist, where it was sold for the treatment of ear-wax, and if you enquired about the availability of, say, an avocado, word would get round and villagers would assemble with flaming torches.

The laws that controlled pub licensing hours could have been established at the Synod of Whitby in AD 664. In one borough they would close at 10.30: across the street in the next borough, 11.00. On market days they'd open at five in the morning, then close at three in the afternoon, and in the Welsh valleys, if, on a Sunday, you asked a passer-by where you could get a half pint of shandy, in a voice of thunder would come the reply, "England".

Trains ran, but for the rock'n'rollers a coach was the more usual mode of transport. The stars, the ones who had passed their driving tests and scraped enough together to buy and insure a car, usually drove themselves from gig to gig, and those who hadn't yet passed their tests, like Billy, would cadge a lift from one of the more seasoned pros, like Marty.

Larry sent Billy off on his first nationwide tour in March 1959 while 'Maybe Tomorrow' was still hot in the singles chart. The tour kicked off at the Regal, Worksop, on the 15th, then went on to the Ritz, Matlock, the Pavilion, Scunthorpe, the Palace, Newark, the Plaza, Wombwell, the Palace, Burnley, the Crescent, Pontefract, and the Empire, Mexborough.

The Palace (or Palace-Hippodrome) in Burnley was an elegant and huge (capacity 2,000-plus) palace of varieties, built in 1907, with 12 dressing rooms and a circle bar.

On the other side of the coin, the Empire, Mexborough, looks as if it was built as temporary storage for some shovels. It was the dog-end of music hall, which had come to be called 'variety'. The rock'n'rollers' tours would often as not be booked for regular variety shows, with three or four of the new heartthrobs bundled onto a bill with a comic, a straight crooner or torch singer and maybe a juggler or ventriloquist.

As Billy said: "There were so many people on those shows that you didn't get much time. Everything was compressed into 30 minutes. But from beginning to end [your own segment] was a real rock'n'roll show, with the current ballad stuck in the middle. And 'Thank you very much, goodnight.'

"But I didn't like talking much in those days anyway."

Like the press, the jazzers and anybody who valued common decency, the old variety die-hards resented the newcomers. You can't blame them. You've been 25 years in the business, you've paid a fortune for your band parts, your shoes are by Anello & Davide, your suit's cut by Anthony Sinclair and your hair's crafted by Wig Creations. Along comes an adenoidal nobody: three months ago he was working in a shop, he can't tap-dance, doesn't know his stage left from his fly loft and he gets top billing. Where's the justice?

The comics were occasionally snarky, but it didn't matter because the audience, waiting to see Billy, Marty, Vince or Cliff, wasn't listening.

On this first tour, Billy was third on the bill, after the comic/compere Bobby 'That Crazy Ball of Energy' Dennis and before Jill Day, a glamorous actress and singer from TV's *The Jill Day Show*, who closed the first half.

The Wiseguys, a piano/bass/guitar trio who did spiced-up versions of 'Baby Face' and 'I Can't Give You Anything But Love', opened the second half. They were followed by Vince Taylor, another "crazy ball of energy" but in a more literal, more worrying, more sinister sense.

Vince Taylor eventually became a kind of legend. He was a proper rocker, from Los Angeles, California (in fact he was born in Isleworth, Middlesex, but the family relocated to the USA when he was a kid). He became enamoured of rock'n'roll, returned to the UK, and scored himself a record deal with Parlophone.

In 1959, he wrote and recorded 'Brand New Cadillac', the song which, after a good while, emerged as a 'cult classic' covered by, among many others, The Clash, The Fall and Van Morrison. When work dried up in the UK, Vince relocated to France, where *les Yé-Yé* girls and *les blousons-noirs* took him to their *coeurs*.

By the early seventies, drugs and mental illness had taken their toll on Vince so that sometimes he believed he was a god and sometimes a being from another planet.

"I met him a few times in the mid-sixties and I went to a few parties with him," David Bowie told Alan Yentob. "He was out of his gourd. Totally flipped. The guy was not playing with a full deck at all. He used to carry maps of Europe around with him, and I remember him opening a map outside Charing Cross tube station, putting it on the pavement and kneeling down with a magnifying glass. He pointed out all the sites where UFOs were going to land."

Vince Taylor became one of the inspirations for Bowie's Ziggy Stardust, and as such he made his mark on history rather more effectively than he did by performing on the same bill as The Wiseguys and Billy Fury at the Wombwell Plaza in March 1959.

On March 23, after the Mexborough show, Billy seems to have joined another tour at the City Hall, Manchester, this one featuring The Mudlarks (a brothers and sister singing group from Luton made up of Jeff Mudd, Mary Mudd and Fred Mudd), Don Lang (the frantic speed-singer from TV's *Six-Five Special*) and, topping the bill, Diana Dors.

And thereby hangs a tale, or at least an inadequately substantiated rumour.

Diana Dors was a pneumatic actress, born Diana Fluck, the name changed, at her mother's insistence, because one day it would be in lights and a letter might fall off. She was hailed at various times as Britain's answer to Marilyn Monroe, Britain's answer to Jayne Mansfield and Britain's answer to the atomic bomb. Essentially, she was every man's ideal barmaid: blonde, buxom and pally. She once posed on a gondola in Venice wearing a mink bikini – the gondolier thought it was mink anyway, and the press said it was mink, although later it turned out to have been rabbit fur.

She had a stormy marriage with her publicist, Dennis Hamilton. They went to America, where Dennis's alcoholism and general unpleasantness – undoubtedly exacerbated by Diana's fairly public affair with Victor Mature's stunt man – effectively sabotaged a potential Hollywood career. In 1958, back in England, they separated, after which Diana found herself rather less well off than she'd imagined. Dennis had been helping himself.

Then a few months later, in January 1959, the ravages of alcohol and general dissolution brought Dennis to an early death, and Diana found herself taking responsibility for his dog, Crackers. Which is where Billy Fury first enters the story.

Diana's London flat was in Kensington, not far from where Billy was staying with Larry Parnes. She used to take Crackers for walks in Hyde Park, where Billy used to walk Larry's dog (Larry loved animals and kept the ashes of two of his Alsatians, Prince and Duke, in pride of place on his mantelpiece until the day he died).

In very much the same way, one imagines, as when Roger and Pongo meet Anita and Perdita in *101 Dalmatians*, Billy and Larry's dog got chatting to Diana and Crackers. As twilight fell, they found a sheltered spot and...

And the upshot was that Billy eventually adopted Crackers.

The story has its flaws.

Dennis died in January 1959 and Billy, according to a report in the *Daily Mirror*, took possession of Crackers in mid-February 1959. Outdoor frolics can be fun in summer but, even if the underwear is mink, only the fiercest ardour can sustain winter drizzle.

And, anyway, the *Mirror* report suggests that Diana never had much to do with Crackers. After taking possession of the mutt, she handed it over to a friend, who handed it over to Perrin Lewis, an 18-year-old dancer, who tried to hand it over to Billy.

Billy told the *Mirror*: "I'd love the dog, but I share the flat with my manager, Larry Parnes, and it's up to him to decide."

Larry said: "It's not up to me – it's up to my charwoman. I've had her for five years and I don't want her driven out of the house by a boisterous dog."

If there was any romantic strand to the story, the love-interest was almost certainly not between Billy and Diana Dors but Billy and Perrin Lewis, the dancer. She worked at the Windmill, the nude *Revuedeville* in Soho.

"Everybody was in love with my friend Perrin," said fellow-dancer Polly Perkins. "Tommy Steele wanted to marry her, so did Billy Fury. She was beautiful; the girls from the Windmill entered her into a Brigitte Bardot lookalike contest. They were like that, the girls."

When Crackers proved far too boisterous for Larry's charwoman to tolerate, he was sent off to Liverpool and stayed with Billy's parents.

Perrin Lewis ended up marrying neither Tommy Steele nor Billy Fury, but poor, mad Vince Taylor, the man who inspired David Bowie to jam good with Weird and Gilly and the Spiders from Mars.

CHAPTER SIX

"SERIOUS HAIRCUT; COLLAR UP AT THE BACK; HANDS IN THE GUNSLINGER POSITION..."

"It's a three-way thing," said Frank, a Billy Fury fan now in his seventies. "It's not just talent that makes a star, it's the fans responding to that talent. And both the fans and the star are made by the times they live in. If Bing Crosby was alive today, he wouldn't be as much of a star as he was in the forties because the times have changed. He'd still have the same talent – he'd still be as good a singer – but even if he could adapt his voice to suit modern music, the times are different, the fans are different, they want different things. The star, the fans, the times – the three are inseparable, really."

There was never any such thing as a 'typical' Billy Fury fan, but one or two vague generalisations can perhaps be made.

Boys on the whole weren't allowed to be 'fans'. Not then, anyway. They could dig the music, they could copy the clothes, the facial expressions and the poses, but they didn't mob for autographs or get dreamy over pictures in *Valentine*, and they certainly didn't scream.

Even some of the stars were iffy about the screaming. "I didn't get it," said Joe Brown. "I thought why don't they shut up and listen? I never understood it until one day I was late and had to come in through the front. Billy had to go on instead of me and close the first half. I'd never felt such an electric atmosphere in the theatre. 'Cos I'd never seen him from the front – the only time I'd seen him was when I was playing for him or from the side, waiting to go on."

Sam Hardie, the pianist with Kingsize Taylor & The Dominoes, told Spencer Leigh, "I remember seeing Billy Fury at the Liverpool Empire. I thought he was dreadful. He was caressing the microphone and I was embarrassed about it. I suppose by booing him I was showing off in front of my girlfriend, but a lot of others were booing him."

Often the boys just got plain jealous.

"While Billy was strutting, giving the chicks their big thrill for the night," said Joe Brown, "the blokes were sitting there simmering and swearing and threatening to kill him. It made me glad my act was about rock'n'roll and not sex.

"Being a sex symbol could cause problems. Some bird takes a Teddy Boy with a lethal quiff to see Billy Fury. He might want to wait outside the stage door to get Billy. He had a terrible time at the Glasgow Empire. They were throwing whisky bottles, anything they could find at Billy".

So the fans, in the early days at least, were girls, mostly a bit younger than Billy, born perhaps between 1943 and '48.

That desperation in the 10 years after the war to get things back to 'normal' had a strange effect on the lives of those young women. 'Normal', it was assumed, meant they all wanted the same thing – a husband, children and a nice house to clean.

Their needs were overlooked, their ambitions denied, their importance discounted. In surveys, a woman's socio-economic class was judged not by what she did but by what her father or husband did. As late as the seventies, a woman applying for a mortgage would often as not be required to have the application counter-signed by a male relative.

All descriptions of social and political trends referred only to the male of the species. When the press talked about 'juvenile delinquents', the examples were boys. When existentialists talked of 'alienation', it was always men who were 'alienated'. If women showed the same symptoms it was put down to PMT.

When rebels without a cause eventually identified the cause against which they were rebelling, usually it was the stifling conformity that girls were trying to impose on them. In John Osborne's landmark play *Look Back In Anger*, thought by many to be era-defining, Jimmy Porter, the angry-young-man protagonist, gets angry mostly because his wife is ironing his shirts.

Girls' schooling was rubbish. It was still widely believed that educating a woman was a waste of time and money, so the girls' syllabus often featured plenty of 'home craft' because, as one government report put it: "The main weight of the shopping, the cooking, the making and mending, the furnishing, the minor household repairs, the fuelling and heating and even the gardening and poultry keeping, above all, the budgeting and catering, is likely to fall on the housewife."

Lots of cookery classes and needlework, then, not forgetting that "the prospect of courtship and marriage should rightly influence the education of the adolescent girl. Though the general objectives of secondary education remain unchanged, her direct interest in dress, personal appearance and in problems of human relations should be given a central place in her education."

Or as *Valentine*, the 'love comic', put it, "No normal woman can fail to experience the thrill of triumph when the eyes of all the men are fastened intently on her as she enters the room."

In 1959, 271,778 girls left school. Just 3,310 of them went on to university. That's roughly 1%. A 'career' for a girl meant something to fill in the time between school and getting married – maybe a couple of years, and if it was more than six or seven you should start to worry.

"Quite a lot of girls back then dreamed of being air hostesses," wrote Lorna Sage. "Being an air hostess hadn't yet been revealed as waitressing-in-the-sky but was somehow connected with team spirit, patriotism and the WAAF officers who mourned the pilot heroes as they pushed mimic planes about the headquarters bunkers in war films. In peacetime, there was more chance of marrying a pilot; or a first-class passenger might at any moment intuit from the way you poured his coffee that you had a sterling spirit and poise to play his helpmate on solid ground somewhere in Surrey."

The very first frame of the very first strip of the very first issue of the teen magazine *Jackie* pictured an air hostess saying, "Four proposals in a week isn't bad going, huh? One in San Francisco, one in New York, one in Bermuda, one in Monte Carlo and who knows what's in store for me in London?"

Failing air hostess, anything that gave a woman the opportunity to have "the eyes of all the men fastened intently on her as she enters the room" would do: model (obviously), nurse (doctors), secretary (boss), teacher (male teachers, young but tragically widowed fathers), hotel receptionist (rich clients), vet's assistant (vets, ditzy men with out-of-control Dalmatians).

In real life, of course, it hardly ever happened. In real life you became secretary to a bloke with rattling dentures, or a machinist in a factory with nary a suave customer in sight. And eventually you realised that, since your chances of marrying an airline pilot or a hospital doctor were negligible, you might just as well focus your dreams on something equally unobtainable but much, much more real. A face you could know. A voice you could hear. Something like Billy Fury.

Lynn in Westcliff-on-Sea wrote:

"I'd sure like Billy to be my guy,
His ginchy blue eyes make me sigh
The way he looks just makes me tingle
And I rejoice that I am single."

Unfortunately – or perhaps fortunately – in pre-internet days the fans' chances of catching a glimpse of or even hearing their heartthrobs was severely limited. The wireless – the BBC – had an agreement with the Musicians' Union and Phonographic Performance Limited that restricted the number of records they could play in a given week. Only a small percentage of the records would be pop, so you were lucky if a month's solid listening rewarded you with one brush with your heart's desire. You had a better chance with Radio Luxembourg, the only station (illegally) broadcasting non-stop pop (with adverts) to the UK. It was an essential accompaniment to homework and a trusted friend late at night, under the bedclothes. But the signal was erratic and Sod's law said that every time a favourite record came on, it would dissolve into static.

You could spend a useful Saturday morning in the listening booths of record shops, playing your favourite over and over until you'd learned the words or, more likely, got kicked out. Threepence in the juke box at your local coffee bar would buy a couple of minutes' pleasure. Buying the single, if you had a record player in the first place, meant forking out 5s

7d (£4.27) – more than a week's pocket money. Actually seeing their faces, their hair, clothes, eyes and poses was a matter of waiting for a package tour to show up at your local ABC or Hippodrome. Otherwise you had to make do with smudgy photos – invariably the same posed press shots – in magazines and comics like *Valentine*, *Roxy*, *Mirabelle*, Marty (named after Marty Wilde), *Picturegoer* and *Photoplay*.

This was how Judith Wills first fell in love with Billy. In her book *Keith Moon Stole My Lipstick*, she reproduces a breathless diary entry, recounting the epiphany.

"I'm in the newsagents at Botley Hill. I've just got off the school bus and I have a shilling and I'm going to buy some sweets. I wait to be served and in front of me is the loveliest face I've ever seen. On a magazine called *Marilyn*. This is it – love at first sight. I don't know who it is, but I have to buy the magazine and find out. Billy Fury. He's a singer. He has a record out. I'm going to save up to buy it, then a record player. If there is someone this gorgeous in the world, then life might be worth living after all."

Thank God, then, for the telly.

Larry Parnes prided himself on having contacts with influential telly people. Having already fixed Billy up with *Strictly For The Sparrows*, in January 1959 he got him exposure on two ITV teenage pop shows – *Cool For Cats* and *The Jack Jackson Show*.

Cool For Cats was one of the earliest attempts to do pop on TV and to solve the pre-MTV problem of what you show on the screen while you're playing the records. It provided the never-very-adequate of neatly choreographed dance routines. Rock'n'roll fans, even pop fans, were never particularly impressed by clean-limbed, regimented youngsters in implausibly wholesome clothing doing little jazz walks and chassés. Somehow it seemed as if somebody was missing the point.

The show was presented by Kent Walton, a silver-tongued wrestling commentator, then in his early forties. His Canadian accent added a slight note of transatlantic authenticity to the proceedings, but otherwise he was seen as a teacher who pretends to be your friend but is liable to snap at any minute.

Joan Kemp-Welch directed – worth mentioning for the benefit of readers planning a 'Women's Contribution to the Early Development of British Television' essay as part of their media studies coursework. (Compare and contrast with Rita Gillespie, see below.)

The Jack Jackson Show was a more successful attempt to translate Jack Jackson's pop and comedy radio show to TV. As well as pop stars like Billy, it featured what would later have been called a posse (usually Libby Morris and Glen Mason) who covered songs or lip-synced to other people's records for comic effect.

Much better than either, but still not quite there, was *Six-Five Special*, which first aired on BBC TV in February 1957 at, as the name suggests, five-past-six.

Six-Five Special was a mishmash of pop, light entertainment, youth club worthiness and misplaced jollity – a cross between *Top Of The Pops*, *Blue Peter* and Alan Partridge. It regularly notched up ratings of 12 or 13 million. It seemed to be informed by a conspiracy not to take this teenage business too seriously and to do everything possible to play down any suggestiveness or sexuality.

On *The Ed Sullivan Show* in the USA, Elvis had been shot from the waist up lest his gyrations caused unwanted pregnancies. No such precautions were needed on *Six-Five Special*. BBC employees, both staff and freelancers, were contractually obliged to hand in their pelvic flexibility at reception. As Lonnie Donegan once said, "It's a wonder show business ever survived the BBC at all."

"Welcome aboard the *Six-Five Special*," said Pete Murray the DJ/geeky older brother/trendy vicar who hosted the show. In patrician tones he announced, "We've got almost a hundred cats jumping here, some real cool characters to give us a gas, so just get on with it and have a ball." Never has the disjuncture between script and delivery been more marked.

Vouchers for long playing gramophone records were offered as prizes to the couple who 'cut the coolest capers'. A pair of Hungarian wrestlers was featured in the 'Sports Section'.

"If you're going to rock'n'roll properly," said Pete, "you're going to have to have your muscles in pretty good shape." In response to which, most spirited 13-year-olds decided to smoke more.

Mike and Bernie Winters provided light comic moments. Bernie had sticky-out teeth and a gormless face. Mike was the straight man who sometimes played clarinet.

There was also an extract of Little Richard, some boxing from Freddie Mills, jazz from Kenny Baker and a movement from Beethoven's 'Pathétique' Sonata, all intended, apparently, to give us the gas.

None of the shows – not *Cool For Cats*, *Jack Jackson* or *Six-Five Special* – held a candle to *Oh Boy!*, often described with much justification as the only TV pop show ever to get it right.

Jack Good, the show's producer, was in his late twenties. Oxford educated, he'd been President of OUDS (Oxford University Dramatic Society) and had appeared on the West End stage before signing up with the BBC.

Jack had been the driving force behind *Six-Five Special*, but in January 1958 he left the BBC to seek greater opportunity and much, much more money at ABC, one of the ITV companies (the BBC had been paying him £18 a week – ITV upped it to £100). There he was given virtual *carte blanche* to re-invent pop TV.

Oh Boy, initially broadcast live from the Hackney Empire and was everything that *Six-Five Special* should have been – fast, slick, dark, dirty and all music. Jack gave his stars – Cliff Richard, Marty Wilde, Billy Fury, Tony Sheridan – detailed direction to maximise their theatrical impact: legs apart, toes in, look down on this line, up on this line, head back as it goes into the middle-eight, now sneer.

"There's no question we were being groomed," says Marty Wilde. "Almost like we were Chippendales. Oh that doesn't sound good!"

"My attitude was that of a director for an actor," says Jack. "I wanted something more than just wiggling about. I wanted flash and danger. That was my big thing. You've got to look dangerous, you've got to look like you'll break out of the whole thing, smash the cameras and walk out the studio."

"It was Jack that was creating this image," said Sheila, one of The Vernons Girls, who provided backing vocals and speciality numbers. "He'd say, 'Now move, Billy. I'm doing the crotch shots,' and he was down underneath, literally going, 'I want another crotch shot.' We thought it was hilarious."

Billy needed little direction.

"He was a real good guy, not a fake performer at all," said Jack. "I immediately took a shine to him because he was so shy, so genuine."

"Jack gave me free hand on most of the songs," said Billy. "But all the stage movements – my looks – he helped with. My movements came from the awkwardness I felt being in front of people. Also [I was influenced by] people I saw in the movies – Rod Steiger, James Dean, anyone who was rebellious like Marlon Brando."

To keep the pace suitably frantic, songs tended to get cut down to the bare minimum of verse, verse, middle eight, verse and out, no repeats, no guitar solos, no extended intros or outros. Backing was provided by the team responsible for Billy's first record – Lord Rockingham's XI.

Oh Boy! was sexy but, better still, it possessed a quality that at the time was foreign to the rest of the BBC's output. It was common. It was vulgar. It was rock'n'roll.

Jazz critic Tony Hall, one of the show's presenters, told the *TV Times* in 1958: "I saw the two trial shows and thought they were the most exciting things I've ever seen on television. The lighting, the camera work was great, and I thought the music was swinging more than most of TV's attempts to present jazz."

"The secret of its success," he said, years later, "was actually that it was done in black and white [not that there was any choice in the matter – colour TV didn't happen in the UK until 1967]. The lighting made it special."

Pools of light, often reduced to a single follow-spot, picked out the stars in the blackness of space – a scheme devised by the show's director Rita Gillespie and the lighting director Jimmy Boyers.

"Jack Good stirred up all the enthusiasm on the music side," said Tony Hall, "and Rita made the show look so exciting."

Like millions of others, Andrew Loog Oldham, the Rolling Stone's first manager, spoke of the show with awe: "*Oh Boy!* was a weekly communication of sex and energy, with words and rhythm that proved to me there was more to life than what was dictated."

Everybody had favourites. Even Tom Driberg, the Labour MP for Barking, spoke highly of "the wonderfully Dadaist Marty Wilde". On the other side of the division were team (Abstract Expressionist?) Cliff Richard.

"There was always a sense of rivalry," Marty Wilde says. "Always. It's natural. Whether it was Cliff Richard or Billy. We just went out there to do our best and if we went down well, we would try to eclipse each other."

It was the same on tour. "We toured in a big bus and they [the stars] were quite friendly," said Brian Gregg. "But the moment the sparkly jackets went on and the barnet was done, they'd change."

"There'd be about six or seven artists on the bill," said Joe Brown, "and they literally had fist fights over who would play 'Hound Dog'."

Larry Parnes seemed to have felt the rivalry more keenly than the stars themselves. He wanted his boys to be on *Oh Boy!* more than anybody else's boys were on *Oh Boy!* and he wanted them to sing the songs that he wanted them to sing and wear the clothes that he wanted them to wear. This put something of a strain on relations between Parnes and Good.

The first salvo came in October 1958 when the show had been no more than a month on air. Jack booked Marty Wilde, but apparently didn't want him to sing 'Misery's Child', the B-side of his latest single, deeming it "unsuitable for the programme". Larry threatened to pull Marty from the show.

There was also a more general complaint that Jack was giving Cliff Richard better songs than he was giving Marty, and that Cliff was getting more publicity. Things came to a head with a spat over a mohair suit. Larry wanted Marty to wear it on the show, Jack didn't. Larry caused a scene. Jack had him escorted from the studio.

When Larry threatened once again to withdraw Marty from the show, Jack called his bluff, dropped Marty, and focussed all of his attention on Cliff as the main star.

Understandably, Marty was put out and tried to terminate his relationship with Larry, whom he blamed entirely. "My father is consulting our solicitors about legal aspects of the contracts," he told the press.

Eventually Marty patched things up with Larry, and Larry (allegedly over a boozy lunch) patched things up with Jack. Three months after the spat, Marty was back in the show.

A week later, Valentine's Day, 1959, Larry got his new boy into the running order, too. Cliff was off sick with laryngitis, so Marty was cock of the walk. He duetted with Alma 'The Girl With The Giggle In Her Voice' Cogan. Shirley Bassey belted out a couple of show stoppers. The Mudlarks and Don Lang, who'd been with Billy in the Diana Dors show, popped up. And the new boy, Billy Fury, hunched his shoulders, curled his lip, made smoke eyes at the camera and caused young women, and some men, all over the country to spill their Saturday tea down their nice clean jumpers so they had to change before they faced up to the relative disappointment of their Valentine's date.

"I don't know what's the matter with you tonight?" said their mums.

"There's nothing the matter."

Oh, but there was.

Vernons Girl Ann Simmons told Spencer Leigh: "I remember Billy joining *Oh Boy!*. What a gorgeous looking boy he was – slim, shy and an adorable adorable person. He had a lovely voice and I think we all fell in love with him."

Margaret, from Maidstone in Kent, fell in love with him that night, too. "I was never that keen on Cliff or Marty", she said. "I always thought Cliff was a bit phoney and Marty looked like the chap who looked after our dog when we went on holiday. Ever so nice and friendly but… you know. I remember my mum was doing some knitting and she'd asked me to look at something in the pattern and then Billy came on and I said, 'Hang on a minute, mum.' I wouldn't call it love exactly. He just looked so dangerous. Slightly scary. And very…"

"My dad liked his football results," says Linda Shawley, a fan from Blackpool, "and I used to say, 'don't switch over, don't switch over. Billy's coming on'."

Oh Boy! turned the singer Ian Dury, then 17, into one of Billy's (few) male fans. "I first dug Billy from seeing him on the telly in 1959," he said. "Serious haircut; collar up at the back; sharkskin or lamé jacket; hands in the gunslinger position; hooded eyes, and double handsome without being a wimpish outing. In 1964 I did a 10 foot x 8 foot painting of him for a youth club in Mornington Crescent, which I have never heard of since."

"Everybody at school was a Marty fan or a Cliff fan," said Joan from Leeds. "It was like two gangs. And I always felt I was a bit younger than them. I was, what, 13 or 14. And I liked people like Alma Cogan, which wasn't very… you didn't say 'cool' in them days, did you? Then I saw Billy on the telly and on the Monday I went into school and… it made me feel special. Different. 'Who do you like, Cliff or Marty?' 'I like Billy Fury.' It was like I had a boyfriend who was better than either of theirs."

"Billy was wonderful, wonderful," Jack Good said. "He was the best rock'n'roll star that we had and it is a terrible shame that I saw him so late in the career of *Oh Boy!*"

Oh Boy! did indeed have just three months left to run. Billy appeared six times.

The last *Oh Boy!* ever features Cliff and Marty and another of Larry's stable, Dickie Pride, harmonising on 'Three Cool Cats', Don Lang being frantic, Peter Elliot crooning 'When I Grow Too Old To Dream' and finishes with Cliff and Marty duetting, just like they're old mates, on Buddy Holly's 'Early In The Morning'.

The high point comes just four minutes into the show. Billy sets the screen alight. He's channelling Elvis, but entirely devoid of the 'don't really mean it' smiles that Elvis had, by then, taken to adopting as a way of convincing the grown-ups that he wasn't going to spread some sort of multiracial communism by providing young people with spontaneous orgasms.

Billy meant it.

He's on two cameras. A close-up camera to his left is tilted up at an angle so that he can look down at it with a slight air of disdain. The camera to his front, shooting just above the waist, has the massed Vernons Girls in the background, a choir of hoop-skirted backing vocalists. As Billy goes into the bridge, the lights change, extinguishing The Vernons Girls and putting Billy alone against black – a common *Oh Boy!* ploy that confirmed the divinity of the stars. After the bridge, cut to the close-up camera, tighter still now. It's black and white of course, but you can tell this man is made not of flesh but of gold. He shines. And yielding flesh could never be sculpted into cheekbones like those.

The song is 'Don't Knock Upon My Door', the B-side of his new single, 'Margo'. "Don't knock upon my door" he sings to his rejected lover. But you can tell he knows she won't be able to stop herself. She'd probably deploy plant hire to get to him.

When he flirts with the camera, it's not boy-next-door flirting. It's the kind of flirting that makes the seams of your clothing and his clothing mysteriously melt, and buttons explode like little fireworks. And there's no need in it either. He doesn't need sex. Why would he? He is sex.

Chapter Seven

"YOU WOULDN'T WANT YOUR GIRLFRIEND ANYWHERE NEAR BILLY FURY..."

Larry's predilection for righteous indignation, together with his inability to spot the line between "being appropriately assertive on your client's behalf" and "pissing important people off" was always a problem. Just as it had almost ruined relations between Jack Good and Marty, on more than one occasion it came close to scotching Billy's relations with the BBC.

In fact, Billy's relations with the BBC never quite got on to an amicable footing. In the early years at least he earned a reputation for being unreliable, for being trouble. This was not all Larry's fault. Billy himself could at times be, let's say, flaky.

The first difficulty came in May 1959, not long before the last ever *Oh Boy!*. Billy was booked for a radio show called *Singalong* to be recorded at the Aeolian Hall in Bond Street, where the BBC had a couple of studios and a suite of offices. Accompaniment would be provided by the BBC house band, called, for the purposes of the show, The Squadcats, the pop wing of The Squadronaires, a well-respected jazz ensemble.

Billy (or possibly Larry) didn't want to be accompanied by The Squadcats. He wanted to bring his own band. The BBC said no. Larry put his foot down: if they didn't let Billy bring his own band, then Billy wouldn't show up at all. The BBC sent a stiff letter in response, asking Larry to "reconsider this decision and to see that Mr Fury attends, failing which we shall consider you to have committed a breach of contract. In this event, the Corporation reserves its rights to take such action in the matter as it may be advised."

As a compromise, the BBC suggested that Billy could sing with no backing, just self-accompanied on guitar. Memos flurried.

This was the first of Larry's and Billy's many set-tos with the BBC and each time it was Patrick Newman, Booking Manager (Variety), who had to deal with the flim-flam and finagling.

This first one begins with a memo from the aforesaid Patrick Newman to (Miss) M. J. Quinault in Contracts, reporting that he'd spoken to Mr Parnes' office and had come up with another compromise. Billy would agree to be accompanied by The Squadcats if he could bring his own guitarist with him. A second contract was issued.

"Please also add a pencil note on the artist's card," wrote Newman, "to the effect that we are probably saddled with this for future bookings. Really – these odd gentlemen with odd names. I propose to discover a new girl singer and I shall call her Dementia Praecox – she should be a *succès fou.*"

As it turned out, Billy didn't perform at all. Though booked to rehearse at 1.00, he and his guitarist didn't show up until 2.15, by which time The Squadcats, who had a booking in Bournemouth that evening, had left the studio. In his defence, Billy said that he had shown up at 1.00, but a commissionaire had told him nothing was happening until 2.15.

In the end, Larry and the BBC agreed to cancel the contract without payment to either Billy or the guitarist.

'Margo', arranged again by Harry Robinson and recorded at a funereal tempo by musicians who sound as if they're playing for a very tired stripper at three in the morning in an otherwise empty club on the outskirts of Grimsby, just about scraped into the Top 20.

The B-side, 'Don't Knock Upon My Door' – the song he'd nailed on *Oh Boy!* – is much better. It cracks along with swooping backing vocals from The Vernons Girls and an eccentric low-register piano solo. Harry Robinson was good at B-sides.

Though Billy's recording success was falling a little short of whirlwind, his live performances had developed the power to frighten horses. As well as working on his voice and his moves, he worked on the attitude.

On his way to the stage, says Brian Gregg, "he'd often whizz past me. And I'd hear this volley of abuse come from him. The first time, I thought he was swearing at me – effing and blinding – a bit strong. But through working a lot with him, I realised it was a way of making himself feel aggression – and it came out over the footlights.

"I stood behind him so many times waiting to go on: a bag of nerves, no confidence at all. The comedian would be out front and they'd announce, 'Ladies and Gentlemen, the guy you've all been waiting for – Billy Fury.' And as he said his name, he stood up, took a deep breath, and it was amazing. He seemed to grow about four inches and Ronnie Wycherley turned into Billy Fury."

The bravado and aggression would evaporate as soon as Billy left the stage. Then he'd turn back into Ronnie – nervous, insecure, asking everybody, "D'you think it was all right?" But for those 20 minutes or so under the lights, he was the best.

"Whatever Cliff Richard once did in his act to provoke the outcry that it was 'too sexy' has nothing on some of the things that Billy Fury does," said an *NME* reviewer. "Indeed some of his antics during a 'love scene' with the microphone were downright disgusting."

Over the summer, Billy joined Marty Wilde's show at the Palace Theatre, Blackpool, backed by Colin Green on guitar, Tex Makins on bass, Alan LeClair on piano and Bobby Woodman (aka Bobbie Clarke) on drums. "It was Billy who got the crowd going," said Bobby Woodman. "Onstage he turned into this sensuous sex machine – but offstage he was a shy, quiet guy."

"Many teenage girls work themselves into a state of frenzy when watching Fury's action on stage," said Mark Crossways in *Picturegoer* magazine. "The cause is one number in Fury's act – an Elvis Presley original called 'Mean Woman Blues'. Fury twists his mouth into a vicious shape and glares into the spotlight. He looks defiant. Slowly, to the throb of guitars, he sings the opening bars. Then with deliberate calculation, he winds his left leg around the microphone, tilts it back, softly caresses the base with his right hand. He has developed his technique, for he knows the exact moment to leap back from the microphone. His next move increases the tension among the female element of the audience. With hunched shoulders and agonised expression, he undoes the zip of his yellow jacket. Down, down it comes, while the screams increase in volume. With one swift movement, he casts the jacket aside and grabs hold of the microphone. His previous exhibition seems tame in light of what follows. Over goes the microphone until it lies full-length on the stage – with Fury on top of it."

Sex before marriage was wrong.

This message was thundered from pulpits, assumed in classrooms, stressed by concerned politicians and journalists, and rammed home even in teenage comics and magazines.

"'No I can't, it would be wrong,'" said the heroine of a *Mirabelle* story.

"'You can, darling. And you will…' Slowly, but surely, he drew me into his arms, his dark eyes holding mine. I felt almost hypnotised. His heart was thudding against mine, as he bent my head back and his mouth came down hard on mine. What could I say? What could I do? 'Yes' I whispered, 'Oh Trevor, yes…'"

But, in the same issue, came this stern warning from Jenny, a reader.

"'Why should we wait?' Fred, Jenny's boyfriend, pleaded. 'We know we were meant for each other, so why can't we be happy now?'

"'He seemed hurt by my apparent coldness, as he called it, and accused me of not loving him. So, I gave way and let him have the proof he wanted. When I got pregnant he simply disappeared out of my life. Of course, now I see that boys will say anything if they think it will make their girls more willing. I learned my lesson the hard way. Girls be warned!'"

The terrible consequences for any unmarried teen who "gave" way to temptation were clear. In this life they'd catch terrible diseases and have babies cursed by the dread stigma of illegitimacy, and in the afterlife they'd go to hell.

"When do you start to say No?" asked one correspondent in *Honey*. "The sooner the better. Sounds hard, but facts often are, especially the facts of life. Begin answering in the negative before it gets too difficult. If a boy asks you to go for a drive in the darkest and most desolate spot in the vicinity, tell him you don't like lonely places. Don't wait till you're parked with him in a forest or on a lonely stretch of moorland. Petting, like chess, requires strategy. Wherever you are, conscience, common sense and instinct will tell you when to be gently discouraging. The time to start saying no is at least two moves before you think it is going too far."

"Sexual excesses are both a symptom of national weakness and a powerful secondary cause of it," said *English Life And Leisure*, a sociological study from the early fifties. "As in so many other fields of activity, the best hope for the future would appear to be to concentrate on the young people who have not yet contracted bad habits."

The report went on to recommend cleaning up "eroticism in newspapers", stopping adults telling and enjoying dirty jokes, more censorship of films ("a single scene can do widespread harm") and making contraceptives less available.

In the UK, until 1968, the Lord Chamberlain had dictatorial power over what could and could not be shown in the theatre. Musical performances were below his radar, although at a local level in England and Wales groups of worthies known as Watch Committees, appointed to overlook general policing, also had the power to close theatres if they suspected that the people inside were perpetrating filth or mayhem.

The Blackburn Watch Committee, for instance, was incensed by the news that after seeing the film *Rock Around The Clock*, "rhythm-crazed" youngsters in nearby Manchester had trampled the flowers in a municipal garden. They banned the film outright in their own town, thus preserving common decency and the hardy annuals of Corporation Park. Another of the committee's bans, this time on The Rolling Stones in 1964, remained in place until 2008.

"We could all have been arrested at one point or another," says Marty Wilde. "We took our style from Elvis. If Elvis was doing something like grabbing the microphone and whatever or bending backwards, then Billy and I would copy him. Billy and Cliff and myself were all copying Elvis because he was so influential and played such a pivotal part in our careers."

Nobody *was* arrested, though. Not for microphone grabbing and bending backwards, anyway.

Some of Billy's more avid fans found that just the sound of his name could set them squirming – a phenomenon frequently observed by the young Chris Eley.

"He was a real threat. You wouldn't want your girlfriend anywhere near Billy Fury. I remember vividly travelling home on the school bus from my secondary school in Truro on a Friday. And the girls would be in such a frenzy of excitement, cooing and giggling and, 'Guess who's on

71

on Saturday. It's Billy Fury.' I can never remember them being like that even when The Beatles came along."

In October 1959, under the headline "Does BILLY cause too much FURY?" journalist James Wynn rehearsed the arguments for and against Billy's onstage rock'n'roll filth in the *New Musical Express*. "Many feel that's he's the most exciting visual rock'n'roll artist Britain has produced for years. [...] Fury's non-admirers, however, aren't appreciative of what they term 'over-exaggerated movements'."

Having observed some of Billy's "sexy stage antics" at a concert, Mr Wynn was of the opinion that "parts of his performance were downright disgusting." At another concert, however, he conducted a few brief interviews to gauge the mood, first with the 'fellows' in the audience: "Generally, they thought that his 'love scene' routine with a microphone was crude and totally unnecessary. But they had no complaint with his prowess as a singer.

"I put a similar question to several teenage girls; they were quite happy about his presentation, but didn't comment on his singing other to emphasise their opinion that he is 'great'."

At the end of the piece, James Wynn mentions that, "Billy left for a six weeks tour of Ireland last week-end. The Irish are an excitable people, which tends to suggest that they'll go for Billy's power-packed electric style in a big, big way!"

Up to a point.

In Ireland, Billy was booked to support Bridie Gallagher, the twinkle-eyed 35-year-old 'Girl From Donegal', who had shot to fame in 1956 with her recording of 'A Mother's Love's A Blessing'. Clem Cattini, Billy's drummer on the Irish tour, described her as the "nearest thing you could get to a nun". Billy is on record as having a penchant for older women. Bridie Gallagher wasn't one of them.

The tour started well enough in the north, and even though Billy was doing nothing to compromise his reputation as a sensuous sex-machine there were no complaints.

"His act was certainly explicit," said guitarist Jim Sullivan. "Billy had obviously seen the early Elvis films and had learnt from the way he moved – but he took it a step further, doing all the gyrations and curling his lip. Then he would be down on the floor with the microphone stand, rubbing his body against it and – of course – the more he did it, the more the girls screamed and the more he liked it."

Then the tour crossed the border and opened in Dublin.

"And that's where the trouble started," says Brian Gregg, the bass player. "It was all, 'You're not in England now; you're in a Catholic country and you can't do that sort of thing.' On the first night they brought down the curtain on us – and of course the audience went nuts."

"The kids who'd paid to see me were marching up and down outside the theatre kicking up a big fuss and waving banners," said Billy. "But the manager paid no attention.

"They dug me in Ulster, but brother, when I got to the south I was in dead trouble. Just before I went on one night, the manager told me that he'd had complaints that my act was indecent. I told him I didn't know what he meant by indecent. 'It's far too sexy – you'll have to stop that sort of thing.'"

Word got back to the boss. Larry Parnes took the next plane over and remonstrated with the manager, telling him that Billy had been doing the same act all over the UK to full houses and had no complaints. But the manager would not, or could not, be swayed – Billy was out of the show.

The sticking point was almost certainly Bridie Gallagher. Billy closed the first half. His antics put the audience in a whirl of sexual hysteria. In the interval they all rushed out to surround the stage door in hopes of getting a piece of clothing, a lock of hair, a scrap of skin or little bone, some saintly relic to preserve for always. By the time Bridie came on at the end of the second half to sing 'A Mother's Love's A Blessing' only old women in hats, priests and drunks too far gone to move remained: and the ranks of empty seats bore eloquent testimony to the truism that though a mother's love might indeed be a blessing, Billy Fury was a sensuous sex-machine.

"It was a dreary show and somebody had to do something to make it exciting," Billy said later. "I got banned from that terrible show, which was a very good idea."

Offstage, in Ireland and elsewhere, the sexual temperature was always turned much lower.

"Basically, I'm a very shy person," Billy said, "I hated talking to anyone because I was too shy to even speak – but once I was singing, I was fine. I think with being so retiring, it gave me a way of letting off steam, to lay it on a bit heavily."

"We were shy," says Marty. "Neither of us were loud people. He was similar to me in many ways and that's why we got on so well. We were reserved. Maybe some other artists on the tours weren't, but we were both shy. But not to the point of being stupid. We had similar backgrounds – he came from a working-class family and so did I."

Billy wasn't yet 20. He never acquired some of the more sophisticated habits money and fame often bring.

"He was a very keen Airfix plane builder," says Vince Eager. "Larry had this massive – must have cost a fortune – marble-top Italian coffee table, which was great for two things – playing Scalextric, which we really loved, and also it was great for building kits on. So, Billy did a lot of building Airfix kits. He had about 60 or 70 of them at one stage. It was unbelievable. The balcony from the apartment overlooked Gloucester Road and one night Billy decided to have a bit of fun and he got his lighter, and I didn't realise how flammable these things were, but he just set fire to them and threw them off the third-floor balcony into Gloucester Road. Billy had this very – it was girlish in a way – giggle. He always used to laugh with his tongue between his teeth. He was pointing and saying, 'Look at that.' And laughing.

"The other one we did off the balcony was when we'd both had an argument with Larry. Larry had a great collection of 78 rpm records in his big sound centre and Billy took them out and proceeded to throw them like flying saucers off the balcony towards the buses that were going up and down Gloucester Road."

Possibly in revenge for this act of vandalism, Larry made Billy record 'Angel Face'.

Billy never had any sort of "artistic control" clause written into his contract, either with Decca or with Mr Parnes. He sang what he was told to sing.

'Angel Face' was a Doc Pomus/Mort Shuman song. They wrote, among others, 'Little Sister', 'His Latest Flame' and 'Suspicion' for Elvis. 'Angel Face' is far from their proudest moment. It had been a minor hit for James Darren in the US charts. Billy's version, released in September 1959, produced by Jack Good and arranged, again, by Harry Robinson, was almost a parody-soppy song, with heavenly choir and lyrics dipped in the sherbet fountain ("Oh, if you were here once more in my embrace, I'd kiss away each tear from your angel face, angel face, angel face, angel face."). Billy, as he said himself, years later, sounds "like a little boy".

It didn't make the Top 40.

Once again, the B-side, 'The Time Has Come', written by Billy, is infinitely better.

The November release, 'My Christmas Prayer', could have been made by Bridie Gallagher. The competition that Christmas included Adam Faith's first hit 'What Do You Want?', Cliff Richard & The Shadows' 'Travellin' Light', Neil Sedaka's 'Oh, Carol', Tommy Steele's 'Little White Bull', Marty Wilde's 'Bad Boy', Harry Belafonte's 'Mary's Boy Child' and Frankie Laine's 'Rawhide'. "Oh Lord the snow is falling/And the whole world kneels to pray/Oh tomorrow brings the dawning/Of another Christmas Day," Billy sang, laying on the Humbrol enamel but knowing it would never fly.

That Christmas, back in Liverpool, Billy's parents had been reading in the papers about how their lad had been banned in Ireland and criticised in the *Melody Maker* for doing "that sort of thing".

"My dad was in a fair old state," Billy told the *People*. "I said, 'Dad, I just don't know what I'm doing wrong.' 'Well,' says my dad 'you show me your act and I'll tell you.'

"It was weird swinging out for my dad in the front room in Haliburton Street. He made me do the act again and again and when he was sure that I wasn't holding out on anything, he told me where I should tone down my movements.

"I think the real crazy rock days are over."

Luckily, he was wrong.

Chapter Eight

"...BUT I THOUGHT I WAS GOING TO DIE SOON."

Billy's shyness, the reserve, could sometimes slip over into morose introspection.

This fact did not go unnoticed by others, including Larry's young secretary Muriel Walker, who was a general confidante to the boys.

"I used to deal with the mums a lot," she said. "They were always worried. I remember one day, Billy sat down with me in the office and started asking me whether I thought that if you had a partner and they died would you meet up with them in the afterlife. He was very serious about this. I said, 'Well, what if they died and you got married again – that could get very complicated.' He was very worried by this. Lovely boy, though – one night he could be singing to thousands of screaming girls and the next he would be quite happy to come home with me for a bowl of spaghetti."

He brooded a lot about death and always had. In all his years on the road, no graveyard was ever passed unnoticed.

"When I was 13 or 14, I overheard the doctor tell my mother that I would never pass a medical test. In fact, he was talking about National Service but I thought he meant I was going to die soon."

"It was hip to say you wouldn't live very long," said Brian Gregg. "It was called 'doing a moody'. We thought Billy was doing this."

Death was big in pop. 'Splatter Platters' were all over the place.

'Tell Laura I Love Her', by Ricky Valance (not to be confused with Ritchie Valens, more of whom in a moment), is a song about a young man, Tommy, who, in order to make enough money to buy his beloved Laura "flowers, presents and most of all a wedding ring", enters a stock car race. Unfortunately, his car turns over in a ball of flames. He lives just long enough to whisper the title of the song a few times. The song gave Ricky Valance the honour of being the first Welshman to make number one in the UK record charts. He stayed there for three weeks in October 1960.

'Endless Sleep' was Marty Wilde's first big hit in 1958. In it the protagonist argues with his girlfriend who then throws herself into the sea and an endless sleep. The sea seems to be encouraging the young man to join her. Possibly at the end he saves her and they live happily ever after, but it's ambiguous.

In 'Ebony Eyes', by The Everly Brothers, a soldier on leave is waiting at the airport for his girl to arrive "through the dark ebony skies" on Flight 1203. The plane is overdue. "Then came the announcement over the loudspeaker, 'Will all those having relatives or friends on Flight 1203, please report to the chapel across the street.'"

In another track, Betty met Jimmy at the candy store. He turned around and smiled at her, you get the picture. Betty's parents forced them to break up because he came from the bad side of town and was not only a member of a motorcycle gang but was the actual 'Leader Of The Pack'. Obediently, Betty dumped him. Jimmy was aggrieved. As he drove away on his motorcycle – in inclement weather conditions (and possibly with inadequate tread on his tyres) – Betty begged him to go slow. He took no notice, with fatal consequences. The song gave The Shangri-Las a US number one in 1964.

See also 'Teen Angel', 'Dead Man's Curve', 'Terry', 'Black Denim Trousers And Motorcycle Boots', 'Johnny, Remember Me', 'Running Bear' and so on and so on. As we'll discover later, Billy Fury's contribution to the death pool included 'Don't Jump' and, indirectly, 'Nobody's Child'.

Theories can and have been spun to explain the popular fascination with death that seemed to reach some sort of climax in the late fifties and early sixties: that it was some sort of deep post-war post-traumatic stress spasm; that it was related to the shadow of the hydrogen bomb that convinced a whole generation they'd never see 30; or that, on the other hand, enjoying the romance of death as a remote but scarily exciting prospect was a luxury in which those living in what promised to be a time of unprecedented peace and prosperity could afford to wallow.

In sexually repressed times, the fifties as Victorian England, death was often a useful metaphor for sex. One is the destruction of life, the other the creation. Both (if done properly) involve an abnegation of control and loss of the self. A near-death experience and an unfulfilled love affair both lead you halfway to paradise.

Vampire films were big in the late fifties, too. The man (or in some cases the woman, but let's stick with standard hetero/missionary position bloodsucking for now) penetrates the woman. Blood is involved. He sucks the life out of her, yet she remains among the living, her individuality removed, a pale shadow of her former self. Happens all the time.

At the end of the film *Sleeper*, Diane Keaton asks Woody Allen, "What do you believe in?"

"Sex and death," says Woody. "Two things that come once in a lifetime. But at least after death you're not nauseous."

The real and highly publicised death that came to rock'n'roll in 1959 produced a paradigm shift. It was like having sat around in the pub talking about sex for a couple of years, somebody went out and did it. Death raised rock'n'roll from a fashion, or at best a genre, to the stuff of myth and legend.

When the ancient Greeks sat around the fire late at night, they told tales of Troy and how Achilles slew Hector. The Anglo-Saxons alliterated stirring stories of bold Beowulf, his steadfast stamina, spirit and spunk, and the death of the grim and grisly Grendel.

And old rockers remember Buddy and Eddie, and the day the music died. Though the stories have been told a hundred thousand times, it is without apology that we repeat them here, for Billy seemed never more than a heartbeat away from joining them. From the moment he was admitted to Alder Hey Hospital with rheumatic fever, the possibility that Billy was "living on borrowed time" haunted first the man himself and then his fans.

In February 1959, Buddy Holly embarked on a *Winter Dance Party* tour in the USA, along with Dion & The Belmonts, Richie Valens and J.P. 'The Big Bopper' Richardson. General Artists Corporation, who'd organised the tour, cheesepared. The itinerary looked as if it had been designed by bouncing a ball around a pool table, with treks of 400 miles or so between some of the gigs. Travel was by antique school bus with defective or no heating. Scott of the Antarctic had toastier times in his tent.

Somewhere near Ironwood, Michigan, Carl Bunch, Buddy's drummer, got frostbitten feet and was carted off to hospital. Richie Valens and The Big Bopper both came down with flu.

On Sunday, February 1, the package played Green Bay, Wisconsin. On Monday they travelled 350 miles to play the Surf Ballroom, in Clear Lake, Iowa. The next gig was in Moorhead, Minnesota, another 370-mile jaunt.

To save his toes, Buddy decided to avoid the frozen bus and hire a plane instead, a little four-seat Beechcraft Bonanza with pilot for less than $150. Richie and The Big Bopper took the two spare seats. The plane took off at 12.55 from Mason City Municipal Airport and, five minutes later, crashed into a cornfield. There were no survivors.

The parts of the world that had heard of Buddy Holly and the (smaller) parts of the world that knew about Richie Valens and The Big Bopper mourned.

And the businessmen of rock'n'roll looked on in wonder as Buddy's latest release, 'It Doesn't Matter Anymore', which had been a slow starter, went to 13 in the US and number one in the UK, the first of 15 Top 40 hits the dead musician enjoyed over the next five years.

Decca also rushed out a greatest hits LP, which stayed in the album charts, on and off, until the mid-sixties. In the rock'n'roll business, it appeared, sex might buy you a limo or two but death buys you a Caribbean island. Still does.

What's more, dead stars never turn into shadows of their former selves. They never dismiss their early work – invariably the best work – as 'kid's stuff' and embrace their country side, or release a song cycle called Existential Overtones, or take up the lute. They never get fat. They never play Vegas. They don't go to prison for unspeakable crimes. They stay perfect and revered.

There's no evidence to suggest that Larry Parnes, perhaps coming home early one day to find Vince Eager and Billy Fury chucking gramophone records off his balcony, thought, "A little push, a tragic 'accident', a post-mortem release, a yacht in Treasure Cay Marina."

And even if the thought did occur, he never followed through.

Buddy Holly's posthumous career was much bigger in the UK than in the USA, possibly because the British prefer their pop stars to be dead, but more likely because he was one of the few American rock'n'rollers who'd actually been here.

The films – *Rock Around The Clock, The Girl Can't Help It, Loving You, Jailhouse Rock* – gave the UK infrequent glimpses of what was going on across the Atlantic, fleeting celluloid moments of impossible glamour and breathtaking excitement. But real flesh and blood sightings were rare.

In February 1957, Lou and Leslie Grade imported Bill Haley, the man whose 'Rock Around The Clock' had brought such desecration to the floral displays of Manchester's municipal gardens, to play 20-something UK dates.

"He pounds his guitar without mercy," reported *The Times*, a surprisingly early, if not enthusiastic, organ of rock journalism. "His pelvis wiggles, not with care (as does that of his rival Mr Presley, the alligator whom Britain is to see later) but with the *purest joie de vivre*. His saxophonist, Mr Rudy Pompilli, delights to lift not simply the bell of his instrument but the whole golden contraption above his head as he puffs out his cheeks and pumps fierce eldritch squeals into it. Mr Al Rex, the contrabassist, is not satisfied with the conventional, erect stance: in order to thrum the best he sits astride it, as if it were some hobby horse."

In March the following year, Buddy came over and played 24 dates in 24 days. Des O'Connor was MC on that show, and even sang a few songs himself, including the music-hall favourites 'Oh, You Beautiful Doll' and 'Shine On Harvest Moon', as a warm-up for Buddy; proof that, despite the fears of rock'n'roll riots, audiences were a good bit more restrained back then than they were by the time The Clash came along.

Then came the first whiff of brimstone.

In memory if not in fact, Jerry Lee Lewis arrived at London Airport in much the same way as Count Dracula arrived in Whitby. Three years earlier he had been expelled from Bible college for playing the Devil's music. One year earlier he'd had a UK number one with 'Great Balls Of Fire' and a number eight with 'Whole Lotta Shakin' Goin' On'. 'Breathless', his current release, was riding high. His songs were the horniest, sneakiest, dirtiest rock'n'roll anybody had ever heard.

Jerry Lee was absolute proof of the rumours that rock'n'roll could, and was, rotting the morals of the nation's youth. At the time, the rumours were airily dismissed by more liberal commentators, but now, looking back, many 75-year-olds are happy to admit that it was 'Great Balls Of Fire' that did it. After one listen, their moral compasses went haywire and their thoughts turned to pre-marital sex, flick-knives and motorcycles.

Jerry Lee got off the plane accompanied by a young woman.

"I'm Myra, Jerry's wife," the young woman told an inquisitive journalist.

"And how old is Myra?" asked the journalist.

"She's 15," Jerry hurriedly replied, as if that would be perfectly acceptable. It subsequently turned out that Myra Gail Lewis was in fact 13. Jerry was 22. And Myra was Jerry's first cousin once removed. And she was Jerry's second wife. And when he married her, he was still married to his first wife.

"Go away," Myra Gail hissed at a *News Of The World* reporter through a crack in the door of their hotel room. "Go away, Jerry and I are in bed."

Lewis had been booked to play 27 gigs. He was cancelled after three and the bad press followed him back to the USA, where his career sank into the doldrums.

"...they were packed off themselves, drummed out of the country for their hillbilly customs of courtship and marriage," wrote Lorna Sage. "There was a lot of huffing and puffing and moral panic over their lack of shame, their backwardness. We imagined her bouncing on the five-star bed in her baby doll pyjamas. 'Just want to be your teddy bear,' Elvis sang."

After that, the promoters played it safe. When Paul 'Diana' Anka came over and Connie 'Lipstick On Your Collar' Francis toured with Nino (The Wonder Dog) and the Six Flying De Pauls (Australian Tumblers), nobody got arrested.

Then Gene Vincent, from Norfolk, Virginia, the most perfect rock'n'roll star ever invented, got off the plane, loaded with guns, knives, whisky and attitude.

Gene wasn't quite as dead as Buddy Holly was by now, but he came close. Pale, gaunt and ghoulish, with saucer-zombie eyes, he sang with a lily-scented whisper that rose to a graveyard wail and he walked with a limp, one leg sheathed in metal, the result of a near-death experience with a motorcycle (or a clash with enemy forces in Korea depending on who you believe). He seldom drew breath without a wince of pain.

'Be-Bop-A-Lula', his first release back in 1956, went to number seven in the *Billboard* chart. The follow-up, 'Race With The Devil', went to 96. Subsequent releases, 'Bluejean Bop', 'Crazy Legs', 'Git It' and 'Say Mama', are spoken of with quiet reverence as a Platonic ideal to which all other records should aspire, but none of them sold much at the time.

By 1959, the big gigs didn't want Gene Vincent anymore. He was playing roadhouses. He toured Japan. And the US tax man was after his share of the money that Gene had made in 1956. He was a desperate man. He'd try anything. So, when management suggested a European tour might revive his career, he allowed himself to be loaded onto a plane.

Gene's plane touched down on December 6, just before seven in the morning, but a clutch of fans had set their alarms and turned out to greet him. They were joined by Jack Good and several Vernons Girls. Jack and Larry Parnes had shared the cost of shipping Gene over. Larry had crafted a package tour around him. Jack had TV plans.

Three hours later, Gene was singing live on the BBC radio pop show *Saturday Club*. That evening, backed by Joe Brown & The Firing Squad, he played the Granada Theatre, Tooting, London, in a Larry Parnes promoted *Marty Wilde Show*, with Marty, Billy, Vince Eager, Dickie Pride and others from the stable.

"Gene and I didn't get off to a good start," says Marty, "because I had the misfortune to appear with him on his first British gig. For some stupid reason, Larry wanted me to top the bill. That was a crazy thing to do. He absolutely tore them apart. It was bedlam. Afterwards I thought, 'I hope that never happens again.'"

"I backed him at the Granada," says Joe Brown. "He was a strange man. The first time I saw him he was drunk in a corner with a gun in his hand."

Gene had a lot of guns and airport security wasn't as tight back then. Four years later, he was arrested in Notting Hill, London, for pointing a gun at his third wife Margaret, who was British. She forgave him. The magistrate let him off with a £20 slap on the wrist for possession of an illegal firearm.

The day after Tooting, Gene travelled to Manchester to start rehearsals for Jack Good's new TV show, the less successful follow-up to *Oh Boy!* called *Boy Meets Girls*. The boy was Marty Wilde. The girls were Vernons.

Jack later blamed the show's lack of oomph on his wife, who, he claimed, had persuaded him that rock'n'roll was on the way out and he should adopt a more middle-of-the-road approach. "I can't tell you any more because I have a big erase machine in my head that has wiped out all my memories," he said.

The BBC had a big erase machine, too, and though there may be telerecordings of *Boy Meets Girls* mouldering in somebody's shed, they are yet to emerge.

Jack even tried to chuck a metaphorical bucket of cold water over Billy. "I fully agree that anything suggestive should be avoided," he told the press. "Though of course these things are partially in the minds of the individual viewers. Frankly there are one or two things that Billy Fury does that I would rather he didn't. I have in fact suggested so to Bill, who does tend to get carried away by his performance."

But the faraway smiles on the faces of those who remember the shows are enough to confirm the rumour that Billy took no notice.

One good thing that came out of *Boy Meets Girls* was a new look for Gene Vincent, which became the new look for rock'n'roll. Gene had worn black trousers and a red and black sweater at his first UK shows. Jack Good knew better than anybody what rock'n'roll should look like and it looked nothing like a red and black sweater at his first UK shows.

"Gene wore a leg iron," Jack said, "so he hobbled a bit. I was a Shakespeare fan, so hobbling to me meant Richard III. I even thought of giving him a hunchback, and I'm glad I didn't. Then I thought, 'He can also be moody like Hamlet', so we'll dress him in black from head to toe and put a medallion round his neck."

And not just, but black *leather*, thereby creating a rock'n'roll icon ten times more persuasive than fat Elvis's jumpsuit or The Beatle's collarless Pierre Cardin jackets. Indeed, black leather – 'the Gene Vincent look' – became the trademark of Vince Taylor in his subsequent career.

It was the look The Beatles went for in Hamburg, before Astrid made them existentialists and Mr Epstein made them loveable. On their first visit to Hamburg they bought leather jackets and on the second the trousers to go with them – "and we looked like four Gene Vincents, only a bit younger, I think," said John Lennon.

It was the look adopted by Elvis for his 1968 comeback special – and subsequently assumed by Father Ted and Father Dougal in the *Three Ages Of Elvis* tribute act they entered for the Priest's *Stars In Their Eyes* contest.

It was the look purloined by Bernard Jewry when, having dispensed with his Shane Fenton persona, he became Alvin Stardust.

And so on...

The package tour that Larry built around Gene was eventually given the snappy title, *A Fast-Moving Anglo-American Beat Show*. To justify the name, he'd need at least one other American. Norm Riley, one of Gene Vincent's revolving carousel of managers, suggested the kid from *The Girl Can't Help It*, the one with hunched shoulders and the orange Gretsch guitar who had so inspired Billy.

Eddie Cochran was from Minnesota, but the family moved to Bell Gardens in Los Angeles not long after he hit puberty. By the time he was 16 he had a record deal, and was playing sessions and writing his own material. He was 17 when he got the gig on *The Girl Can't Help It*, playing his own song 'Twenty Flight Rock'.

Elsewhere 'C'mon Everybody', 'Summertime Blues', 'Somethin' Else', 'Teenage Heaven', 'Weekend' are literate, witty teen anthems that clearly defined the aspirations of his fans – the male ones at least. If one day they found themselves knocking on the door of a fine-looking girl, with a car – albeit a '41 Ford not a '59 – parked out front, went out to party where the house was shaking from the bare feet slapping on the floor (because when you hear the music you just can't sit still), and then rounded off the evening by driving up to Lookout Hill with the car-top down, they knew they were in teenage heaven. And if you didn't get there you always had the option of complaining to your congressman (and he said, quote, "I'd like to help you, son, but you're too young to vote.")

The records were all sonic adventures, pushing the limited technological envelope with double tracking, slap-back echo, harsh compression and mighty reverb.

And to cap it all, Eddie was arguably better looking than Elvis and was certainly sharper dressed (although to modern sensibilities the idea that a double-knit jumper with a shawl collar could ever have been considered 'sharp' seems dubious). He could also play guitar like he was ringing a bell. And he was friends with Gene.

Offers were made. Eddie, spooked by Buddy Holly's death, had concerns about flying, but when Larry told him that in the UK artistes rarely flew to gigs, preferring to enjoy the luxury of British Rail and the speed and efficiency of the advanced network of roads, some of which had two lanes and lay-bys with pie-stalls, he was reassured.

The tour kicked off on January 24, 1960 at the Gaumont, Ipswich (East Anglia's largest theatre) and ended, three months later, with six nights at the Bristol Hippodrome, closing on April 16.

Gene and Eddie were permanent fixtures, with a rotating support mostly drawn from Larry's stable. On the first night, they were joined by Vince Eager, Tony Sheridan and The Viscounts. By the time they got to the Birmingham Hippodrome, on March 17, the bill included Billy, Joe Brown and Georgie Fame. Gene was accompanied by The Wildcats – Big Jim Sullivan, Tony Belcher, Brian 'Licorice' Locking and Brian Bennett – who, it said in the programme, appeared "by kind permission of Marty Wilde".

Bravely facing down any accusation of vested interest, Jack Good reviewed one of the Gene/Eddie shows for *Disc* magazine.

"Then at last came Gene Vincent. Dressed in black from top to toe, Gene is like a demon possessed by the beat. His face pours with sweat, contorted to an agonised smile, his huge eyes staring at a vision only he can see. Vincent is the most extraordinary, eccentric and terrifying spectacle on the stage today. The volume of the screams, together with that of the band, drowned Gene's voice, which is – the final contradiction, in this mass of contradictions – a soft, fluid and beautiful instrument. But it didn't matter. To watch him was enough... and knowing how ill he was, for me it was too much."

Another vivid account of the show comes from the actor Peter Bowles, who, working at the Bristol Old Vic, caught it towards the end of the tour at the Bristol Hippodrome. He was particularly impressed by Eddie.

"When he came on, the stage was in complete darkness and the spotlight came on as the music started – but it was on his bum; he was wearing a pair of tight-fitting red leather trousers, never seen before. And the spotlight was just on his bottom, gyrating. This was wicked. Sexy. The audience was screaming. The other thing I particularly remember about his performance was that at one point he said to the audience, 'I'm gonna do something I've never done before. I've never done this before and I'm gonna do it now. I'm a gonna do it for you. I'm gonna... I'm gonna...' And we all thought, my God, he's going to drop his trousers! And he said, 'I'm a-gonna... smile!' The audience went absolutely mad! Extraordinary!"

While Eddie sexed it up for the USA, Billy gave his all for team UK.

85

The *Liverpool Daily Post* described Billy "creeping around the floor and performing the strangest of contortions", and wondered what Billy's mates from the tugboat would think of his gold lamé suit. The piece concluded, "the only man fit to review the show at the Empire last night would be a psychiatrist."

"The girls used to go wild when Billy was on stage," said Joe Brown in his autobiography, "screaming and jumping all over the place. But their boyfriends: they'd just come to see Gene Vincent. So, while Billy was strutting his stuff, giving the chicks their big thrill for the night, the blokes were sitting there simmering and swearing. 'Bloody kill him' they were all threatening.

"There was this one night, Billy came rushing out of the theatre intent on a quick getaway to find that the roadie hadn't unlocked the door of the car. Girls were grabbing bits of him and blokes were throwing punches at him. It was pandemonium. Billy put up an arm to protect himself and accidently walloped some girl in the face. At which very moment there's a flash and some amateur photographer's racing down's down the street screaming 'Scoop! Scoop!' followed by a furious Billy, some rent-a-roadie, screaming girls and swearing fellas."

Eddie and Gene both liked a drink, and though, compared to Gene's, Eddie's carousing barely put him in the professional league, when hell needed raising he was happy to help out with the heavy lifting.

On tour, the British contingent, though not averse to the odd shandy, looked on with amazement as night after night Eddie and Gene filled their legs with scotch.

"Eddie was so drunk at the Liverpool Empire," said Jim Sullivan, The Wildcat's guitar player, "that we weren't sure that he would make it to the stage. It had one of those microphones that came up from the floor. We positioned Eddie so that it would come up between his body and his guitar and he could balance on it."

Gene could be a nasty drunk. Billy learned to keep clear of him.

"He'd say, 'Wanna meet Henry?' and pull out his switchblade. One night, he cut up the road manager's suit... while he was still wearing it."

Eddie was a far more mellow presence, who liked to take the edge off things with a spliff or two. Billy had – according to many sources – been smoking weed since his tugboat days. Eddie introduced him to resin. Cannabis remained Billy's friend for the rest of his life and may (see later chapters) have even kept him alive.

Birth of a legend. Marty, Ronnie and Jimmy Tarbuck, the Essoldo 1958.
LIVERPOOL ECHO

The Liverpool cowboy's first EP, 1959.
ALAMY

Billy's 22nd birthday (Larry lied about his age – in icing).
MIRRORPIX

"Angel face."
CHRIS ELEY

Billy and the Furettes.
ALAMY

The A Team: Gene, Joe, Billy, Eddie.
ALAMY

"Hands in the gunslinger position."
CHRIS ELEY

"Serious haircut, collar up."
CHRIS ELEY

Lennon, fawning for once in his life.
CHENISTON ROLAND

Bridie Gallagher's worst nightmare.
CHRIS ELEY

Billy, playing nicely with the other boys on the set of *Play It Cool*.
ALAMY

Making movies.
CHRIS ELEY

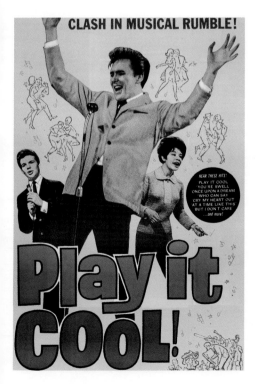

"It was a really bad, bad movie."
ALAMY

"Hi, Baby, what's happening?"
CHRIS ELEY

"Standing in one spot gyrating the hips was never the most cinematic dance, anyway."
CHRIS ELEY

"Man, we've had a terrific season here." Billy with The Tornados in Great Yarmouth.
CHRIS ELEY

Billy sandwich! With unknown beauty (left) and Maggie Stredder (right).
CHRIS ELEY

With Lee's chihuahua.
CHRIS ELEY

On the road.
CHRIS ELEY

Secret love – Lee Middleton.
LEE EVERETT- ALKIN

Thank Your Lucky Stars.
CHRIS ELEY

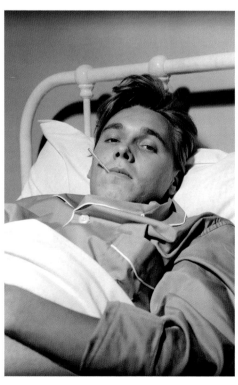

"Don't die, Billy! Don't die!"
ALAMY

Hal Carter, Billy's tour manager and later his manager, was on the tour, doing his best to satisfy Gene's demands for pizza (at the time, an exotic delicacy unknown outside of specialist Soho outlets) at 11 at night, in Wales.

Maurice Berman, a reporter for the *Melody Maker*, provided a glimpse of Billy's life on the road through a phone call to Billy when the tour hit Newcastle. Hal Carter was close by, standing in for Larry and carefully vetting the call.

"'We're touring with Gene Vincent and Eddie Cochran,' says Billy.
'Who's going over best?'
There was a slight pause and another man's voice answered.
'Billy is. He's too modest to tell you.'
Billy took the phone back.
'No, we are all going over well.'
'Who was that?'
'Hal Carter, my road manager. He's standing next to me and can hear you. Am I still in the hit parade? I haven't seen the *MM* yet and I'm worried.'
'Where are you staying now?'
'I don't know.'
'How do you find your way home then?'
'My manager brings me home. I call him my shadow.'
'Manchester' whispered the manager behind Billy.
'We are appearing at Manchester next week,' said Billy dutifully.
'Television,' said the manager, sotto voice.
'I'm doing a dry run next week for Jack Good's TV show. Jack chose my record 'Colette'.'
'What do you do all day in Newcastle?'
'I get up at 11, have breakfast, then read a lot of comics...'
'No, no,' said the manager in a hoarse, urgent voice
"'Well... they're classic comics taken from films. Then I read comics like *20,000 Leagues Under The Sea*. I also read horror comics...'
'No, no, no!' shouted the manager, now frantic. 'He reads books!'
'Well I do,' said Billy 'but I only get so far then I get fed up. Then I play a lot of records. Then it's time to go to the theatre.'
'No sport?'
'No.'
'No girls?'

'NO.' said the manager. Then, 'Gold lamé suit.'

"'Oh yes. I have a gold lamé suit'."

Halfway through the tour, Eddie's girlfriend, the songwriter Sharon Sheeley, who'd written Ricky Nelson's monster hit 'Poor Little Fool' and co-written Eddie's 'Somethin' Else', flew to the UK to be with Eddie on her 20th birthday. Some sources suggest that Eddie wasn't too happy about this, even though the pair were supposed to be 'unofficially' engaged.

Hal Carter was pretty adamant that at some point Billy and Sharon hooked up. It's impossible, of course, to establish the truth of this, but it's not difficult to imagine the scenario. It's late night in a drab hotel. They're two heterosexual, pretty young people far away from home and a little bit lonely. They both possess the full complement of hormones. Eddie's drunk. Billy's a sensual sex machine. Under the circumstances, it's hard to imagine why they wouldn't have done it. Most people would.

After the last Bristol show, Eddie, Gene and Sharon were eager to get back to London. Eddie and Sharon had a flight to catch back to the USA. Gene had commitments in France.

"We'd been using a minicab all week and asked the driver what it'd cost to take them to London," said Hal Carter. "He said he'd find out and get back to us but instead of going to his firm, he asked a friend of his to borrow him his car and came back and told us £25."

The three and their tour manager Pat Thomkins got in the car. On Rowden Hill, just outside Chippenham, it blew a tyre and hit a lamp-post.

One of the first police officers on the scene was a young Wiltshire cadet called Dave Harman.

"The driver and roadie were virtually unhurt, but Eddie, Gene and Sharon were all lying on the grass injured. It was quite clear that Eddie was in a bad way."

All three were rushed to hospital. Sharon suffered a broken pelvis. Gene broke ribs and his collarbone and sustained further damage to his already weak leg. Eddie was the worst casualty with, among other injuries, severe head trauma and possible brain damage.

Billy, Dickie Pride and Larry Parnes arrived at St Martin's Hospital in Bath at six in the morning but Eddie didn't regain consciousness. He died at 4.10 that afternoon.

Vince Eager joined them at the hospital. A few days earlier, Eddie had played him a new song called 'Cut Across Shorty'. "He said it would be his next release, with another of his songs, 'Three Steps To Heaven', on the B-side." But on the steps of the Bath hospital where Eddie had just died, Larry Parnes announced to the press that by a strange irony, Eddie's next release was called 'Three Steps To Heaven'.

"He exploited the situation and I fell out with him over that," said Vince.

'Three Steps to Heaven' had been recorded in California earlier that year. It was released soon after Eddie's death and went to number one in the UK, with 'Cut Across Shorty' as the B-side.

A well-known footnote to the story concerns that police cadet, Dave Harman. He made sure that Eddie's guitar, the orange Gretsch, was safely impounded at the station. From time to time, however, he'd take it out of its case to give it an airing. He taught himself a few chords. Later, he changed his name and formed a band called Dave Dee & The Bostons, which changed its name to Dave Dee, Dozy, Beaky, Mick & Tich, whose 1968 hit 'The Legend Of Xanadu' was a million-seller.

It's an ill wind.

CHAPTER NINE

"...ONE OF THE GREATEST ROCK AND ROLL ALBUMS OF ITS ERA."

In June 1960, Larry launched a mini tour, *A Tribute Show To The Late Eddie Cochran* – "each artiste will perform one of Eddie Cochran's songs" – just five venues but week-long gigs in Glasgow, Liverpool and Cardiff. At the start of the tour, he issued a press release announcing that part of the proceeds from each show would go to Eddie's family.

Gene Vincent, who after a couple of week's recuperation in the USA had returned to carry on touring in the UK, appeared in the first couple of shows. After that Billy took over as the headline act.

Before Eddie's death, at the end of March, Billy had at last had a Top 10 hit with 'Colette', another song he'd written back when he was on the tugboats.

"Between tides, I found I had time to spare so I went to a local cinema," he told Keith Goodwin for the *New Musical Express*. "There was a French film showing – I forget the title – and the heroine was a pretty girl called Colette. I found a stub of a pencil in my pocket and rummaged round on the floor until I found an old cigarette packet. Then, while the film was still going on, I began to write the lyrics in the dark."

"Don't forget Colette – it rhymes, I thought," he told the *Evening News*. "£3,000 I made out of that. But it's the mood that counts, see. If you go home and say you think you'll write a song, you'll never write it. You have to feel something."

"Billy was a very good songwriter," Marty says. "Better than he ever thought, better than he ever dreamed. At the time, I didn't give it a lot of thought, but when you review those early songs like 'Colette' and 'Margo' and all those other songs, he was well on the way. It was maybe an area that he didn't follow through as much as he should have done. We were all too busy doing things, we didn't have a lot of time. Larry was working us so hard and we were touring all over the place."

Vaguely reminiscent of Buddy Holly's 'Peggy Sue', 'Colette' is sung throughout in Everly Brother's-style two-part harmony. Live, on *Boy Meets Girls*, Marty Wilde provided the harmony. On record it was Ann O'Brien – another Vernons Girl.

"Jack Good had seen me and Mary Redmond doing an Everlys' song," said Ann, "and Billy asked me if I would sing with him. I said, 'Oh yes, I'd love to.' Billy sang it to me and asked where I could put some harmonies. It was recorded at Decca Studios in West Hampstead and I got an envelope with £7 cash in it."

Billy made £3,000, Ann was grateful for £7. Rick Wakeman made £9 for the iconic piano introduction of Cat Stevens' 'Morning Has Broken'. Such is the lot of the session musician.

Billy seemed to be trying to corner the market in heartbreak songs. He was fond of 'ow' rhymes – appropriate perhaps for any hurting song. Compare and contrast "you broke a v*ow*, I'm lonely n*ow*" from 'Colette' with "Don't fool with other guys, don't paint the t*ow*n, you'll get a big surprise, I won't be 'r*ou*nd" from 'Margo', and "Rise in the mornin', you're not ar*ou*nd/Searchin' all over, you can't be f*ou*nd" from 'Maybe Tomorrow'. "Ow", he sings, and the armies of heartbroken fans think, "That's just how I feel".

'Baby How I Cried', the B-side of 'Colette, sung with a Johnny Ray intensity, is exactly the kind of song a jilted lover might play endlessly in a darkened bedroom while their mother knocks on the door saying, "It's a lovely day out, you know. Why don't you take your sister up the park?"

On the back of a Top 10 hit, Jack Good suggested that an LP might be appropriate and Decca agreed, albeit to a modest 10-inch one rather than the full 12-inch standard size.

Jack set about recreating the sound he had in his head.

Actually, it wasn't in his head. It was already on record.

In 1954 and 1955 at a series of sessions at the Memphis Recording Service on Union Avenue, otherwise known as Sun Studio, recording engineer Sam Philips invented the sound of rock'n'roll, most notably using Elvis Presley on vocal and acoustic guitar, Scotty Moore on electric guitar, Bill Black on stand-up bass, and sometimes either Jimmie Lott or Johnny Bernero on drums.

Decca Studios, in Broadhurst Gardens, West Hampstead, London NW6, were getting on for four and a half thousand miles from Union Avenue, Memphis. Nevertheless, Jack gave it his best shot and the result, *The Sound Of Fury*, is nothing short of magnificent.

Billy composed every track himself. It wasn't the first time an artiste, even a rock'n'roll artiste, had self-composed an entire album. By 1960 Chuck Berry already had three of them under his belt, but all the same it was a rarity.

In an interview in April with the *Evening News* (during which the pompous reporter repeatedly refers to Billy's composition 'Colette' as 'Nicolette') Billy talks about his *modus operandum*: "What I do is get an idea when I'm depressed – usually 'cos one of my girls has let me down – and scribble a lyric and sing the whole thing into a tape recorder. It never gets on paper you know until a chap at the music publishers puts it there. Then they send me back an arrangement which I can't read, so I just record it the way I thought of it anyway."

The reporter goes on to say that Billy must have had a lot of feelings because he's had no less than 18 girlfriends in 12 months (not including a "'blonde' he found in his car boot in Leeds").

The 18 "girlfriends" Billy admitted to is almost certainly something of an underestimation. Sometimes Mr Parnes was called upon to help him out of his romantic entanglements.

"Our relationship," said Larry, "is not of artiste and manager. We are more like mates."

Billy seemed to agree: "He even helps me with my girls. It's when they get a bit of a drag, see. Like this chick kept phoning me. So Larry wrote me out a script and I read it to her over the phone. Boy – it was good! The last line went something like, 'Goodbye, I still love you but this is how it's got to be. Bless you.' Girls have caused me bother. I suffered love heartache and all that. But it helps me compose."

Though generally known for his shyness and reticence, Billy was never backward in coming forward when it came to matters of the heart, as he told journalist Donald Zec. "'Then there was Doreen. I was really smitten on her, y'know. Just like Elizabeth Taylor she was. But she was engaged to someone else. I broke it up, it was a horrible thing to do.'

"'It could have happened to anybody,' says Parnes earnestly. 'It worried Billy so much he hardly ate that day – and wrote '[The] Time Has Come'.'

"A beautiful, vivacious girl named Anne was the next to fall for the melodious sound of Fury.

"'She was a model with smashing lips, y'know,' Billy recalled with a crooked grin. 'The sort you wanted to kiss all day long.'

"'Did you?'

"'Yeah – except when I was 'aving me dinner.'"

Jack Good picks up the story. "He'd say, 'I've just written something can I play it to you? And he'd play it quietly to me. The whole man was before you. And I thought, we must record this. I bullied Decca into letting us record these tracks. Their confidence in us was, I suppose, shown in that we had a budget for just five musicians and Billy had to fly in his own vocal backing group and we were given two three-hour sessions to make 10 songs."

A rough tape recording of Billy demoing *The Sound Of Fury* songs has miraculously survived. The tape recorder is not state of the art; the best guess is that it was Jack Good's machine and the tape was recorded at Jack's flat in Chiswick. Somebody, possibly roadie Hal Carter, provides harmony on one track – but otherwise it's all Billy, self-accompanied on guitar. He adds modest comments between the songs, addressed to the musicians who'll eventually be playing on the session, delivered in his little-boy-lost voice: "Hello? These are the... these are the songs fellahs, and... er... let's see... yeah... I'm just gonna give you a rough idea... I don't know... I don't know where the solos are or anything... ahem... that'll have to be worked out in the session, but this is how they go roughly... erm... the first one's called 'Well, All Right'."

The recording quality is less than pristine, but the intimacy of those tracks makes them almost better than the album itself. The voice, without echo, artifice or affectation, has an innocence about it, reinforced by the straightforward naivety of the lyrics and the simple strummed chords. A few years later a studio-recorded version of the demo might have been released, unadorned, as the work of a singer-songwriter. Indeed, its directness gives it almost the quality of folk music – except that this is a lad from Liverpool singing about having his heart broken rather than a graduate from Carshalton whining about colliery explosions. As Jack put it, "The soul of Billy Fury was in that record."

Not all the tracks on the demo tape ended up on the album. A song called 'Cheating With Love' wasn't properly recorded until 1963. Even then it remained in the vaults, and eventually became one of Billy's posthumous releases, in 1989. Other songs had their titles changed. 'Well, All Right', became 'Alright, Goodbye', presumably to avoid confusion with Buddy Holly's 1958 release, 'Well... All Right'. Similarly, for reasons less clear, 'What I Need' became 'It's You I Need.'

On the first issue of the album they're all properly credited to "Fury", but, confusingly, some re-issues and compilations credit the songs to "Wilberforce". This was a pseudonym later adopted by Billy – perhaps part of a plot designed to prevent Mr Parnes taking his slice off the top of the royalties. William Wilberforce was a renowned anti-slavery campaigner.

The demo was handed to pianist Reg Guest, who sketched out some arrangements, and on April 14, two days before Eddie Cochran's accident, Billy took a couple of days off the tour to go into the studio.

He was joined by Reg Guest on piano, Joe Brown on guitar and Andy White (who later played on one of The Beatles' early sessions when heretical doubts were cast on Ringo's competence) on drums.

There were two bass players, Alan Weighall on bass guitar and Bill Stark on stand-up bass, playing simultaneously. Usually this is explained as an attempt to recreate Bill Black's slap-bass technique in which the strings are snapped and smacked against the fingerboard, a percussive effect to make up for the lack of drums on most of the Sun records. In fact, scoring identical lines for acoustic and electric bass became a relatively common studio practice in the sixties and seventies. The acoustic bass can provide a slap and a grunt to the bottom end: the bass guitar adds clarity and welly.

Backing vocals were provided by the Four Jays, a Scottish comedy/ close harmony group (not to be confused with an early incarnation of The Fourmost that had the same name). The members of the group all had names beginning with J – John Morgan, Joe McKinley, John Dickie and John Chalmers – hence 'The Four J's'. The band had featured, usually fairly low on the bill, on package tours of the time, but broke up soon after *The Sound Of Fury* sessions when one of them won the pools.*

Jack's instructions to the musicians were to make it sound as much like a Sun session as they could. "He asked Reg Guest to play like Floyd Cramer [Elvis' piano player on many sessions after the Sun era] and told me to do my Scotty Moore [Elvis' guitar player]," says Joe Brown. "We did a run-through of each number and then a take. Practically everything was done in one go."

Joe Brown copped his very first guitar off the bloke who played in his Uncle Joe's pub. It cost him £1. He was 10 years old. Listening to his playing on *The Sound Of Fury* convinces you that he must have spent every waking hour since immersed in Chet Atkins, Merle Travis, Franny Beecher, Scotty Moore, Cliff Gallup and all the other guitar heroes of country, rock'n'roll and rockabilly (not to mention heroes peripheral to country and rockabilly but nonetheless crucial, like George Formby, Charlie Christian, Max Wall, Les Paul and 'Two-Ton' Tessie O'Shea) and absorbed their spirit, their rhythm, their licks and their turnarounds. His playing isn't an imitation of the style. It has absolute fluidity and authority. He's cracked this one. He knows how to make a solo fly, and, even more impressively, knows how to land it with satisfying assurance.

The entire album, as Joe says, was recorded in a day, most of the tracks in one take; although 'Turn My Back On You' may have been previously recorded in January and possibly re-recorded at the April session, and possibly may feature Big Jim Sullivan rather than Joe on guitar (the guitar sound is distinctly different, but deciding which version ended up on the album can lead to earnest discussions about matrix numbers so is best avoided).

"We did squeeze out of Decca some rehearsal time in the rehearsal hall beforehand where Reg Guest wrote down the chords for the three guys who read music and we worked out what we would do roughly," said Jack. "So, when it came down to it, we had to accept stuff that sometimes you'd like improved on. But it did have spontaneity. It did have simplicity. Billy's voice, we made sure, was always there, not smudged over by loud backing."

---

* Many thanks to Chris Eley and Roger Dopson for providing that intricately researched nugget of information on the sleeve notes for the CD of the demos.

The whole is an object lesson in less-is-best. Three of the tracks are less than two minutes long, and another two clock in at no more than a whisker over – 20 minutes' running time all told.

It's a great deal more than a mere copy of Elvis' Memphis sessions. Thanks largely to Reg Guest's piano, the overall sound is much more bluesy than anything Elvis did at Sun, moving away from Memphis up to some smoky club on the South Side of Chicago. Billy, too, is something more than an Elvis tribute act, pulling in influences from all over the place – from Johnny Ray, from Eddie Cochran, from Ray Charles, from Hank Williams.

Jack, as already mentioned, was a Shakespeare scholar, who later in his career turned *Othello* into an excellent rock musical called *Catch My Soul*. The title of Billy's LP is more than likely inspired by *Macbeth*, Act 5, Scene 5, "Life's but a walking shadow, a poor player/That struts and frets his hour upon the stage/And then is heard no more: it is a tale/Told by an idiot, full of *sound and fury*/Signifying nothing."

The sleeve is a black and white shot of Billy on stage wearing his gold suit – acquired just that year for 35 guineas (£36.75) – in a pose aping the shots of Elvis in *his* gold suit, used on the cover of *Elvis' Golden Hits – Volume 2*, released in the previous year. Billy's eyes are directed to the left and up. He looks peeved, as if, maybe, a stage-hand up in the flies is trying to put him off by pulling faces and flicking Vs. It is possible that Decca was hoping for a shot of him looking furious, in keeping with the title of the album, or at least 'moody and smouldering', but had to settle for slight irritability.

"I look like I've got a gobstopper in my mouth," was how Billy liked to describe it.

The album sold well, making Top 20 in the album charts (but failing, like everything else, to shift the soundtrack recording of Rodgers & Hammerstein's *South Pacific* from the number one slot, to which position it had been bolted week in, week out for 18 months, and in which position it would doggedly continue to remain, with just a handful of exceptions, until September 1961.)

New Musical Express was particularly impressed with the novel idea of a rock'n'roller writing his own material. "How many teenage stars can boast that they wrote all of the songs on their first LP?" it asked.

"Sooner or later," Billy said in the article, "I want to learn to read and write music. Right now, I'm purely self-taught. I play guitar, a little piano, and I'm also just picking up the rudiments of bongo playing. But I'm certain that if I study the technical side of music it will be a big help to my career."

He never found time to commit himself to studying the "technical side", which is perhaps a blessing. It's doubtful whether 'Billy Fury, virtuoso bongoist' would have brought the same pleasure he did as a singer.

The Sound Of Fury has endured as a great classic, indeed *the* great classic of British rock'n'roll. Jack and the engineers did their lad proud.

The record does have the intimate feel of the Sun sessions – the impression that the musicians are all gathered close around a single mic, eyeballing each other, exchanging nods and smiles, having a good time. The only sense of space is provided by the slap-back tape and chamber echo the studio had on tap.

But there's also the question of attitude. Jack and the musicians are taking the music seriously. They don't sound like jazzers slumming it. They recognise that there's more to this beat music business than three chords and some honking. They're not taking the piss.

Respect for the album continues to build.

"If Billy had done nothing but that classic 10-inch album," says Chris Eley, "he would still be revered today."

Keith Richards, in a 2015 *Rolling Stone* interview, said, "Billy Fury did one fantastic album that I've lost. He got it together once. One really good album. Songs he'd written, like people do now. He got some people he knew to play together and did it. His other scene was the hits, heavy moody ballads and the lead pipe down the trousers. But *The Sound Of Fury* is one of the greatest rock'n'roll albums of its era, and one I swear by."

In a 2008 *Daily Telegraph* poll, journalist, producer and manager Paul Morley chose *The Sound Of Fury* as one of his top 30 albums of all time. DJ John Peel called it "the only authentic British rock'n'roll album around at that time."

Unfortunately, "the only authentic British rock'n'roll album around" came just after the music was on the wane.

In the first few months of 1960, the word on everybody's lips was 'bay-beh' – an impersonation of Adam Faith's pronunciation of 'baby', the hook of his million-seller 'What Do You Want?' The track with its pizzicato strings and light, bouncy rhythm, was definitely not rock'n'roll.

In 1960, Lonnie Donegan, who used to sing murder ballads with laser-beam passion, released 'My Old Man's A Dustman'. Cliff Richard, sloe-eyed sex god of *Oh Boy!*, had achieved his first number one the year before with 'Living Doll', a song of female oppression sung with a gentle country lilt. He enjoyed his second number one in 1960, with 'Please Don't Tease', a medium-tempo youth club foot-tapper, and his third with 'I Love You', a boon to insomniacs. Everything, it seemed, had gone soft.

The same was true in America. Chuck Berry was doing five years, later commuted to three, for "transporting a minor across the state line for immoral purposes". Little Richard had renounced secular music and was studying for the ministry in Huntsville, Alabama. Elvis, his hair shorn and sideburns shaved, was a GI in Germany. Jerry Lee Lewis was still in disgrace. Buddy was dead. Eddie was dead.

Real rock'n'roll had all but vanished from America's airwaves.

"All they played was them Bobbies," said Jerry Lee. "Bobby Vee, Bobby Vinton, Bobby Rydell, Bobby Darin. If your name was Bobby, you were in with a sporting chance."

"Isn't the 'rock' party over?" Donald Zec of the *Daily Express* asked Larry. "Aren't the agonised 'Arrys in the leather jerkins, tight jeans and long sideburns just about all washed up?'

"Not at all," Larry replied. "If I had another six artistes on my books I could sell them all. What has happened, though, is that they've all had to change their style. They've grown up now. In the old days, they were just coffee-bar cowboys making peculiar sounds. All they needed was a guitar, a dominant background and plenty of echo. The fellow didn't even have to speak, and as long as he looked clean under the spotlight it didn't matter if he needed a wash. Now the kids want toffs – not scruffs. The T-shirt is out – gold lamé is in. Take Billy Fury. He's got three-dozen stage suits and shirts to go with them. He's got a gold lamé suit, a deep purple velvet jacket and a red and gold shirt interwoven with silver tinsel [one must never forget that Larry Parnes started his career in the rag trade]. And that's the sort of style I demand from my other boys."

British TV seemed to have caught the Bobby bug, too.

Boy Meets Girls, Jack Good's follow-up to *Oh Boy!*, finished its run on March 5, 1960. Just over a month later *Melody Maker* carried the front-page headline "Jack Good Back With A – Wham!"

Wham!, hosted by Keith Fordyce, was as fast moving as *Oh Boy!* and introduced the innovation, later adopted by *Ready, Steady, Go* and *Top Of The Pops*, of making the audience an integral part of the set. The first show went out on Saturday, April 23 at 6 p.m., in direct opposition to BBC's *Juke Box Jury*.

At first the signs looked good.

"It's going right back to rock'n'roll," said the *Daily Express* preview. "The opening show features singing guitarist Joe Brown, Billy Fury and Little Tony. One innovation is 'The Fat Noise'. This is a new musical combination of four trumpets, two trombones, a tuba, four saxes, three guitars, a bass guitar, two sets of drums, a piano and a Salvation Army-type bass drum. 'It will provide the fattest, roundest sound that has ever come to television,' says Jack."

Another innovation was competition. Viewers were asked each week to vote (on a postcard, please) for their favourite act. It was nearly always Billy.

Then came the apocalypse. On June 4, ABC television, the company behind *Wham!*, announced: "ABC thinks there is no longer a public for teenage rock'n'roll type programmes."

They pulled the show.

The last transmission was on June 18. The following week it was replaced by *Holiday Town Parade*, a variety show with a seaside theme, and, as a sop to 'pop' fans, the 5.30 slot was filled with *The Tin Pan Alley Show*, featuring MOR and big band singers – Michael Holliday, The Kaye Sisters, Ronnie Hilton and The John Barry Seven – in whose company even a Bobby or two would have seemed dangerously hip.

CHAPTER TEN

"...BUT WHEN HE PUT THE GOLD LAMÉ SUIT ON, IT WAS LIKE THERE WAS SOMEONE ELSE INSIDE."

On May 19, 1960, Decca released 'That's Love', the Bobbiest of all the songs from *The Sound Of Fury*, as a single. It went to number 19.

Earlier in the month, Larry had decided that Billy, now that he was an established star and a headlining act, needed a backing band all of his own. Possibly because he knew where the top talent of the time was to be found, or because he wanted Billy to feel at home with his new playmates, or because he reckoned scousers would be cheaper than cockneys, he travelled to Liverpool and hired the Wyvern Social Club at 108 Steel Street (later called the Blue Angel) for auditions.

"All the Liverpool bands were down there," said Adrian Barber, guitar player with Cass & The Casanovas, "because this was Larry Parnes, man, the big-time promoter! But we all hated him, we hated his acts. He was the epitome of the cliché British show-business guy: the mohair coat, always smoking a cigar. They used to call him 'Parnes, Shillings and Pence'. But it was a gig you know? So we all showed up."

The Silver Beetles, formerly Johnny & The Moondogs, and before that The Quarrymen, turned up late and nearly missed their slot.

"When we arrived at the club, our drummer [this was long before Ringo] hadn't shown up, so Johnny Hutchinson, the drummer with Cass & The Casanovas, sat in with us," said George Harrison. "I don't think we played particularly well or particularly badly."

They didn't get the gig. According to Lee Middleton, more of whom in a few pages time, "Billy said they'd be trouble, and I think he was right. Lennon would not have been an easy man to have in your backing group, would he?"

There is a photograph from that day, taken by Cheniston Roland. Billy, sitting, has pen and paper, while Lennon leans in towards him, making what looks like a request for an autograph. Billy looks glazed, shocked maybe or stunned. It could be that Lennon had made some inappropriate remark. Or it could be that Billy was having a terrifying presentiment of things to come. Lennon later told Brian Gregg that he thought Billy was "the best rock singer in the country." And at that time, Billy was everything that Lennon wanted to be. The toppermost of the poppermost.

"John Lennon asked me if they could sing a couple of their own songs," said Larry, years later in an interview with Bob Azurdia. "He said, 'We don't really want to be a backing group but we will do anything to get work. Would you listen to our own songs?' I said, 'We're going to be late but we'll stay behind for a quarter of an hour and listen.' They played me three or four of their songs, songs that later became big hits, and I remember saying to John Lennon, 'No disrespect to your drummer but you need another drummer, somebody with a little more drive and bash. He's a good drummer, but he is not for your outfit.'

"John Lennon said, 'Please give us work, we really need it', so I said, 'If something comes along, you'll be first [band I'll] phone.' Something did come along, a tour in Scotland, six weeks with Johnny Gentle, and I got in touch with John Lennon and that's how it happened. Johnny Gentle used to phone me several times a week saying how good they were and I should get up to see them. I didn't have the chance or the time to do that."

With or without The Beatles, "the epitome of the cliché British show business guy" was coining it. He had installed himself and his organisation in a 2,000 square foot suite of offices overlooking Oxford Street. The "trickle-down" theory, so popular in the eighties, that if the rich are allowed to get richer their wealth will magically "trickle down" and make the poor a little bit richer too, was as fraudulent in Larry's time as it was in Mrs Thatcher's.

"As far as Billy was concerned, his clothes, flat, car, petrol – all that was taken care of," said Hal Carter. "So £20 was on top of that, just pocket money. The second year it was £40, and so on. They (the stars) weren't overpaid, sure, but they were looked after."

Larry made sure all the lads had nice wheels and arranged photo-ops of the stars with their cars. Johnny Gentle had a two-tone Ford Consul, Vince a two-tone Triumph Herald, Dickie Pride a beat-up red Sprite, Duffy Power a cream Consul with red and white upholstery and Marty Wilde was driving his "cream and red American Ford Fairlane with the assurance of a veteran". He was a married man with a baby on the way by this time. "I've had my go with sports cars," he said. "They're all right for the enthusiast, but now I want a family car."

"Well, y'see," said Larry, "the cars themselves are worth £10,184. 'Course Marty's American job, costing £2,660, bumps up the figure. And then I've just insured all 10 stars for a sum total of £205,000."

Billy's first car was a blue MGA coupe. "It's a marvellous car," he said in April 1960. "The needle goes right round to the red bit. No. I haven't taken my driving test yet – a friend's giving me lessons."

As soon as he'd passed his test he started hankering for something faster – an Aston Martin or an E-Type Jag. "I never want to be passed in a car, and neither do a lot of other drivers," he said at the time. "They seem to dare me to overtake them when I try to pass. I get a kick out of that sometimes. I might catch up with a car on a bend. My sense tells me to slow down, but my foot won't come off the accelerator. The tension builds up – will I be able to make it? That's when I capture the scared feeling."

For a time, he talked of becoming a racing driver, but, in the end, decided, "Quite frankly it's far too risky a business. My friends and associates have all advised me against it."

By December 1961, he'd managed to pick up four speeding fines.

"Sometimes I'd have to phone up and get insurance for the boys' cars," says Muriel Walker, Larry's secretary. "I'd say, 'Under 21, rock'n'roller, sports car,' and they'd laugh."

"The lowest insurance I could get for a sports car would be £500 a year," Billy said.

The average annual income at the time was just under £1,000.

"The lowest premium I can have on any car, even a Mini, is £180. So I've settled for a Humber."

The white Humber Super Snipe cost close to £2,000. It was the sort of car that, despite its vaguely American styling, a raffish bank manager might have parked outside his golf club. "It's a smart car and very comfortable, but not as fast as I'd like."

He later added a Lotus Super Seven to his collection – a two-seater that looked Grand Prix ready and made a satisfying growl. "Anyway, from now on," he said, "I'm going to be very careful on the roads."

A year later in Great Yarmouth, he was done for speeding again. This time he pleaded mitigating circumstances, claiming that two girls had waited until the early hours at the stage door to get his autograph. They were supposed to be home by 10.30. Their dads, they said, would kill them. So, Billy hurried them home in his Humber. Which is why he was doing 43 mph in a built-up area.

Fined £50 and banned for a month.

Meanwhile, Gene Vincent continued his apparently never-ending progress around the country. Billy sometimes joined him.

On the same night as the last ever *Wham!*, June 18, Gene walked onto the stage at the Theatre Royal Nottingham. He'd been playing there a week, on a bill with Vince Taylor, Duffy Power, Lance Fortune and Nero & The Gladiators.

With tears streaming down his face, and in a mumbling, barely coherent voice, he read out a telegram he'd received from his wife Darlene telling him that his 18-month-old daughter, Melody, had contracted pneumonia and died.

Some people in the audience tittered, thinking it was part of the act. Others assumed that Melody was a dog, and reflected on how an Englishman, in such circumstances, would show a little more pluck and keep the upper lip stiffened. When the awful truth finally dawned, sniffles were heard in the audience, too.

The following day, on doctor's orders, he cancelled the rest of his UK gigs and got on a plane back to the USA. "I've had a rough time since Christmas, but I don't blame anyone for that," he told the press. "I have never really felt fit myself, but to cap that, my wife has been ill, and I've lost, first my best friend, then my baby daughter within two months of each other.

"I'm only sorry I have had to cancel variety dates and a summer season in Blackpool. [...] I hope nobody thinks I have let them down by going back to America. I want everyone to understand that it was the best thing I could do under the circumstances. Believe me, I wanted to finish those variety dates at Liverpool, Birmingham and Cardiff and then move on to Blackpool Queen's."

When he arrived back in the USA, however, he found, to his enduring astonishment and joy, that the tales of Melody's death were greatly exaggerated. She was alive and well and "playing happily at the Vincent home in Vancouver, Washington."

Darlene was completely mystified by the telegram. She certainly hadn't sent it. Gene decided it must have been some sort of hoax – although what kind of monster would be so cruel as to do such a thing?

Hit Parade magazine was quick to scotch the front-running theory that the telegram was a ruse designed to get him out of the tour. "But, whatever the truth, Gene to many people is a king of rock'n'roll, and no nasty rumours or stories will remove him from that throne."

Larry Parnes was having none of it, and put the whole affair into the hands of his lawyers.

Gene had been on the road a long time, spending endless hours in cars and trains, enduring dressing rooms, sleeping in inadequate hotels. He was in pain a lot of the time and grieving the loss of his friend. Heavy drinking and threatening people with guns and knives can take it out of you too. Under the circumstances, the prospect of "variety dates at Liverpool, Birmingham and Cardiff and then moving on to Blackpool Queen's" may not have seemed as attractive as he claimed. He wanted to go home.

All the same, faking your own daughter's death to get out of a contract takes a special kind of chutzpah. Rock'n'roll.

Summer was the time when all the pop stars came off the road, packed their buckets and spades, and enjoyed longer bookings at seaside resorts. A lot of them congregated in Blackpool. In 1960, Adam Faith was at the Blackpool Hippodrome. Tommy Steele and Cliff Richard both did short seasons at the Blackpool Opera House. Joe Brown was at the Queen's Theatre, Blackpool. Marty Wilde was at the Bournemouth Pavilion.

Shirley Bassey at the Bournemouth Winter Gardens. Frankie Vaughan at the Brighton Hippodrome and Billy Fury at the Britannia Theatre, Great Yarmouth.

The show was billed as "Larry Parnes presents the First Ever Anglo-American Summer Show, The Billy Fury Show, Meet The Beat". It starred Billy along with Vince Eager, Dickie Pride and Johnny Gentle (but no Silver Beetles, whose contract came to an end after the seven-date Scottish tour). Larry was running through Americans to justify the "Anglo-American" handle (one had died, the second had scarpered), so he hired Davy Jones (no relation to the Monkee), a singer and entertainer from Harlem, New York, who'd moved to the UK the year before and was trying to make a name for himself.

Billy was backed not by any of the bands that Larry had auditioned in Liverpool, but by The Beat Boys, a band of no fixed personnel. Even those who were there at the time find it hard to remember who backed whom at what gig, and what name they were using at the time. Best guess is, perhaps, Kenny Packwood on guitar, Brian Gregg on bass, Clem Cattini on drums and Georgie Fame on keyboards.*

In the souvenir programme for the Great Yarmouth show (priced at a shilling), Billy lists his hobbies and interests as "taking long walks" and "soft drinks". Someone has shaved a year off his age, too.

That was the summer that Meg Cummings, a Billy fan, had a close encounter – or was it a lucky escape? "We spent two weeks in Great Yarmouth and stayed in a caravan for the first week and a guest house for the second. It was next door to the house where some of the guys from the show were staying.

---

* Names came and went. For a short time, it was rumoured that Clive Powell, who became Georgie Fame, was given the name Lance Fortune. Later it was taken away from him and given to somebody called Christopher Morris who, as Lance Fortune, released the record 'Be Mine', which went to number four. And if Larry Parnes' friend Lionel Bart, the man who wrote 'Living Doll' and the musical Oliver!, had had his way, Clive Powell/Georgie Fame would have been called Bertie Beamish. Similarly, Bernard Jewry, who later became Shane Fenton and later still Alvin Stardust, started his career as a roadie for Shane Fenton & The Fentones, but got promoted to the 'Shane Fenton' role when the original 'Shane Fenton' (whose real name was Johnny Theakstone) died of complications resulting from – and here's the link with Billy – childhood rheumatic fever.

"One night a friend and I had a few too many drinks and had to return to the caravan. As we walked or probably staggered along the prom, lads in cars kept offering us lifts and we were getting a bit fed up.

"When we heard a voice say 'Get in,' we were just about to tell them to go away when we saw that it was Billy in his Humber Super Snipe. We jumped in and he asked us what on earth we had been doing.

"I was so sozzled that I kept poking him in the back and gabbling on about all sorts of nonsense. I said I liked his car and he told us that Larry had bought it for him and that it was a horrible monster of a thing and he hated it.

"He dropped us at our caravan and I invited him in for a drink and he said, 'Some other time – get to bed.' He told us that he had things to do. The next day we read in the evening paper that his car had been stolen and crashed."

The last bit is tricky to unpick. Did Billy later crash the car because he hated it, then reported it stolen to evade the consequences? Or was the driver not Billy at all, but a car thief who bore an uncanny resemblance to Billy, and (it gets less likely the longer it goes on) offered drunk young women lifts in his stolen car without any intention of taking advantage?

Meanwhile, Jack Good had found a song.

"I had a demo of Bill Giant's 'Wondrous Place' and it struck me immediately that it had to be done by Billy."

Bill Giant and his writing partner Jeff Lewis were two hopefuls working out of the Brill Building in New York, the 'song factory' where, at one time or another, Carole King, Neil Sedaka, Neil Diamond, Burt Bacharach and a few dozen other songwriters all went to work.

The song had already been recorded as an album track by Jimmy Jones, who'd had a couple of hits with 'Handy Man' and 'Good Timing', both of which featured his ability to effortlessly slip in and out of falsetto.

It was a minor-key piece, spooky but sexy.

"We both agreed that we wanted a steamy bayou thing," said Jack, "shades of Elvis Presley's 'Crawfish'. It was a wonderful stage number and Billy was terrific on stage. He was so quiet but when he put the gold lamé suit on, it was like there was someone else inside."

Billy recorded the track in June 1960, nailing its bedroom intimacy as well as the psycho-drama. The tempo suggests a pre-dawn stroll on a moonlit beach. Though the lyric says that the 'Wondrous Place' is in his "baby's arms", the music and performance suggest that the embrace is that of a ghostly visitor, "her tender hands on my face/I'm in heaven in her embrace/I want to stay and never go away/wondrous place."

The Jimmy Jones version had an ethereal choir and strings pushing the spookiness and Jimmy lays back on the beat, soulful and a little bit Sam Cooke. Billy's version is stripped down – you can barely hear much more than the two basses (acoustic and electric playing in unison again) and the brushed drums. He carries the mood all by himself, his voice drowned in reverb. At the end of each verse, the backing cuts out for two bars and the vocal for one. For three and a half agonising beats there is nothing but Billy's intake of breath, faintly vocalised on the last repetition as a "ca" sound.

The *NME* called it "tough, powerful and striking". Bridie Gallagher might have put it in the class of "that sort of thing", and not without justification.

Never has so much sexual longing been contained in the grooves of a bit of plastic.

Live, it was even sexier than the record.

"I saw Billy Fury in the early days before I got into music," said Dave Berry, the singer whose sinuous antics with a microphone on his big hit 'Crying Game' corrupted willing teens by the thousand. "The first time I saw him do 'Wondrous Place', he was using a tight, white spot and holding a cigarette. In the breaks, he tapped the cigarette and the ash fell on the floor. He looked great in that white spotlight."

'Wondrous Place' peaked at number 25, proving there never was any sense or justice in the charts.

Anyway, pop was on the move again. Those who thought the Bobbies were bad enough were completely dumbfounded by the advent of the Ackers.

CHAPTER ELEVEN

"DECCA GOT REALLY HEAVY WITH ME AND SLOWLY SWAYED ME TO THE BALLADS."

On September 30, 1960, *the New Musical Express* asked: "Will Dixieland kill rock?"

"That's the latest topic circulating through the British music scene," it went on. "For the first time ever, jazz has become 'pop' music. And, in Britain, locally-produced brash, revivalist, New Orleans-style trad jazz performed by the likes of Acker Bilk, Chris Barber, Kenny Ball, Terry Lightfoot and Ken Colyer, has spread out from the cellar clubs and art college Saturday night raves and into the charts, where it now stands shoulder-to-shoulder with rock'n'roll."

The New Orleans jazz revival – youngish, white, British men trying to play trumpets and banjos like old, black, American men – had been around since the end of the Second World War. Before the advent of rock'n'roll, it beamed passion onto the dance floor in a way that the standard strict-tempo combos never could. It was music that weekend bohemians in oversized sweaters and cats-eye eyeliner could jive to; music that the hipper Cambridge undergraduates could argue about over the sherry. "Buddy Bolden", they would say to each other, and nod enthusiastically.

Then it went mainstream.

As early as 1956, 'Bad Penny Blues', a boogie-shuffle by Humphrey Lyttelton & His Band, produced by Joe Meek, had edged into the Top 20. Then 1959 brought raids from Chris Barber's 'Petite Fleur' and 'Lonesome'. In 1960 'Summer Set', by Mr Acker Bilk And His Paramount Jazz Band (the "Mr" was obligatory), made number five at the same time as Billy's 'Colette' was languishing at number 22; and by the end of that year barely a week went by without a braying trombone, a wailing clarinet and a spanked banjo clogging up the charts.

Most perplexing of all was 'A Stranger On The Shore' by Mr Acker Bilk with the Leon Young String Chorale, which wasn't trad at all but a haunting melody played beautifully by Mr Bilk with deep emotional vibrato. It went to number two in the UK chart. Even more perplexingly, it reached number one in the US charts, a near-unprecedented achievement.

Trad also got, or seemed to get, an inordinate amount of BBC airplay. It's not hard to see why; the BBC was the senior guardian of the nation's morals, and trad was the kind of thing that members of the Ramblers Association liked to listen to.

The most accurate guide as to who was in and who was out in pop – at least as far as *Daily Express* readers went – was the annual Royal Variety Performance. In 1960, it had featured Lonnie Donegan, Adam Faith and Cliff & The Shadows. In 1961, it was strictly trad, dad. Her Majesty The Queen Mother was treated to not one but three trad bands: Mr Acker Bilk's, Kenny Ball's and The Temperance Seven. And not a single proper pop singer in sight.

The trad boom, like the Bobbies, was essentially an indication that pop had lapsed into a confused slough in which Roy Orbison, Sam Cooke, Gene Vincent, Ray Charles, Cliff, Marty and Billy had to share the tightly rationed minutes of BBC needle-time with, as well as the Ackers, Charlie Drake's 'My Boomerang Won't Come Back', Joe Loss & His Orchestra's 'Wheels-Cha-Cha' and Andy Stewart's 'The Battle's O'er', a Highland lament.

Larry Parnes and Jack Good observed the carnage that was being visited on their stock-in-trade and decided to go with the flow – or at least pretend to. The 'Trad Boom', be it illusory or real, was not to be ignored.

They put together a new monster package, with no less than 15 of Britain's finest rock talents including Billy, Joe Brown, Dickie Pride, Johnny Gentle, Duffy Power and Georgie Fame, and, covering their bets, billed it as the *Rock And Trad Spectacular*, "The New Noise of 1960, Starring Billy Fury and his company of 50". It opened in London in front of a celebrity audience that included Adam Faith, Marty Wilde, Lionel Bart, Cliff Richard's mum and dad and Tommy Steele's wife, sister and parents.

"I want the show to be fast-moving," Jack Good had said, and was as good as his word. The acts came and went in a blur.

Even Billy Fury, with his top billing as star of the show, was restricted to three numbers. Nevertheless

"Billy nearly stopped the show," said the *NME* review. "Or at least some of the young ladies in the audience did. Several ran to the pit rail threatening to climb on to the stage. Two succeeded in getting into the orchestra pit before being carried out, struggling, by attendants. Fury twisted, grunted, growled, rolled, pouted, glared – and won the biggest screams."

The putative trad element was provided by "Jimmie Nicol and his 15 New Orleans Rockers" (Jimmie Nicol was the drummer who later depped for Ringo on a Beatles tour of Australia when Ringo was having his tonsils out). The music they played was "more Glenn Miller than New Orleans", but the piano player wore a bowler hat like Mr Acker Bilk, and according to the mood of the times, that was pretty much enough to make it count as trad.

The tour started in late September 1960, and slogged around the country until December. Billy didn't quite make it to the end. When the tour reached its last gig at the Newcastle Empire, he collapsed with "chest and stomach trouble and his doctor ordered him a complete rest".

At the same time, Mr Parnes and Decca began to seek a new style for Billy. It would have been too much of a shock to the fans to hear him say "Play that thing, Mr Bilk" in a hot-jamboree take on 'I Wish I Could Shimmy Like My Sister Kate', and Billy could never be a Bobby, but luckily another alternative had presented itself.

On March 5, 1960, Elvis was honourably discharged from the army and was back in civvie street. His first post-army UK hits, 'Stuck On You' and 'Mess Of Blues', gave encouraging signs that he was returning to rock'n'roll form.

But Colonel Parker, his manager, and his record company were keen for him to try a new direction. Having spent two years doing PE and loading cannon shell into tanks, he was in better physical shape than he had ever been, or would ever be. And he'd been taking singing lessons, working on his breathing, opening his throat, improving his diction.

The first evidence of the new Elvis came with 'It's Now Or Never', a reworking of 'O Sole Mio', the 19th-century Neapolitan song that was invariably found on the setlists of strangled tenors.

Elvis, while approaching the verses in an encouragingly 'Love Me Tender'ish way, gets slightly *Rigoletto* in the choruses, and, in the final repeat, goes the full 'Nessun Dorma'.

'It's Now Or Never' went to number one on both sides of the Atlantic.

Wary observers saw the approach of power ballads and ducked.

Elvis' next UK release was less operatic, but no less worrying. It was a version of the 1927 standard, 'Are You Lonesome Tonight?', a waltz, already covered by everybody from Al Jolson to the Carter Family. The original sheet music had a 'recit' passage – a talking bit – in the middle, which was used on some recorded versions but not others. Jolson, who ever since 'My Mammy' and 'Sonny Boy' could never resist a recit, did it. And so did Elvis. "I wonder if you're lonesome tonight," he says, with feeling, after the first tremulous romp through the melody. "You know, someone said, 'the world's a stage'…" And intellectual quiz fans all over the UK reached for their buzzers.

'Are You Lonesome Tonight?' again whizzed up to number one.

Larry Parnes and Decca watched and learned, and it was decided, just as the early Elvis had been such a successful model for *The Sound Of Fury*, this new Elvis – the passionate balladeer and sensitive lover – would provide the template for Billy's future career.

Billy initially resisted.

He'd made his preferences clear in an interview for the *New Musical Express*, published not long after the release of *The Sound Of* Fury, under the headline "FURY PLANS TO SING THE BLUES".

"'In time, I would like to develop into a blues singer. For this album, I have included two blues numbers, and some songs with a country and western flavour. I was happy with the overall result, particularly with the blues songs 'Phone Call' and 'Since You've Been Gone' – and now my ambition is to record an EP of standard blues numbers. I like the blues, and particularly Ray Charles, for whom I have a great admiration. There is so much feeling in Charles' music and, like him, I *feel* everything I am singing."

Though he'd had Top 10 hits in the USA, Ray Charles was still not widely known in the UK at that time. Even Charles' 1959 release, 'What'd I Say', which musicians and the in-crowd spoke of in awe and was part of every rock'n'roller's basic core repertoire, never found its way to the UK Top 100 (although a Jerry Lee Lewis cover made the Top 10 in 1961). Possibly Billy had been introduced to Ray Charles' oeuvre by Eddie Cochran, who had recorded his 'Hallelujah I Love Her So'. But his ear was always alert to new sounds, and his record-buying habits were developing along the road less travelled: imports by little known country and blues artists, proto-soul singers and pretty much anything made for the 'race' charts in the USA. His mum mentions being embarrassed when Billy sent her out to buy a record by Nappy Brown (Napoleon 'Nappy' Brown was a fifties jump-jive singer), because it involved speaking the words "Nappy" and "Brown" in the same sentence, out loud in a public place. Billy knew about Jimmy Reed before Keith Richards had learned to bend strings. He acquired records by torch singers and jazz singers, Ella Fitzgerald, Dakota Staton, Damita Jo.

It was clear that Billy had assumed, or hoped, that this was the way his career would develop: recording the songs he wanted to record in the way he wanted to record them, surrounded by sensitive, sympathetic friends. "But later Decca got really heavy with me and persuaded me I was going in the wrong direction and slowly swayed me to the ballads."

'A Thousand Stars' was a harmless enough start. It had been written in 1953 by Gene Pearson, an 18-year-old doo-wop singer, and was released the following year by his group The Rivileers, with Gene on lead vocal. It didn't chart.

Six years later, the song had been picked up by Jim Lee of Indigo Records, a California-based label, for one of his signings, the 15-year-old Kathy Young, with local group The Innocents on backing vocals. It went to number three on the *Billboard* chart.

The Rivileers' version is smooth doo-wop at its very best, although Kathy Young, bless her, sounds like a 15-year-old doing terribly well in a talent contest.

Billy's version is produced by Charles Blackwell, just turned 21, who'd learned the arcane mysteries of the recording studio from Joe Meek. He lays on lush strings and an angelic choir straight from Joe Meek heaven (a place with acoustics like the Wookey Hole). The song is still doo-wop, a million miles away from 'O Sole Mio', and only a few baby steps from Billy's rockabilly comfort zone. It's clear, though, that Billy's exploring new vocal possibilities, less nasal, more open-throated. He could never have approached the Mario Lanza tenor that Elvis was aiming for on 'It's Now Or Never' – tenors need athletic breath control and Billy's childhood illness had already kicked any possibility of that out of the window – but he had something else.

"Billy was a stylist," says Marty Wilde. "I was too. I look on Elvis as a singer and Eddie Cochran, Buddy Holly, Billy Fury and myself as stylists. We were stylists rather than singers. Singers were separate. Roy Orbison is a singer. The important thing is, if Buddy Holly came on you would know it was Buddy Holly. And if Billy Fury came on, you knew immediately it was Billy."

Like 'Are You Lonesome Tonight?', 'A Thousand Stars' has a talking bit, although nothing as fancy as Shakespeare references. Instead of singing, Billy speaks the repeat of the middle eight: "Each night I count the stars in the sky, hoping that you're not telling me lies." For a man never quite comfortable speaking on stage, it was a tricky moment to pull off live. Usually he made a joke of it. "Each night I count the stars in the sky," he'd say. "Bloody hell, there's hundreds of them."

The B-side was 'Push Push', a cover of a song co-written by Phil Medley (who also wrote the more esteemed 'Twist And Shout') and Bert Russell (not the same person, one assumes, as the philosopher Bertrand Russell, but one can never be sure). It's Latin flavoured, with bongos and gimmick-timpani. The lyric, "Push push, you've got to give a lover some, push push", would probably have won a BBC ban if they'd ever considered playing it in the first place.

But they didn't.

The BBC still had a grudge against Billy. He'd been in their bad books ever since he'd made the fuss about bringing his own guitarist to the *Singalong* booking and then had the nerve to show up late. "Please add a pencil note on the artist's card," the memo had said. And, "Really – these odd gentlemen with odd names."

Billy hadn't had a BBC booking since, and he needed airplay, not just for his new single: Decca, on its Ace Of Clubs label, had put together a greatest hits album, *Billy Fury* – 10 tracks including 'Maybe Tomorrow', 'Margo', 'Colette' and 'Wondrous Place' – all nicely packaged for the

Christmas market with a picture of Billy dressed in a fancy weskit like a Mississippi gambler. Without airplay or publicity, both single and LP would wither on the vine.

So, towards the end of 1960, Larry wrote to Donald MacLean (Music Organiser, Light Entertainment, BBC) asking why Billy never got booked for *Saturday Club*, the Saturday morning radio show hosted by your old mate Brian Matthew. Was he banned outright?

Maclean prevaricated, dodging the question of whether he was banned, merely noting that he had looked into the matter and "all the relevant producers remarked that in their opinion a significant part of Billy Fury's success was attributable to visual aspects – that, in fact, sound radio does not do him justice and vice versa."

At the beginning of 1961, after 'A Thousand Stars' had begun to see some chart action, Larry wrote again, this time to Jimmy Grant, one of the "relevant producers".

"Just a line to ask you if you can possibly see your way clear to playing Billy Fury's record of 'A Thousand Stars'," he says, before going on to point out that Billy's voice has "matured" and referring to the "little difficulty" of the *Singalong* booking. "I really would appreciate it if you could release the 'ban' so to speak and perhaps play his record or have him appear at your earliest convenience."

It took another six months before Billy was allowed off the BBC's naughty step. On June 21, 1961, they booked him for *Parade Of The Pops* at a grudging fee of 10 guineas (£10.50).

Not that he was short of work. In the *NME* Poll, he was voted the nineteenth best 'Male Singer In The World', the ninth best 'British Vocal Personality', the eighth best 'British Male Singer' and, most prestigious of all, in the section where readers were asked to nominate the artist they'd most like to see in the mighty *NME Poll-winner's Concert*, Billy was number two (significantly, one place ahead of Cliff).

When the *Rock And Trad Spectacular* went back on the road in February 1961, Billy was therefore, with some justification, no longer billed as "Britain's newest teenage idol" but as "Britain's greatest teenage idol". He and his "company of 50" advanced from Romford, to Colchester, to Hull, then north to Scotland (Aberdeen, Dundee, Glasgow). In March, they zig-zagged from Taunton, to Leicester, to Southampton, to Cheltenham, to Ipswich, onwards and onwards, finally ending the tour on May 8, seven months after it had started at the Bristol Hippodrome. Wars have been shorter.

'Don't Worry', the next single, put Billy back into his Elvis box. He deploys his new "mature" voice but adds, as Elvis had begun increasingly to do, careful consonants. "Do your memories stray to a bright-t-t summer day?", sings Elvis on 'Are You Lonesome Tonight?', and Billy comes right back with "Don't-t be ashamed-d, it-t might-t happen to you" on 'Don't Worry'. The Elvis vibe is enhanced by a Floyd Cramerish piano intro and The Four Kestrels doing Jordanaires things in the background, but the whole is much enlivened by Charles Blackwell's orchestral arrangement, which involves little yelps from the violins and a bizarre baritone (or maybe bass) saxophone solo in the middle that puts one in mind of Tubby the Tuba.

The B-side, 'Talkin' In My Sleep', with Fats Domino-esque piano and a honking sax solo, is better. Billy, closer to his comfort zone, sounds as if he's enjoying himself.

Despite which, and despite the violin yelps and Tubby the Tuba on the A-side, the record, released at the beginning of March 1961, gathered dust in the record shops for two months before finally hauling itself up to number 40, most probably off the back of the howling success of his next release.

Chapter Twelve

"...AND HE'S NOW A MATURE, DEPENDABLE ARTIST."

1961 was the year that Gerry Goffin and Carole King first struck gold.

Gerry and Carole had met as college students in New York. Carole got pregnant, Gerry did the decent thing. She was 17, he was a couple of years older. They dropped out of college, got jobs and started writing songs in the evenings. Carole played piano and wrote the music: Gerry wrote the lyrics. They knew pop. They understood pop. They oozed pop.

At high school, Carole had dated Neil Sedaka, who subsequently had a hit with 'Oh, Carol'. In reply, Carole (with Gerry and Howard Greenfield) wrote and recorded 'Oh, Neil', which didn't do much business but got attention. It was a start.

They were hired by Don 'The Man With The Golden Ears' Kirschner, President of Aldon Music, who eventually shoved them in a tiny room equipped with a piano, a desk and a typewriter and told them to write some hits. They obliged.

In 1960, The Shirelles, four teenagers from Passaic, New Jersey, had a minor hit with 'Tonight's The Night', a barely euphemised account of a girl's decision to do it. Don Kirschner told Carole and Gerry to write them a follow-up.

The result, which had the girl from 'Tonight's The Night' wondering, even as she's doing it, 'Will You Love Me Tomorrow', went to number one in the USA and remains one of the best pop songs ever written. It's a song that can be subjected to drunken karaoke and magically survive with its dignity intact.

Goffin and King's list of hits in 1961 alone is formidable. As well as another number one, Bobby Vee's 'Take Good Care Of My Baby', they scored lesser chart entries with Bobby Vee's 'How Many Tears', The Drifters' 'Some Kind Of Wonderful', Gene Pitney's 'Every Breath I Take', The Shirelles' 'What A Sweet Thing That Was', The Crickets' 'Don't Ever Change' and a clutch of others, among which were two songs for Tony Orlando.

Tony was a young singer who later had massive success with 'Bless You' and then, in the seventies, with the group Dawn singing 'Candida', 'Knock Three Times', 'Tie A Yellow Ribbon Round The Ole Oak Tree' and other bright confections that made the seventies such a stirring decade.

Those two early Goffin and King songs didn't do much for him, though. One made the lower reaches of the Hot 100, the other was a complete no-show. Neither song would be remembered at all, certainly not in the UK – except maybe by dedicated Tony Orlando fans – were it not for cover versions by Billy Fury.

'Halfway To Paradise' is a song, maybe, about what the boy in 'Tonight's The Night' would have felt if the girl had decided not to do it after all. Tony Orlando sings it with oddly contorted vowel sounds, as if he's simultaneously trying to unscrew a recalcitrant lid from a pickle jar. But Dick Rowe at Decca saw something in it and brought it to Billy's attention. A session was booked for April 9, 1961, this time with a new production team in place: Dick Rowe supervising, Mike Smith producing and Ivor Raymonde as musical director.

Raymonde was a versatile chap who'd also worked as an actor, appearing in an early episode of *Hancock's Half Hour*. In his long and magnificent career he provided some of Billy's best orchestrations, wrote 'I Only Want To Be With You' and 'Stay Awhile' for Dusty Springfield, and provided string arrangements for Ian Dury's *Laughter* album, including those for the delightful final track 'Fucking Ada'.

Coincidentally, Ivor was also father to one of the Cocteau Twins. Just the one, mind.

Mike Smith, then in his mid-twenties, had been working for Decca since his demob from National Service in the RAF. He'd set up the mics and worked the knobs for Mantovani's shimmering strings, Winifred Atwell's 'other piano', the mambo maracas of Edmundo Ros and the spine-stiffening stylings of forces-sweetheart Vera Lynn. When he was promoted to producer (with a two quid a week pay rise to £11), one of his first artistes was Bridie Gallagher, the Irish sweetheart who'd crossed paths with Billy in Dublin.

"I really enjoyed being with Billy Fury in the studio," Smith told Spencer Leigh for the *Independent*, "and 'Halfway To Paradise' sounded right from the moment it started. Dick Rowe had picked the song; Ivor Raymonde had written the arrangement; and my contribution was keeping everyone sober. Billy was managed by Larry Parnes and I remember Larry telling the bass guitarist to 'tighten his strings'. That became a running joke at Decca."

Georgie Fame, by then practically a seasoned pro, also happened to be in the studio when Billy was recording 'Halfway', and he was slightly astonished to see this shy young man he knew from the road stand at the mic in Decca's big studio, with the assembled ranks of strings, brass, woodwind and percussion letting rip behind him, singing with passion, commitment and all the confidence of Sinatra.

A few months after the 'Halfway To Paradise' session, Mike Smith was the producer for The Beatles' Decca audition. Afterwards Dick Rowe asked him to choose between The Beatles and another group. Mike chose the other group (apparently on the recommendation of his optician, who happened to be managing them) and thus went on to produce a string of hits for Brian Poole & The Tremeloes.

'Halfway to Paradise' was released in mid-May.

"It's not an out-and-out rock disc, although the beat flavour is there," Billy told *NME*. "It's the sort of record that I hope will find acceptance with adults as well as teenagers."

'Halfway' took time to establish itself, snailing into the Top 40 at the end of the month, and finally making the Top 10 at the end of June. Having got there it held on for 15 weeks, peaking at number three, denied the number one spot by Eden Kane's 'Well I Ask You' and Helen ("Anyone can sound like me/on a 45 played at 33") Shapiro's 'You Don't Know'.

It was, however, the ninth best-selling record in 1961, beating Elvis' 'Are You Lonesome Tonight?' by one position and leaving Cliff Richard's best shot, 'Theme For A Dream', panting for breath at number 27.

It was also voted number two in the 'Best British Disc of 1961' category in the *NME* Poll. And, oddly perhaps in the year of Chubby Checker's 'Let's Twist Again', it won a Carl Alan Award, "the Oscar of the dance world", in the category 'Most Popular Record For Dancing'.

'Halfway To Paradise' became, to all intents and purposes, Billy's signature tune, the song he was obliged to emote his way through, at every opportunity, for the rest of his life. Understandably, his feelings towards it mellowed.

"He hated it," says Lisa Voice, his partner for the last years of his life. "I won't say what he used to say, but basically he couldn't stand singing it again."

Some songs – very special songs – worm their way into the national consciousness and stay there. People born years after Bill Haley had died still find it impossible to hear the phrase "See you later" without appending "alligator". And, even if you don't say it out loud, if somebody says "I'll tell you what I want", you can't help doing a mental Spice Girls' "what I really, really want".

For a year or so, "You're such a half-witted parasite", sung in a voice somewhere between a Billy Fury impersonation and a jeering snort, was a common playground insult.

Ten years later, in an episode of Dick Clement's and Ian La Frenais' sitcom *Whatever Happened To The Likely Lads?*, Bob Ferris (played by Rodney Bewes) is sitting in the pub with Terry Collier (played by James Bolam), reflecting on a failed venture.

He comments: "As Paul Anka put it at the time, 'So near, and yet so far away'."

"It was Billy Fury," says Terry.

"Paul Anka," says Bob.

"It was Billy Fury," says Terry, getting cross now.

"No, it wasn't. Paul Anka. Quid on it."

"'You're only Halfway To Paradise'. Billy Fury. 'I want to be your lover, but your friend is all I'll stay.'"

119

"What does that mean?" says Bob. "'Your friend is all I'll stay?'"

"'I want to be your lover'," says Terry, forcefully now. "But you'll only let me be your friend."

The pub's landlord, wiping a table nearby, turns and, in an unreconstructed seventies way, says, "Oi. You two fairies. Out."

With a Top five hit under his belt, Billy Fury was big time.

Now apparently forgiven by the BBC, bookings on *Saturday Club* and *Parade Of The Pops* began to come through and his rate went up from 10 guineas to 12 guineas (£12.60).

In September, he hosted his own show on Radio Luxembourg.

The Blue Flames (so named – according to drummer-legend Clem Cattini – after the farts they lit "to keep themselves warm" on the freezing tour bus) seemed by now to have been installed as his backing band. As we've said, trying to pin down the line-up of any of these backing bands (Joe Brown's Bruvvers, Marty Wilde's Wildcats, etc.) at any given time is a fool's errand, but at this point The Blue Flames seem to have featured Georgie Fame on keyboards, Colin Green on guitar, Tex Makins on bass and Red Reece on drums.

'Halfway To Paradise' was still hanging on in the Top 10 when the next single was released. It was an uncompromising choice of song.

To show off the "more mature" voice that Larry had boasted about, on the Radio Luxembourg shows Billy had been supplementing his usual pop and rock repertoire with the odd standard – 'Slow Boat To China', 'When I Fall In Love', 'Am I Blue'– and it was from this Big Book of Standards that the new single came.

In 1925, Joseph Gade, a Danish violinist, composer and conductor, was worried about the terrible things he read in the news.

"One day the papers were filled with sensational descriptions of a crime of passion, a jealousy-murder, which made such an impression on me that I could not stop thinking about it," he wrote. "During my morning walk across the fields, however, I came to the sensible conclusion that the horrifying drama was really none of my business, so it faded gradually into the background. Nevertheless, the word 'jealousy' stuck in my mind as a title to which notes began to attach themselves. When I got home I sat down at my desk and after a few hours 'Tango Jalousie' was finished."

Gade was conducting the orchestra at the Palads Cinema in Copenhagen at the time, and writing music to accompany the silent films. He fitted his new tune to the big Hollywood movie then showing, *Don Q*, starring Douglas Fairbanks and Mary Astor. The tune was less than an instant hit, but the sheet music was published elsewhere in Europe and in the USA.

In the 1930s, a version, recorded by the Boston Pops Orchestra, sold a million. Vera Bloom, an American lyricist, added breathless words: describing the loss of peace, a "surrender" to the "charm" of jealousy, it's effect bringing pain but also "ecstasy". By now, 'Tango Jalousie' was known by its more familiar title, 'Jealousy'.

Slightly less obviously SMBD lyrics were added by the English poet Winifred May, a woman who, under the pseudonym Patience Strong, wrote sentimental verses for the *Daily Mail* and *Woman's Own*, some of which were painted on milk jugs or embroidered on samplers.

Dozens of versions of the song have been recorded over the years, some with the Vera Bloom lyrics, some with the Winifred May. Theoretically it's a song for a big tenor, Placido Domingo or Richard Tauber or, at a push, Elvis showing off his 'It's Now Or Never' chops, but there are several other role models to choose from. Frankie Laine sings it in his customary manner, like an Elk celebrating its own lung power. Vera Lynn does it as if it's a surprising round-off to a thank you speech given for winning the jam-making prize. Leslie 'Hutch' Hutchinson could enter his version for an elocution exam.

Billy goes for the passion, laying it on thick and making a meal out of every vowel and consonant. "My life was hell, every moment we were apart," he sings, with an affecting shake on "were".

"My heart was on fire with desire for you," he sings, enjoying the triplet and almost making "heart" rhyme with "fire" and "desire".

For the final chorus there's a key change, up a semi-tone. And there, melodic variations take him up to an E and then to an F#, nowhere near the high A that Elvis nails at the end of 'It's Now Or Never', but all the same it's a perfectly pitched note, delivered with full-chested authority, a bona-fide money note that brings a tear to the eye and joy to the heart.

The only song around at the time that could match passion like that was Roy Orbison's 'Crying'. Otherwise red meat had become a rare commodity. Cliff was serving up the frighteningly anodyne 'When The Girl In Your Arms Is The Girl In Your Heart'. The Highwaymen were riding high with 'Michael Row The Boat Ashore'. Elvis' best shot was 'Wild In The Country'.

'Jealousy' went to number two, Billy's highest chart position of his career, and was only kept from the number one spot by the twang of Hank Marvin's guitar on 'Kon-Tiki' (even though there's a fluffed note at 1.05).

His third LP, *Halfway To Paradise*, released in September, was essentially another greatest hits. On the Decca budget label, Ace of Clubs, it offered 12 tracks for just over a pound – two-thirds the price of a regular LP.

'A Thousand Stars', 'Don't Worry' and 'Halfway To Paradise' were on there, together with their B-sides and a few bonus tracks.

'You're Having The Last Dance With Me' is an 'answer' song, the 'question' being The Drifter's huge 1960 hit 'Save The Last Dance For Me', written by Doc Pomus and Mort Shuman.

Actually, it was the second response to the original song, the first being Damita Jo's 'I'll Save The Last Dance For You'. In Billy's answer to the answer, he is requesting, not to say aggressively demanding, that she (Damita Jo) reneges on her agreement to save the last dance for The Drifters and has the last dance with him instead. And if there was any doubt in the earlier versions that "last dance" and "take you home" are thinly disguised euphemisms, it becomes crystal clear in this one. "My love is stronger by far than his small love could ever be," Billy sings.

'Would You Stand By Me?', another Pomus-Shuman song, sounds as if it could be an 'answer' to their 'Stand By Me', the big hit for Ben E. King, covered by everybody from John Lennon to Florence & The Machine and was adopted as the title of a movie starring River Phoenix. It isn't, though. It isn't really much of anything – a humdrum tune and some so-so lyrics. Possibly Pomus and Shuman wrote it, shoved it on the reject pile, then recycled the 'Stand By Me' idea for the infinitely better Ben E. King song.

'Fury's Song' is one of Billy's own. The lyric forms the basis of a 'see how many references to other Billy Fury songs you can spot' quiz for the fans: "I'll forget sweet Colette," it goes, "you'll have to go, bye-bye Margo, Maybe Tomorrow there'll be no sorrow."

"Backing is imaginative," said Allen Evans' review of the LP in *NME*, "varying from a small group to a string-filled orchestra with a girl group adding a lot. Billy croons well throughout."

By the middle of October 1961, 'Jealousy' was high in the Top 10, 'Halfway To Paradise' the single was still selling healthily enough to be hanging around just outside the Top 20 and *Halfway To Paradise* the LP was at number five in the album charts.

'I'd Never Find Another You', his Christmas release, was, like 'Halfway', another cover of a Tony Orlando record, written by Goffin and King.

'I'd Never Find Another You' is a sentimental ballad approached with a full-on rock'n'roll attitude. Here was a man reassuring his girlfriend that he will never leave her. "So, why's he sound so cross about it?" you wonder. Because he's mean, moody and magnificent. Obviously.

NME describes it as a "medium-pace rock-cum-Latin beat" running behind "the most attractive melody".

"Billy's versatility as a singer capable of tackling anything from out-and-out rock'n'roll to sentimental ballads has really come to the fore this year," it said, "and he's now a mature, dependable artist."

It was 1961. The Bobbies were still riding high. "Mature" and "dependable" were desirable qualities in a pop star. Besides, the business model still insisted that nobody could make a lasting career out of the teen market. The long-term business was with the mums and dads. "Mature" and "dependable" meant bankable.

"It was a bit of a joke with us," said Terry Dene. "He [Billy] said to me, 'Well, we've got to sing these syrupy songs,' and I said, 'Yeah, I know Billy but they've become hits haven't they?' It was a bit of a downer because he wanted to get out and do his thing.'"

"He had these ballads in his repertoire," said Georgie Fame, "but what he was really into was [American legend] Etta James. He loved Etta James."

Billy publicly denied that he was abandoning rock'n'roll. "The reason I have been recording ballads recently is simply to see if the fans would retain their interest in my career if I varied my material."

But, all the same, he added: "One of my plans for the future is to wax some more standards in a modern vein. I'd also like to record with a big swing-style band."

'I'd Never Find' stayed in the Top 40 for 14 weeks, nine of them in the Top 10.

It was also the song that first alerted Chris Eley, later editor of the *Sound Of Fury* fan club magazine, to Billy's magnificence. Chris came a little late to the party, largely because he lived in the wilds of Cornwall.

"I heard Billy and Elvis on radio in '61. I can't remember the songs. And then in January '62, just as I was turning 13, I was at my grandfather's and he had a black and white telly. We had no electricity at home, so I had to go and see the TV there, which was infrequent, and it was *All That Jazz* [a 1962 series made by ATV television]. And there I was, and I was mesmerised because up until that time all my idols were cowboys. My idol was Clint Walker [star of TV cowboy series *Cheyenne*]. It was all westerns. But I started to change, obviously – adolescence. Billy came on *All That Jazz* and I was – wow! I'd heard him and now I could see him and although it was very restrained because all the girls had to sit and really behave themselves and there was hardly a bloke in the audience, I thought – wow! He was singing 'I'd Never Find Another You', and my grandfather went, 'Rubbish, turn it off,' and you didn't argue in those days. But, all of a sudden, I didn't want to be Clint Walker anymore, I wanted to be Billy Fury."

A month later there was an EP, with four brand new tracks.

'I Love How You Love Me' is a cover of the Barry Mann/Larry Kolber song that Phil Spector had produced for the Paris Sisters.

'Please Don't Go' is a big begging song with triplet piano and dramatic stops for extra sobs.

The other two songs were written by Billy. 'If I Lose You' is a barnstormer sung with great grit and determination.

The oddity is 'Don't Jump'. Billy, jilted, stands on a cliff top, having decided to end it all. He's fairly determined to go through with it, but still can't help noticing that "it's a long, long way to fall".

Then he hears a soft voice. The soft voice, however, calls only for a moment before being replaced by several men, some with deep, froggish voices, chanting "Billy don't jump, Billy boy don't jump. No woman's worth the trouble. You can always find another."

Their intervention causes his resolution to falter: "I'm gonna, then I wanna, then I will and I won't, 'cos it's a long, long way to fall."

And in the end he decides, for the time being anyway, to abandon the suicide attempt because there is a possibility that he will, indeed, "find another".

The moral, dissuading potential suicides? Speak froggish.

His run of chart success was broken by a cover of Gladys Knight &
The Pips' 'Letter Full Of Tears', his first release of 1962. The press hailed
this as a new departure for Billy – an exploration of the choppier waters
of "rhythm and blues".

"He's been including a few R&B items in his stage act for quite a
time," said *NME*, "but this is his first venture on disc. It's a gamble which
could well have come unstuck. For Billy was on fairly safe ground so
long as he continued to wax ballads of the 'I'd Never Find Another You'
and 'Halfway To Paradise' calibre because he has established a second to
none reputation as a purveyor of this type of material. But R&B is an
entirely different matter."

'Letter Full Of Tears' was probably not what Billy understood as being
R&B, but the press – even the music press – seemed to use the term to
cover any music by black American artists ranging from Howlin' Wolf to
The Supremes. 'Letter Full Of Tears' is up towards The Supremes end of
the spectrum.

Billy never liked it anyway. "I had an awful lot of trouble with this
song," he said, years later. "I didn't want to do it because it wasn't my
style and I find the vocal really difficult to do and I was really pressurised
into doing it. And I didn't really like the arrangement."

The public shared his reservations. The record stalled at number 32.

The magnificent follow-up, 'Last Night Was Made For Love', stayed in
the Top 20 from May to September and defined the summer, with Ivor
Raymonde's trombones and triplets screeching out of beach transistors
and fairground tannoys.

NME called it "a most appealing tango" and gave it a "one hundred
per cent recommendation".

"If you dug the Billy Fury on 'Jealousy'," said the *Record Mirror*, "then
this is your meat."

"Last night was made for love", Billy sings, "but where were you?"
And we know we're back with Billy's 'disappointed in love' schtick:
drenched in longing, lovelorn, loveless bedsit music that, in another age,
could have been recorded by Tim Hardin or Morrissey.

It was still generally reckoned that pop, almost by definition, was
ephemeral. The public was fickle. Today rock'n'roll, tomorrow the Twist,
the day after, who knows? The average pop star's reign at the top could
be measured in months if not weeks. The trick was to cash in while you
could and secure your pile for the long retirement ahead.

Billy had reached number two in the charts. He was a headline act, at the peak of his earning power. The sun was shining. Hay must be made.

Between September 1961 and the end of 1962, he headlined three major tours, released four singles and an album and made a movie. To fill the time in between, there were tellies, radios, including another 13 quarter-hour shows for Radio Luxembourg, personal appearances, one-nighters, and, on November 16, he did a *Crackerjack*, the long-running BBC kids TV show in which the guest stars were expected to join in the fun and maybe go home with the star prize, a *Crackerjack* pencil.

The *Star Spangled Night* tour, starring Billy, with Joe Brown, Eden Kane, Karl Denver, Tommy Bruce and The Allisons, kicked off in Cannock on October 17 and wound up in Exeter on December 3. In Cambridge, the queue for tickets started forming at four in the morning and the whole thing was sold out in a day.

This was followed by the *Big Star Show of 1962*, which ran from February 19 to April 16, Billy headlining with Eden Kane, John Leyton and Joe Brown.

Summer brought the comparative ease of a season in Great Yarmouth with Marty Wilde and Karl Denver. Then the *Mammoth Star Show* with Marty, Karl Denver, Mike Sarne and Joe Brown, which opened in Guildford on September 30 and finished at the ABC Stockton on December 7.

Billy took out a day or a week now and then to deal with other commitments, but otherwise it was a constant round of travel, dank hotels, unsuitable snacks, disheartening dressing rooms, half an hour's utter adulation and on to the next town. And in between the package tours, Billy was booked into one-nighters at clubs and ballrooms. He played for dances at the Majestic Ballroom in Barnoldswick and the Rink in Spennymoor. He played Stevenage Football Club and the Royal Lido, Prestatyn.

To say the workload nearly killed him is not a figure of speech.

CHAPTER THIRTEEN

"...SEEING BILLY IN IT MAKES ME REALISE WHY THE BEATLES HAD TO HAPPEN."

"The atmosphere on the road had been just a bunch of young guys having a really good time," Billy said, looking back in 1981. "It was great. You thought that freedom had really arrived.

"But it ended up with you not able to go anywhere. If you went out of the stage door you'd get ripped to bits. I was genuinely frightened that I'd get badly crushed by fans when I was leaving the theatre. You couldn't go anywhere. You couldn't go out for a walk, you had to go at three o'clock in the morning. It got to the point where I used to move into my dressing room at about four in the afternoon and remain there until about one o'clock the next morning, when I'd go back to the hotel. Then you'd move on the next day to the next town and repeat the pattern again. And in the end by trying to gain your freedom, you'd lost it."

"Yeah, Larry worked his acts extremely hard," says Marty Wilde. "The first year I was away from my parents – which on reflection, was terrific

– I was away for about 48 weeks out of 52. It was really quite strange and it was quite tiring. The places we stayed were awful. It was just the way things were in those days. It was a great way of losing weight though. I lost a hell of a lot of weight, I remember that much. I must have lost a stone in that year. Not that Billy had a problem with his weight. And neither did I until I was 77. I got very thin, but I was young, fit. I enjoyed it."

They looked after each other on the road.

"I was on tour with Billy when I lost my father," said Marty. "Hal Carter and Billy looked after me in many ways. I was pretty down about it obviously and they helped me get through that bad patch."

Not all the acts had the same resilience, physical or mental.

"Two years, he [Larry] worked me, without one single night off," says Joe Brown. "Two years. And I just went to pieces. I was a gibbering wreck. And I was sitting on the bed, in my flat in Chiswick, sort of sobbing, and laughing, and crying – I was gone, you know. And me mum rang Larry up and said, 'He can't do any more work, he's got to have a rest. I've called the doctor.' The doctor came. He took one look at me and crossed himself and went out. So, me mum phoned Larry back and said that the doctor had been and I couldn't work. And within 25 minutes there were two Harley Street blokes around – Larry sent them straight 'round – to make sure I wasn't swinging the lead."

In August 1961, Billy was booked to do an off-package one-nighter in a tent in Chippenham, Wiltshire. Journalist Mike Hellicar was shadowing him for *NME*. He arrived at Billy's flat mid-afternoon, to find him moaning because his telly had broken.

Hal Carter, Billy's roadie, drove them, installed Billy in the nearby Pheasant Inn and furnished him with sandwiches and tea while he checked out the gig.

The place was packed, the stage tiny. 'Beefy stewards' had their work cut out keeping fans away from the star. Many fainted and had to be carried backstage. Some pretended to faint so that they could be carried backstage, too.

Billy did a 20-minute set and ran for the car. It was stuck in mud. Fans hammered at the windows. Eventually they got it moving and drove back to the Pheasant where Billy changed and had a post-show cup of tea, then back into the car.

"You be careful how you go round the bend 100 yards down the road," the pub's landlord told them. "You know who the last fellow was to cop it down there."

Of course they knew. It had been not much more than a year since Eddie died.

They got back to London at two in the morning. And the following day they went to Great Yarmouth.

If the acts had had to take an obligatory medical test before being declared fit to embark on the tours, Billy, with his history of rheumatic fever, would almost certainly have failed.

"I always knew Billy had health problems," says Marty. "You had to work your head off. It took its toll on Billy. And although he was pretty fit when I first knew him, he always said he wouldn't live to an old age. When he said that sort of thing, I always ignored him – but he would often say he wouldn't live to an old age. He had a weakness in his body. At the time, I don't think Larry knew it."

On October 24, 1961, the morning after a gig, Billy collapsed in a taxi in Cambridge city centre and was rushed to Addenbrooke's Hospital. He had kidney stones. After treatment, he spent a couple of days in a nursing home, recuperating.

"I've been a bit under the weather for several days," he said. "First, I had a sore throat and then an internal disorder started developing," he explained. "I tried to keep working in the hope that it would eventually wear off, but I just had to give in. And when they examined me, they discovered that I had a small piece of grit in the kidney."

"It happened a couple of times after that," Larry said. "And one time one of the doctors said to me, 'This young man needs to see a heart specialist.' Well, because of his history of rheumatic fever as a boy and his time on the tugboats he had a heart problem."

There was another collapse after a concert in Slough during the *Big Star Show*. Marty and Billy were sharing a dressing room. "Billy suddenly fell forward," he told the *Daily Mirror*. "I caught him."

Larry massaged his heart in an attempt to revive him and they bundled him into a car and took him to a clinic in London. There he was diagnosed – according to the *Mirror* – with fibrositis and bronchitis. He stayed in hospital for a few days, buried in get well cards, cuddly toys and knitted mascots from the fans.

Again, as soon as he was discharged, he was back on the road: the ABC Exeter, the Gloucester Regal, the Southall Dominion, the Worthing Plaza, the Dover ABC, on and on.

In June 1962, he had to cancel a BBC radio recording. This time it was "laryngitis". Larry sent Marty to fill in. This sparked an avalanche of BBC correspondence demanding a medical certificate to prove the laryngitis, and the whole debacle put Billy once again in the BBC's bad books. One memo has a handwritten note added saying – "I'm told you don't want prod[ucers]s to book either Fury or Wilde for 6 months."

Towards the end of the summer season in Great Yarmouth, Billy was taken ill again – with 'measles', later reported as an "illness", probably a recurrence of the kidney complaint. This kept him out of action for the best part of a month and caused him to miss the first week of the *Mammoth Star Show of 1962*, autumn tour.

1962 ended with a "minor operation", three days in hospital and orders not to work for another six weeks. He even had to cancel the ceremonial presentation of a giant teddy bear – a Christmas present from the Midlands branch of his fan club – because he had been "forbidden to do anything which might cause excitement."

Death was an ever-present spectre.

In the previous year when Donald Zec had interviewed Billy and Larry for the *Daily Express*, Billy had led Donald into his bedroom and from a cupboard "he hauled down an old oak chest with three massive brass locks. Inside was a great pile of dough – coppers, silver and notes.

"'Some folks like collecting stamps, y'know – I like collecting money. I wanna see it grow higher and higher and higher.'

"'Understandable,' murmured his manager.

"'I'm gonna leave it all in this will,' said Billy, taking a blue notebook from the chest. "'It's very secret what I've written in here,' he said. 'It's got poems in it and thoughts and things. I'll read you the heading. It says: 'Here is the last Will of Billy Fury. This box contains…' I'd better not go on.'

"'Why not?'

"'Well, it's only got about eighty quid in it so far – not much to write a will about is it?'"

Zec asks Billy whether he's happy.

"'No. I keep asking myself, what's it all for?'

"'What about the happiness you bring to thousands?' asked Mr Parnes anxiously.

"'Yeah, but it's not the same, is it?' Billy muttered.

"'Same as what?' I asked.

"'Discoverin' penicillin,' he said."

Larry had by now moved many of his acts into a large rooming house in Bayswater: Duffy Power was in there, and Dickie Pride and some of The Vernons Girls. Billy lived there for a while but eventually moved out to a flat of his own.

He didn't seem to like it much. He put it about that he was a man on the move, a restless soul who could never settle down. It was good for the image.

"I always had a bit of wanderlust," he told *Disc*. "Even when I worked on the tugboats I was the same [...] I could never settle down. I can't now. I love doing one-nighters because I'm on the move from one town to another. Even one week in a place is too long. As I said, I'm all mixed up.

"I drove up to Glasgow once just to buy a box of matches. I don't know why, I just do things on impulse. I like other people who do the same [...] I can make friends with them."

"Nothing in this place is my own idea," he told the *Daily Express*, showing them round the flat. "My manager designed it and selected the furnishings. All a bit lush for me. See... black carpet. Look, green ceiling. That's unusual. These doors, see, they've got black leather on them. Padded. That glass table is the only one of its kind in the world. Straight from Sweden. It doesn't look much, but it cost £87."

He'd made it. He had the car and the flat with the £87 table and, in 1961, a steady, if secret, girlfriend.

Lee Middleton – proper name Audrey – was a Sheffield girl, a cinema usherette who had married young. It was not a happy marriage and anyway, quite soon the young husband was called up to do his National Service.

Then, one glorious day, rock'n'roll came to town in the shape of Mickie and Alex Most, the Most Brothers, neither of whose real names were Most and neither were they brothers. Lee formed a romantic attachment with Alex and eventually ran off to London to be with him.

An attractive blonde with a friendly face, a wide-open smile and understanding eyes, she and London hit it off. She found work as a showgirl and singer. Like Tommy Steele, Cliff, Adam, The Shadows and nearly everybody else other than Billy, she performed at the 2i's coffee bar, the "Birthplace of British Rock'n'roll".

She lost Alex to Lionel Bart, the *Oliver!* composer, and eventually took up with Duffy Power, which is how Billy got to know her. When she split up with Duffy one thing led to another.

Billy and Lee fitted. Both were northerners. Both were crazy about animals. Billy was shy, Lee wasn't. Billy was a little boy lost, Lee was mum to the world.

"I must admit to not being very taken with him at our first meeting," Lee said. "He wasn't one of the ravers like the other musicians, so we didn't consider him 'cool'. I also thought he was a bit of a poser, which of course he was when he was around his work. One thing he was, though, was very professional. Whilst all the other lads were raving around, he was working on his act, movement by movement, and that was why the others fell by the wayside and he went on to become a 'living legend'.

"Billy was always very aware he had a problem. He was not at all a healthy boy so he could only offer me a 'semi-invalid'. He'd been left with very weak heart valves and had to have special treatment, even with little things like having his teeth fixed, as an anaesthetic was dangerous for him. He was also supposed to avoid stress at all costs. He warned me he would die very young. All he told me made me love him more. I felt like I wanted to take care of him so that he could live to a ripe old age."

In the early sixties, the UK market for teen movies was thriving. An estimated 60% of teenagers went to the cinema at least once a week. Some went two or three times.

Some 30% of the films on offer – 41% after 1961 – were made in the UK. This was the law, or at least a regulation put in place by the British Board of Trade to protect British industry.

The Brits *could* make world-beating films. In 1957, *The Bridge On The River Kwai* won five Oscars. A year later *Separate Tables* won four. But the Board of Trade regulation also meant that our dross didn't have to compete even with America's mediocre. British dross was almost guaranteed domestic distribution. And lack of choice would result in tickets sold and profits made.

Teen movies, both American and British, were and are, with few exceptions, dross at its finest. Then, as now, the requirements of the genre were (tick at least two) sex, drugs, rock'n'roll, alienation, motorised transport, vampires and/or werewolves. The other requirement was a couple of good-looking teens or 35-year-olds dressed as teens, sometimes recognisable as "that bloke out of that thing" or "the woman from the toothpaste commercial".

Thus, *I Was A Teenage Werewolf* starred a 21-year-old Michael Landon (who later became "that bloke out of *Bonanza*") as a teen so alienated that sometimes his face grew hair, along with Yvonne Lime, whose wise choice in upper underwear (enabling full support even when she was hanging upside down) was let down by her hit-and-miss use of leg-coverings. It cost $82,000 to make, took $2 million at the box office and thus inspired *I Was A Teenage Frankenstein* starring Gary Conway (who later became "that bloke out of *Burke's Law*") and a 30-year-old Phyllis Coates.

The American rock'n'roll film – that specialised branch of the teen flick genre – was, as we've already noted, a wonderful phenomenon for the Brit audience, affording rare glimpses of key role models as well as vital instruction in how to dress, stand, walk, talk, dance and get up people's noses. A close-up of Elvis, projected 12 feet high, could provoke discussions about skincare that lasted weeks.

British rocksploitation pics were, by comparison, shabby and awkward. One of the earliest, *Rock You Sinners*, an almost forgotten low-budget B-movie, featured Tony Crombie & His Rockers, Art Baxter & His Rockin' Sinners and several other combinations of moonlighting jazzers who try terribly hard but aren't convincing anybody. Even worse was *Six-Five Special*, a spin-off from the TV show of the same name, which crammed as many acts as possible ("more than 20 top hits!") onto a fictional train bound for the TV studio. The idols sing their hits while trapped passengers try to look spellbound.

When it came to proper star vehicles, nobody, it seemed, quite trusted that rock'n'roll – or even pop – could sell a picture. Accordingly, Tommy Steele's and Cliff Richard's films had cut the pop with starchy song and dance numbers, thereby simultaneously boring the fans who'd come to see their idols and irritating the mums and dads who'd seen Gene Kelly or Fred Astaire do it properly.

Often the pop and the star was a bit of background atmosphere to a steamy seedy drama. Thus in *Serious Charge*, a film addressing vexed themes of out-of-control youth and homosexuality, Cliff sings an early arrangement of 'Living Doll' sat at a coffee-bar table, surrounded by hand-jiving girls, while, over at the pinball machine, more important characters speak over him.

And in *Beat Girl*, a film addressing vexed themes of out-of-control youth and heterosexuality, Adam Faith sings 'I Did What You Told Me' sat at a coffee-bar table surrounded by teen rebels who eat buns and drink squash while a young Oliver Reed squirms to the rhythms.

But whatever the shortcomings of the product, the market's potential was there for all to see. Cliff's *The Young Ones* was the UK's second highest grossing film of 1961.

Larry Parnes wanted some of that. So, deals were made, scripts prepared.

In November, *NME*, commenting on Billy's proposed film debut, said, "You don't have to be the world's greatest actor to get away with movie-making – so long as you have a pretty reliable director."

Billy got Michael Winner.

Winner was 26 and just starting out on a career that later encompassed *The Jokers*, *Death Wish*, *I'll Never Forget What's'isname*, *Death Wish 2*, *Hannibal Brooks*, *Death Wish 3* and *Won Ton Ton: The Dog Who Saved Hollywood*.

He had done a sort of pop film before – *Climb Up The Wall* was a 1960 low-budget, one hour-long B-picture, a version of Jack Jackson's TV show – but mostly he'd done documentaries. His only foray into feature films had been *Some Like It Cool*, in which Jill, an adventurous housewife, introduces her husband Roger and his upright parents to the joys of naturism. The film was low-budget tosh, but it was low-budget tosh with no clothes on and thus turned a huge profit.

In December 1961, Winner got a call from David Deutsch of Anglo-Amalgamated, offering him £2,000 for 12 weeks' work directing a picture called *Play It Cool*, starring Billy Fury. Most of those connected with the *Play It Cool* project, at Anglo-Amalgamated and elsewhere, treated it with all the distaste they should have lavished on *Some Like It Cool*. Jack Davies, who wrote the script, was so ashamed he took a pseudonym and became Jack Henry.

"The executive producer, Julian Wintle, typified the gin and tonic three-piece-suit brigade," said Winner. "He was horrible. He viewed the film he'd been asked to oversee by Nat Cohen of Anglo-Amalgamated as infinitely beneath him. Everybody who was anything to do with it was beneath him."

Billy plays Billy Universe, the naïve and noble singer with a band struggling to get to Brussels to compete in a song contest that they are sure will be their big break. But the weather thwarts their ambitions and Billy ends up in the waiting room of the airport wistfully singing 'Once Upon A Dream' to airport staff and passengers, all of whom look as if they're about to melt with pleasure. Indeed, so devastating is Billy's effect that it's hard to tell whether some of the air hostesses are experiencing repressed desire or grumbling appendices.

But, of course, the object of Billy's affections barely responds at all. She is Ann Bryant (played by Anna Palk), a runaway heiress infatuated with a far more successful, but secretly evil, pop star, Larry Granger.

Ann's dad (Dennis Price), who knows that Granger is evil, in the way that dads do, wishes to prevent his daughter from falling into his clutches. Ann goes AWOL, maybe to elope. So, to help out, Billy and his band take a trip around the clubs of London to look for Ann and/or Larry, but instead trip over top popsters like Helen Shapiro, Shane Fenton, Bobby Vee and Lionel Blair & His Dancers. And it all ends happily.

The New Big Thing in America was the twist, a dance craze popularised by Chubby Checker, but there was some doubt as to whether it would ever catch on in the UK.

Checker's starter records 'The Twist' and 'Let's Twist Again' had both snuck briefly into the UK charts and dropped out again in the previous couple of years. Not until the start of 1962 did the dance begin to take hold. While the film was in production, both records began once again to sell. By February, 'Let's Twist Again' was at number two.

Anglo-Amalgamated, keen to be bang on trend, wanted to shoehorn in some twist numbers. The problem was, says Winner, "The twist had barely reached England. None of the extras knew how to do it. So we had twist instructors from America."

Standing in one spot gyrating the hips was never the most cinematic dance anyway. Some of the extras barely look as if they're moving.

The film was shot at Pinewood, and Winner – according to Winner – kept the shoot a happy one, with banter shouted through a megaphone and *Beano* pranks. At one time the crew smeared the mouthpiece of his megaphone with shoe polish so that it left a mark. Another time, just when everybody was geared up for a frantic twist, the soundman instead played Bach. It kept things jolly.

Dr No, the first Sean Connery Bond film, was being shot on the next soundstage. Theirs was not a happy shoot. The feeling that they were working on an overpriced flop had infected the cast and crew with gloom. Sometimes Connery would wander over to the *Play It Cool* set to bask for a moment in the happier atmosphere and confide in Winner his fears that the James Bond escapade would kill off his fledgling career.

Winner found Billy "a delight". So did everybody.

"Tired publicity men who have seen it all before crowd the floor at Pinewood Studios," said Fergus Cashin in the *Daily Sketch*. "Actors leave their own films and join the crush. Chippies and scene shifters jostle for position. Tea trolley girls fight to serve the cuppas on the set. What's going on? Well, Billy Fury's out there singing."

Billy, it seemed, was the only person having no fun at all.

"I found the film difficult to make. I was up at 5 a.m. and I was wanting to have a good time. Getting to bed at 10 p.m. was bad news and so was learning scripts and elocution.

"I was scared stiff [...] I remember working on night locations at a large London railway station and wondering if I'd ever have the nerve to stand before the cameras. Sometimes I get tongue-tied off screen – and this was much worse."

"Our boy is doing his best to weather the rigours of movie making," said an on-set report in *NME*, "but it's not all honey and roses. 'Nervous strain, oh man, it's fantastic. Concentration day and night, week after week, it's hard work.'"

His co-star, Anna Palk, had barely heard of Billy. "That may sound strange," she said, "but I was schooled in a convent and rock'n'roll was far from the order of the day."

Billy had been bringing her up to speed on jive talk: "Every morning I come on the set and yell to her, 'Hi baby, what happening?' and she yells back, 'Look out, Daddy – everything.' She's learning fast."

Billy didn't mix easily. At lunchtime on the first day of shooting, Winner saw Billy's 'band' – Michael Anderson Jr., Keith Hamshere, Jeremy Bulloch and Ray Brooks – lounged around a table frolicking and joking, while Billy cramped himself on a corner, shyly munching. Winner had to have a word with them, like teacher ordering the more boisterous lads to include the new boy in their games.

One day Billy didn't show up for work at all. David Deutsch, one of the producers, went round to his flat to fetch him and knocked on the door. There was no answer, but he reported looking through the letterbox and seeing Billy scurrying away, like a skint tenant hiding from the rent man.

The film ran over. In late February, Billy had to miss the first couple of gigs of the *Big Star Tour of 1962* to squeeze in a couple of extra days' filming, and was still involved in night shooting in early March. All the same, Winner brought the film in within the £75,000 budget.

The musical director, according to the credits, was Norrie Paramor, Helen Shapiro and Cliff's producer at EMI. He also co-wrote some of Billy's songs. Indeed, Billy's songs are credited to Norrie Paramor, Dick Rowe (Billy's man at Decca) and Larry Parnes in various combinations: 'Once Upon A Dream' is by Rowe and Paramor, 'Play It Cool' by Paramor, 'The Twist Kid' by Paramor and Parnes, and so on.

Norrie Paramor liked a credit and the royalties it brought, and had a reputation for foisting his own songs on EMI artistes. "Oh, I do like to see me on the B-side", they'd sing when his back was turned.

'Once Upon A Dream', released as a single, went to number seven, with Billy's own 'If I Lose You' on the B-side.

The film's release, originally slated for May, was delayed until July, possibly to avoid clashing with *It's Trad Dad*, another popsploitation vehicle featuring Helen Shapiro. It was released into a world that was still getting a pop fix maybe only twice a week on TV, three times on radio and once every six months in the cinema so, understandably, it made money. Billy, Helen and Bobby Vee were all top acts, and teen audiences were "hungry to see something that related to them", as Winner said, "rather than Gregory Peck as a lawyer."

Chris Eley couldn't get enough of it. "I cycled to my local cinema about three or four times during the week it was on and saw *Play It Cool*. And, of course, as a vehicle for Billy, it's fantastic – when he's actually singing. I mean, forget the film, but when he's actually singing, nobody on Earth, not even Elvis – and I love Elvis – had got that electricity. That presence leaps out at you."

The newspapers mostly ignored the film, and those that did deign to mention it did so sniffily. Peter Jones in the *Record Mirror* didn't mince words, "badly written, uneasily directed, not too well acted and patchily photographed." To which a fan replied, "Billy Fury and the supporting cast did the best with the parts they had. I do admit that the story was a bit thin, but so are some other British pop films and these American twist films."

Melody Maker singled out Helen Shapiro's performance of 'I Don't Care' as the high spot of the movie but barely mentioned Billy.

Fan Mick Houghton was underwhelmed: "I saw *Play It Cool* twice [back then you could sit in the cinema and watch the film all day once you'd paid the price of admission]. It was a flimsy affair. 'Once Upon A Dream' was a rather wet dreamy ballad."

Even Larry found it hard to big up. "He worked hard on that film," was the best he could come up with in an interview with *Photoplay*, adding, "and considering it was his first, I thought he did well."

The film hasn't aged well. "*Play It Cool*," said the music writer Jon Savage, "was a very big film when I was young." But looking back… "seeing Billy in it makes me realise why The Beatles had to happen, as Billy was still tugging his forelock. He is very respectful to the figures of authority like Dennis Price who are bossing him around. It is very different from The Beatles who took the authority figures on."

"As the director readily admits," says critic Bill Harding in his book *The Films Of Michael Winner*, "*Play It Cool* and *The Cool Mikado* [Winner's next film] can at best be described as quaint, and at worst as an actual embarrassment. Products of their time and of interest only insofar as they indicate the type of projects an aspiring film director had to undertake in the early sixties. Detailed discussion would be futile, serious discussion almost impossible."

Or as Billy later admitted, "It was a really bad, bad movie."

During the shooting of *Play It Cool*, the police came round to Billy's flat on suspicion that illegal substances might be found therein. There was undoubtedly some justification for their visit.

Billy's shyness, his quiet affability, his lax timekeeping that sometimes morphed into an inability to show up at all, the laconic sense of humour in interviews, his "I keep asking myself what's it all for?" spirit of philosophical enquiry all suggest that he was possibly doing a lot of weed.

When people asked him what he did for relaxation, his customary reply was, "I just sleep."

Billy was filming when the police came round, and Lee Middleton, with whom by this time he was living in pre-marital bliss, was out. The concierge told the police that he didn't have a pass key so the law, feeling that breaking down the door might be a bit extreme, said they'd come back the following day.

The concierge tipped Billy and Lee the wink and they stayed up half the night smoking as much of the stash as they could, then flushed the rest.

When the police arrived the following day, they found nothing, but warned Billy and Lee that the tip-off they'd received was very reliable and they mustn't think that this was the end of the matter. At this point Lee "broke down" and confessed that she had tried marijuana but Billy had made her get rid of it and she promised never to do it again. The narrative of the ditzy blonde going off the rails and being straightened out by a sensible guy was one the cops readily understood and they bought it.

Smiles and handshakes all round. No more bother.

A high spot of the pop year was always the *NME Poll-Winners Concert*. Usually televised, it was a glorious opportunity to see your favourite stars fumble in the face of technical confusion and terrible acoustics. At the Empire Pool, Wembley, home of the 1962 concert, the mush was such that it was hard to tell whether Cliff was singing 'The Young Ones' or telling somebody off for dive-bombing.

It was Billy's third appearance at the show in as many years. The crowd was 10,000 strong. He came on in a silver lamé suit and "twisted through 'Sticks and Stones'."

"After 'Halfway To Paradise'," said *Melody Maker*, "we were treated to the inimitable Fury gymnastics through 'Sweet Little Sixteen', 'I'd Never Find Another You' and 'Just Because'." Then he was given his award ('Most Requested Artist To Appear At The Concert') and "a spontaneous gift of a giant teddy bear from his fan club secretaries."

In May 1962, Larry took Billy to America to try to drum up some interest in him and in *Play It Cool*. He'd sewn up a deal for three American record releases and – reportedly – for various TV shots, including one on the premier pop programme *The Dick Clark Show* in Philadelphia (although the evidence suggests that this might have been the usual Parnesy flannel).

Larry also mentioned that during the trip they would be finalising arrangements for a second film: "It will be made in Hollywood, and should be a colour movie specially written for Billy."

Before leaving, Billy had hoped he'd get to see Ray Charles and Mahalia Jackson and maybe visit a church to hear gospel music at first hand. Chaperoned as he was by Larry, none of that happened, but at a cocktail party in LA he rubbed shoulders with Phil Everly, The Crickets and Tab Hunter. He danced the twist at Peppermint West and The Interlude. In New York he met Jerry Leiber and Mike Stoller (composers of 'Hound Dog', 'Jailhouse Rock' and a few hundred other perfect songs.) And he treated himself to a Martin guitar.

More importantly, Larry had blagged the opportunity for Billy to present Elvis with silver discs for 'Rock-A-Hula Baby' and 'Wild In The Country' and, initially at least, several other hits. "I went to meet Elvis," Billy said, "because the music paper *Disc* had some silver discs for him. I had quite a suitcase to take over with me and got held up in customs because they thought I was trying to smuggle through gold bullion."

The presentation would take place at Paramount Studios in Hollywood where Elvis was shooting *Girls! Girls! Girls!*.

At this time, few Brits had seen the King in the flesh. To the fans in Chelmsford and Chorlton-cum-Hardy, Elvis was like a bird of paradise in a David Attenborough film: impossibly wonderful, but the evidence that it *does* exist can never explain how it *could* exist.

In 1988, Larry talked about the encounter with Bob Azurdia of Radio Merseyside. As always, his grasp of hard historical fact is hazy, but he remembers clothes thread by thread.

"We had a suite in a hotel," he said, "and Billy came out into the lounge. He was beautifully dressed but he was all in black. He had a lovely, black silky-looking suit. I said, 'Billy, you can't go dressed like that. Surely you should put on one of your nice tailor-made suits and one of your lovely shirts with a nicely patterned tie.' He said, 'Okay, to please you I will go and change.' He changed and he looked good in whatever he wore: he held his clothes beautifully.

"We got to the studio and we were introduced to Elvis Presley. We shook hands and Elvis was dressed in black from top to bottom and he looked virtually identical to the way Billy had dressed."

The meeting was brief. Billy handed over the silver discs. They smiled for the cameras – Billy in one of his lovely shirts and a nicely patterned tie, Elvis in black, both in their prime and looking as if they'd just majored in Handsome at a top university. They exchanged a few words.

"He was a very shy, quiet person," Billy said, afterwards, "and unfortunately I was the same. So, when we did meet, we really didn't say much. All we got to say to each to each other was, 'Hi'."

Larry heard it different. "He asked us all about England," he told the *Record Mirror*, "and there is no doubt that he knows what is going on. He asked after a lot of people on the English disc scene, and told me he'd been to see Marty Wilde in *The Hellions* (Marty's western film set in South Africa) no less than five times."

As if.

"Elvis said he was so impressed by Lionel Jeffries in the film."

Lionel Jeffries was a British character actor, best known for playing Grandpa Potts in *Chitty Chitty Bang Bang*."

Elvis was whisked back to the film set. No time, then, to get out the guitars and jam, to chew the fat about the use of slap-back echo, to eat fried peanut butter and banana snacks or wrassle with army buddies, but all the same Billy hung around on set for half an hour or so watching Elvis work.

Afterwards Elvis said, "Billy is okay! A swell guy! He seemed like a very nice boy. We didn't have a chance to talk much because I had to work."

He neglected to add, "But, heck, I'm really glad I got the chance to mention my admiration for Lionel Jeffries."

Larry claimed that Billy was not overawed. Billy disagreed. "When I met Elvis, I was bowled over!" he said. "I reckon he must be the most handsome guy in show biz! [...]."

By now he'd undoubtedly been briefed by Larry to embroider. "What I liked about Elvis was his terribly polite manners and the way he said, 'Hi Billy', as if he had been my cousin or something, and he hadn't seen me for a few months. He not only treated me like a friend, but he was so anxious to know about my discs, different styles, etc. He had heard quite a few of my records, I don't know how but he certainly had."

"And brother is he tall! At least he seemed to tower over everybody else who was standing around."

On this, Larry's interpretation of events concurred for once with Billy's. "Elvis was a very nice guy," he said, "and very genuine. He was so much taller than I thought he would be."

Elvis was just shy of six foot. Billy was no more than a couple of inches shorter. Perhaps our heroes always look taller than they are. Or perhaps the illusion of height is one of the tricks that make a hero a hero. Or perhaps he was standing on a secret box.

"The Americans," said Larry, "were impressed with the rough cut of Billy's first film, *Play It Cool*, which was sent over. We talked about making a film [in Hollywood], but one thing emerged. If he makes it, Billy will do it in England. He's a home-loving boy."

Remove the standard Larryisms and make of it what you will.

Elvis got his silver discs and Billy came home with a demo of 'Because Of Love', an actual Elvis song, slated to be included in the *Girls! Girls! Girls!* soundtrack. Then he scooped the King by bringing his version out first: his appeared in October 1962; the Elvis album in November.

Billy's version is better. Elvis' is Elvis-music, a beautifully designed generic product that served his market well – albeit with diminishing returns – from 1961 to69.

Billy, Ivor Raymonde and Mike Smith put the effort in.

"It's deep down Billy, emoting soulfully about the effects of love upon him – which are considerable," said *Record Mirror*.

Shoot a film, back on tour, quick trip to America, back on tour.

Billy started the *Big Star Show of 1962* backed by the Blue Flames. After a few gigs, Larry noticed that jazzy elements were infecting their playing, and not banjo and trombone jazz either: this was the bad kind of jazz that slipped a sneaky flattened fifth into a perfectly healthy minor chord or, worse still, a flattened ninth into a dominant major. Larry had ears. He didn't need to know their fancy terminology to recognise their Thelonious Monk filth. He fired them.

Joe Meek, the Professor Brainstawm of British pop and producer of Billy's tour-mate John Leyton's gothic hits ('Johnny, Remember Me', 'Wild Wind') said he had a possible replacement. So, Larry and Billy went round to Joe's ramshackle studio/flat on the Holloway Road, London N7, to meet Alan Caddy (lead guitar), Roger LaVern (organ), George Bellamy (rhythm guitar), Heinz Burt (bass guitar) and Clem Cattini (drums).

They played. Billy approved. Larry offered them £25 a week each, took out contracts and unleashed his biro.

They were called The Tornados.

As was so often the case, the weak link in the band was the bass player. When bands form, the bass player often gets the gig because his dad has a van, or because he owns two amps. Stuart Sutcliffe played with The

Beatles because he was John Lennon's friend and because he won enough cash in an art competition to buy a Hofner President bass. Heinz Burt played with The Tornados because Joe Meek was in love with him. He was a German-born looker plucked from the bacon-slicing counter of a Southampton grocery store. Inspired by the movie *Village Of The Damned* – the film in which aliens disguised as very blonde, starry-eyed children take over the world – Joe persuaded Heinz to peroxide his hair.

Clem Cattini was never impressed with Heinz's musical ability and is on record as saying the lad barely knew how to hold the instrument. Nevertheless, the others covered for him, worked on Billy's set and acquitted themselves gloriously.

They bonded with Billy, too. "I consider myself so fortunate in having a group behind me that is comprised of five of my best friends who are enough, musically, to astound the world with their talents," Billy said. "Best thing about our friendship is that we are able to enjoy ourselves together just like any other bunch of fellows. We like to walk in a line down the main street, making jokes, having a laugh or kicking a cigarette packet like the FA Cup depended on it. This is the type of offstage friendship that I enjoy with The Tornados. Backstage we have our fun. Have you heard about our draughts championship whilst on tour?"

Rock'n'roll.

With Billy fronting, they were a smash in Great Yarmouth, too.

The summer season always provided a few weeks' respite from the rigours. "It's great to be in one place for a long time instead of having to pack, travel and sleep between every two shows. I'm having myself a ball here."

He rented a house with "every mod con including an automatic temperature gauge that switches on central heating should it be required" and lived in a sort of domestic bliss with Hal Carter, his road manager.

Marty, also in the show, rented a house nearby with "the craziest little cove", where they could work up a tan.

"We have parties, too. Swingin' parties! People come over here after the show and we have the record player going till it gets light."

"Man, we've had a terrific season here," Billy told *Pop Week*. "We've had capacity audiences every night and they're still coming in their thousands. I reckon more than half a million will have seen the show by now. Some have come six or seven times to the show, which I know by the letters that are handed in at the stage door. It knocks me out."

But heady though the excitements of capacity audiences, swingin' parties, automatic temperature gauges and draughts championships must have seemed to Alan, Roger, George, Heinz and Clem, they were about to conquer a world far beyond Great Yarmouth, beyond Gorleston, beyond Lowestoft, up and up beyond the blue beyond itself.

It all began when Joe Meek, in honour of the marriage of Fury and Tornados, wrote an instrumental, 'Love And Fury', and summoned The Tornados to record it at his flat.

"Joe was a musical moron," said Clem Cattini, "and I don't mean that disrespectfully. Musically, he didn't know anything. But he was a genius in getting sounds out of that studio. The first time I went there, there were wires and cables all over the place. I was frightened to put my foot down in case I got electrocuted.

"On the floor was a spring attached to a piece of wood. That was his echo device. He was innovative in terms of ideas and the equipment he had made himself. For instance, he put Sellotape around the spindle of the tape recorder so it went slower. When you replayed it, the sound was speeded up."

'Love And Fury' is unmistakably the work of – in the most respectful way imaginable – a "musical moron". It has the 'Johnny Remember Me' galloppy-galloppy rhythm and all the instruments are processed by the wires, cables, bits of wood and Sellotape to within an inch of their lives. But the tune is incoherent. No butcher's boy could ever whistle it, or want to. It died.

But then, later in the year, inspiration struck Joe again.

On June 10, 1962, NASA launched a rocket carrying the world's first telecommunications satellite, TELSTAR, which was capable of relaying live TV pictures across the Atlantic.

Two weeks later Richard Dimbleby, the BBC's senior presenter, announced, "Hello, Walter Cronkite, hello United States. On my television screen here in Brussels, I have, on the left-hand side the Statue of Liberty, on the right-hand side the Eiffel Tower. They are both together, it's clear, so go America go, go America go." And, thanks to this miracle of modern science, the British public was able to watch in stunned amazement as the two indistinct pictures flickered on their screens, broadcast live from their respective continents.

Joe Meek watched, too, and brooded.

A tune came into his head.

Since it would be recorded, like all Joe's productions, in a manner as modern in its conception and as scientifically advanced as the satellite spinning up there in the heavens, it seemed only right that the two should share a name – 'Telstar'.

The Tornados were still in Great Yarmouth. Joe sent them a tape of himself humming the tune. He was never much of a hummer and it took a while to turn his meanderings into actual notes. Vaguely prepared, after the show on Saturday July 21, they travelled down to London, and showed up at Joe's studio/flat – some accounts say this was on the Sunday, others the Monday.

They recorded two tracks: 'Telstar' and 'Jungle Fever', the eventual B-side, and left at 3.30 the next day to be back in Great Yarmouth in time for the show, leaving Joe to add some sci-fi sound effects (including, it is rumoured, a heavily processed toilet flush).

The record was released on August 17, 1962, entered the chart a couple of weeks later, went to number one on October 10 and stayed there for five weeks. On the TV show *Thank Your Lucky Stars*, Billy presented "his" group with their gold disc.

In December, 'Telstar' went to number one in the USA, too.

This led to an offer of a US tour for the band, but Larry refused to release them from their contract as Billy's backing band. They could go, he said, as long as Billy went, too, fronting them. Billy had not had a US number one. He had not had a US Top 100 hit. American promoters were not interested in Billy. Thus the tour fell through.

Who knows? More than a year before The Beatles conquered America it could have been 'The Tornados are coming', a roaring trade in blonde Heinz wigs, controversy when Clem Cattini says 'The Tornados are bigger than Jesus', a final concert on the roof of Joe Meek's flat on the Holloway Road. The upside was that Roger LaVern, the Tornado's organist, rather than marrying Yoko Ono, was free to become a major star in Mexico, where he was known as 'El Lobo Plateado' – ('The Silver Wolf').

And anyway, the real history was already being written. The UK chart for the first week of November 1962 has 'Telstar' still celebrating its apparently endless run at number one. Billy's 'Because Of Love', the one in which he wipes the floor with Elvis, is on its way up at number 25. Marty's at 31. Cliff's at 15. Mr Acker Bilk is at 16. And at number 32 – a new entry to the Top 40 – we see 'Love Me Do' by The Beatles.

145

CHAPTER FOURTEEN

"WHY HAS HE NEVER APPEARED AT THE PALLADIUM?"

No book about the sixties can be considered complete without the Philip Larkin quote. You know the one. The poet Philip Larkin reckoned, along with many others, that the great change in sexual attitudes came between "the *Lady Chatterley* trial and The Beatles' first LP" – 1960 and 1963. He also suggested that the change wasn't so much the number of people doing it or not doing it, but the terms of negotiation and, above all, the sense of shame attached.

The dates are approximate. Some factions of the leisured, moneyed elite had always considered sexual continence a little provincial for their tastes. The D. H. Lawrence-bohemian fringe, often naked apart from sandals, had been advocating free love in woods and waterfalls with a religious fervour since before the First World War.

The first signs that attitudes were generally changing came not long after the Second World War with the publication of the two Kinsey Reports. *Sexual Behaviour In The Human Male* (1948) and *Sexual Behaviour In The Human Female* (1953) afforded glimpses into the lucky bag of delights that people dipped into when the curtains were drawn, revealing, for instance, that 92% of men had masturbated, 6% of women had kissed a girl and liked it and 26% of both men and women reported an erotic response to being bitten. This, for many readers, suggested for the first time that there was really no such thing as 'normal'.

After that there was regularly some scandal, statement or report to shake up preconceptions and provide fodder for the tabloids among which were…

The Wolfenden Report On Homosexuality & Prostitution, published in 1957, which eventually led to the decriminalisation of homosexuality 10 years later. Tellingly, though, during the proceedings that led to its publication, for the benefit of the ladies present, the words 'Huntley' and 'Palmer' (Huntley & Palmers was a popular manufacturer of biscuits) were often substituted for 'homosexual' and 'prostitute'.

The *Lady Chatterley* trial, mentioned by Philip Larkin, was the one in which Penguin Books was sued under the obscenity laws for publishing D. H. Lawrence's *Lady Chatterley's Lover*, a novel which describes the couplings of a Lady and her gamekeeper without resorting to Latin. Penguin won the case, and in the three months after the verdict sold three million copies.

In 1963, the Profumo scandal, which mixed sex, politics, aristocrats and spying, as well as providing the nation with gritty reading matter in their morning papers for several months, is alleged to have promoted an "if they can do it, why shouldn't I?" attitude.

And in 1961, the oral contraceptive pill was made available (initially only for married women). By the end of the decade, nearly half the female population had used it.

Sex, it was discovered, could be recreational as well as a marital duty for the purposes of procreation. Who knew?

Even the strict Christian view – that God took a dim view of sex in general and would punish fornicators and adulterers with hell fire – was coming in for reassessment.

In 1963, the Bishop of Woolwich, who'd appeared as a witness for the defence in the *Lady Chatterley* trial, published a book called *Honest To God*, that nobody understood but which seemed to elevate the secular at the expense of the divine. Theologians began to speak of the 'New Morality', a thing of relatives rather than absolutes, perhaps best summarised by Joseph Fletcher, an ordained minister and a Professor at Harvard Divinity School, who wrote:

"It is doubtful that love's cause is helped by any of the sex laws that try to dictate sexual practices for consenting adults. [...] We find nothing in the teachings of Jesus about the ethics of sex, except adultery and an absolute condemnation of divorce. He said nothing about birth control, large or small families, childlessness, homosexuality, masturbation, fornication or premarital intercourse, sterilisation, artificial insemination, abortion, sex play, petting and courtship. Whether any form of sex (hetero, homo, or auto) is good or evil depends on whether love is fully served."

Billy was born, brought up and began his career under the rules of old morality. On stage, he was all brooding, steaming potential, a living embodiment of caged hormones, forced, for the want of any other outlet, to do it with a microphone stand.

He and his rock'n'roll contemporaries thought it best – or were advised by their management to think it best – to play by the rules, to fake innocence and never to admit to pre-marital sex.

"I am deadly serious when I say all my relationships with girls have been platonic," Adam Faith told the *Daily Mirror* in February 1963. "I am not frustrated, although my needs are great. Although I'm lustful – isn't everyone? – I have never gone further than a kiss and a cuddle. I don't think girls scream after me because I sing sexy songs or because I have sex appeal. Girls go after me because I am young and unsure like them. I don't think they want to climb into bed with me or anything like that."

If the timing had anything to do with it Adam was probably wrong. After all, the great poet Philip Larkin decreed that sexual intercourse began in 1963, between the ending of the ban on *Lady Chatterley's Lover* and the release of The Beatles first album, which occurred in March that same year. His point was that, like Bob Dylan surmised, the times were a-changing, and change, for many, was indeed that sudden.

The Beatles had nothing to do with caged hormones ... Not on their side of the footlights anyway. They projected absolute and unassailable sexual confidence. They had done it. Probably lots of times. And they would do it again. Probably tonight. They had no frustration to vent. They did not need to cajole, negotiate, plead or beg.

When Billy sang 'Halfway To Paradise' it was a plea to an indifferent goddess. When The Beatles sang 'Please Please Me' it was an 'I do all the pleasing with you' accusation of selfishness, a 'shape up or ship out' ultimatum. They had no doubt of their ability to please. As they sang in their next release, "I've got everything that you want".

Grown-ups often mistook this effortless self-confidence for mop-top innocence. The Fabs, it seemed, were nice smiley boys, not like that Billy Fury, slowly unzipping his jacket and writhing on the floor.

Beatle fans knew, though. These moptops were messengers from the 'New Morality' sent to remake the world in our own image.

"I fought the war for your sort," says the middle-aged businessman in *A Hard Day's Night*, the first Beatle film. "I bet you're sorry you won," says Ringo.

To Beatle people, sex, jokes, smokes, politics, shoes, slang, history, hair, heroism, trousers, everything was new, everything had been reinvented. Even the language was undergoing reconstruction.

In April 1963, a couple of weeks after the release of that first Beatles' LP, the *Record Mirror* reported criticism that Billy "studiously avoids losing his Liverpool accent and is not capable of speaking for himself when meeting important show business people."

He himself later acknowledged that when he was making *Play It Cool*, "I was very embarrassed about my Liverpool accent because I was the first one down and I was in a land full of southerners. I was very, very conscious of the way I spoke."

By the end of 1963, boys from Charterhouse, Eton and Rugby were rhyming 'hair' with 'fur' and practising key phrases like "this chip butty is gear", "give us a ciggie", and "Gary Crimble", in hope of impressing the 'talent' at the Pickwick and during the coming-out season.

Meanwhile Billy's fans, the ones who had still been at school when they first encountered him in 1959, were now in their late teens and early twenties. Married, possibly, with children. They were not so easily swayed by collarless jackets and elastic-sided boots. They were unimpressed by 'all the long-haired geezers twisting and shouting' as *Jackie* magazine put it. "Because in six months all those scouse faces will be back playing in local hops again and Liverpool will only be remembered for its two football teams and *Z Cars*."

And, of course, Billy Fury.

"When the Beatles first came along," Billy said, "I thought it was quite a raw sound at first. I thought it was a very weak sound as well.

"But I thought the tunes were absolutely amazing. More than exceptionally good. They changed the music industry altogether from solo singers to bands. Which in turn changed the music scene worldwide."

That year the Clean Air Act, banning the use of coal fires in certain urban areas, kicked in. The Beatle world even smelled different.

Larry Parnes was not a happy man.

Marty hadn't had a Top 10 hit since 1961. When Joe Brown's contract came up for renewal, he chose not to renew. Freed of Larry's tutelage, he blossomed, enjoying his first Top 10 hit with the magnificent 'A Picture Of You', then, to prove it wasn't a fluke, following it up with two more: 'It Only Took A Minute' and 'That's What Love Will Do'.

Larry's later signings – Julian X, Peter Wynne and Nelson Keene – had not set the world aflame. The possibility that he might have lost his touch was hard to ignore.

Meanwhile, in January 1963, the band he could have signed but instead fobbed off with a mini-tour backing Johnny Gentle released their second record, 'Please, Please Me'. At the beginning of February, it went Top 10.

The buzz was growing. Everybody in the business, and many outside, knew there was something special about this new group and their funny hair, suits and shoes. Already the question "next big thing?" was being asked.

By summer, they and Brian Epstein's other acts – Billy J. Kramer and Gerry & The Pacemakers – had moved in on the charts, rearranged the furniture and changed the locks.

While Larry had had to go head to head with the BBC to get his boys the recognition they deserved, The Beatles had been given their own weekly BBC radio show, *Pop Go The Beatles*. Five o'clock. Every Tuesday.

Beatlemania was reported not just in the *Mirror* and *The Sketch* but in *The Times*.

When Marty had done the Royal Variety Performance in 1959, it was only as part of an *Oh Boy!* medley, with Cliff and Lord Rockingham's XI. And that was before the show was on telly. The Beatles did four numbers and made it the top TV show of the year.

Billy, still out there, still having hits, was Larry's last hope. And Larry loved Billy. There's little doubt about that. They were never an item in any conventional sense, but Billy needed mothering and Larry loved fussing over him, making sure he was nicely turned out, making sure he watched his manners. And, for his part, Billy was loyal, sticking with Larry all the way through to 1971.

The others acknowledged that Billy was special. "We were all youngsters all trying to make our way," said Johnny Gentle, "but Billy was the one Larry put all his attention into. Billy was the favourite."

March 1963 saw the publication, somewhat late in his career, of the first edition of Billy's own magazine *Billy Fury Monthly* – editor David Caldwell, managing editor Albert Hand. Priced at 1s (5p), it provided several pages of black and white pictures, notes on Billy's doings and a weekly 'phone call' with the editor, full of Bill and Dave banter. There was even an agony column in which Billy advised the lovelorn and confused:

"Dear Billy, I'm wondering if you could give me some advice. I have been going out with a boy named Ray and we are thinking of getting married. I am almost 18. Just lately I have begun to think that Ray is more interested in the Pipe Band and the Boys Brigade than he is in me. He plays the drum in the band and has to go to Harrow once a week and has to do a job every Saturday with the Boys Brigade. Should I ask him to stop going to both? Please don't tell me to join the Band or the Brigade, this is serious. Please help me – Freda."

"Dear Freda, If you love him you'll put up with anything. Try telling him you'd like to go out with him more often. Then see if he likes the pipes and drums or you best."

The magazine's editorial is, more often than not, some hectoring exhortation to the fans to get out there and buy product. "Billy has to put up with one of his smallest hits to date BECAUSE OF THE LACK OF INTEREST BY HIS FANS!! YES – YOU!!. Instead of writing letters requesting Billy's latest single on TV and Luxembourg and on the BBC radio programmes, many of you are quite content to sit back and listen to Billy's latest release at your ease and to let 'someone else' get on with the job!"

And it's peppered with anti-Beatles, pro-Billy propaganda. "Let's see if they can stay around the recording scene for five or more years, and let's also see if, in three years' time they can get every one of their records in the Hit Parade. Furthermore, I wonder if, in three years' time, they can do a summer show for three months and play to a packed audience every night. I somehow don't think they will."

The prediction came true. At no point in their career did The Beatles do a three-month booking at a seaside resort.

1963 was the year of the Parnes Panic.

As the Beat Boom went from strength to strength, Larry's protective instincts grew keener. Nobody was going to do wrong by his Billy. And Larry's single-minded struggle to make sure that, despite the irresistible rise of The Beatles, Billy was going to stay up there, and get the billings and the press he deserved, caused no end of bother.

There were two big rows across the year and countless smaller ones.

The first of the big ones came in February. Ads had gone into the papers announcing a *Top Of The Pops* concert at the Royal Albert Hall, "reflecting four of radio's most popular programmes, *Saturday Club*, *Easy Beat*, *Parade Of The Pops* and *Go, Man, Go*." The show would feature a host of stars including Helen Shapiro, Acker Bilk, Craig Douglas, Danny Williams, Brian Poole & The Tremeloes and Billy.

Although Larry was still very much Billy's personal manager, responsibility for day-to-day bookings seemed, at this time, to have been delegated to the promoter of the Albert Hall show (and Cliff's manager) Tito Burns.

On February 25, Patrick Newman, the BBC's Booking Manager (Variety), wrote to Tito Burns wondering why Billy's contract for the Albert Hall show had been sent back unsigned. Tito, with an air of long-suffering, put him on to Parnes. Patrick contacted Larry, who said that he was perfectly happy to have Billy sign the contract subject to certain conditions being met regarding Billy's billing, the running order and the number of songs he'd be singing.

"Having just looked at the above artist's past history with us," wrote Patrick, in a memo, "it does occur to me that booking him is a somewhat tedious exercise."

Larry assured Patrick that there wasn't really a problem. Compromises could be made. Conversations had. If everybody kept their heads and remained "reasonably diplomatic", "there should never be any difficulties which cannot be settled."

More memos, more letters, more phone calls. Tito Burns insisted that the problems were not coming from his office, and hastened to add that "neither the producer [of the show] nor the booking department [at the BBC] are in any way liable for this almost laughable fiasco."

Larry dug his heels in. If Billy wasn't the star of the show, he was walking.

At the end of the month, Larry bought advertising space in *NME* to declare, "Mr LARRY PARNES would like to announce on behalf of his Artiste BILLY FURY that although he was announced and advertised to appear at the BBC *Top of The Pops* concert at the Royal Albert Hall, London, on Thursday 14th March, due to contractual difficulties it has been found impossible for me to accept this engagement on his behalf. However, BILLY FURY would like all his fans who have bought tickets for this concert, thinking that he would appear, to retain one half of their ticket and send it to L.M.P Entertainments limited, Flat 7, 24 Great Cumberland Place, London W.1. Mr LARRY PARNES will then, at the earliest possible opportunity, book a London theatre and admit BILLY FURY's fans entirely free of charge to a special BILLY FURY CONCERT."

"Frankly I would have thought your announcement slightly misleading," wrote Patrick Newman, "in that it fails to point out the vital truth of the matter, which is that the 'contractual difficulties' were not raised at the right time, and the responsibility for this lies somewhere between you and Tito Burns, as I am sure all parties will agree."

And in that one word "Frankly", there at the beginning of the letter, one can almost hear the whole peevish weight of the BBC's bureaucracy – the big revolving door left fiercely spinning, leather-soled shoes echoing down corridors, an Imperial typewriter being beaten to within an inch of its life.

The post-script to the story came a few months later, when the BBC contracts department received a short note from Larry saying that all future bookings for Billy Fury should come through his office and *not* Tito Burns "because all agency agreements with Burns have been terminated."

The second, not dissimilar spat occurred six months later. Billy had never appeared on ITV's top-rated show, *Sunday Night At The London Palladium*. Adam Faith had done it. Marty Wilde had done it. Cliff Richard had done it loads of times. But never Billy.

In the August 1963 issue of *Billy Fury Monthly*, a fan wrote...

"His discs are fab, his stage act's great,

For him I'll always nominate,

The greatest star ever to appear,

For him I'll always cheer and cheer.

He's better than Cliff, Elvis, Adam and Vee
And he'll soon be KING, you wait and see,
There's just one thing he has not done,
Why has he never appeared at the Palladium?"

In customary hectoring style, the magazine went on the offensive.

"Artistes who have only a tenth of Billy's popularity have been appearing on the Palladium – BUT WHY NOT BILLY? Some say it's because Billy's act is too uninhibited for the Palladium, others say it's because someone at the Palladium dislikes Billy – and the rumours go on and on and on. Petitions are being started by national newspapers, and by magazines like *Mirabelle* etc. But I don't think anyone will take much notice of these. At least they don't seem to take any notice of these."

Judith Simons took up the cudgels in the *Daily Express*. "The 21-year-old lean Liverpudlian, whose crude stage presentation once made him the favourite butt of the anti-rock sneers, is now Crown Prince of British pop.

"But why is Billy still denied the big-time opportunities? Why has he never played the Palladium, either live or on television? Why has he never appeared in a major film? The answer could be that because of his earlier stage efforts some ridicule still attaches to the name of Fury in higher show business circles. This is not dispelled by the ex-tughand's own introvert personality – the complete opposite of Cliff Richard's. Cliff is charming, forthcoming, polite. He speaks clear, standard-English speech. Billy Fury, on the other hand, never gave the right impression to the right people. Confronted with authority, he retreated into glazed gawkiness. Perhaps when he has proved to the show business high-ups that he can project his speaking voice (though his manager Larry Parnes objects to his taking voice production lessons), perhaps when he is less inhibited about expressing his own private personality, this second-class idol will get his ticket to the first-class compartment of his calling."

It was time for the Billy Fury fan club to mobilise its paramilitary wing. "We are having a big MARCH from Trafalgar Square to Associated Television in Marble Arch. Fury fans who think they are fans please come and we'll see what happens. A petition will be handed in, of course, but the outcome should be fantastic.

"Well, whattya say? Just to make sure that at least 2,000 people turn up, will all those prepared to march for Billy please write to the address below, stating their name and address."

The plans for the march were reported in national newspapers – well, the *New Record Mirror*, anyway. But, before the big day, fans began to have second thoughts.

"At first, I was in favour of The Great March, but now I am beginning to think about it seriously and I realise that it will not do the good it is intended to do. Granted it will attract attention, but will the attention be the right kind? Won't it make people think that we're trying to do something for Billy that he can't do under his own steam? We know that we're only trying to help him fulfil an age-old ambition, but what respect are we going to gain for Billy by walking round the streets of London like a party of 'Ban The Bomb' demonstrators?"

Reportedly, 91,000 signatures were collected for the petition addressed to Lou Grade at ATV, but eventually the whole thing was called off, "because the fans of some other artists had indicated their intention to cause riots at the scene. And riots are something the Fury management didn't require."

In September, the Palladium bowed under the pressure (maybe) and booked Billy for September 29, along with the usual mixed bag of acts including ventriloquist Dennis Spicer (whose dummies included Sexy Rexy, a wolf), The Morlidor Trio (a male contortionist, dressed inexplicably as a 'golliwog', who allowed two glamorous assistants to pack him into unfeasibly small spaces and then chuck him about in a heedless manner), and stars of the Royal Ballet, Nadia Nerina and David Blair.

Then the rows started. Billy wasn't getting top billing. Larry pulled him out of the show, explaining to the *Daily Mail* and the *Express* that he had been told at the last minute that Billy would have to "take second place to Nadia Nerina and David Blair [...] I want to make it clear that I am responsible for taking Billy out of the show. Of course, we have no quarrel with the ballet stars – they are wonderful artistes. But this has placed us in an embarrassing position."

"The Palladium was a washout for Billy and I'm on his side," thundered the *BFM* (as true Billy Fans had come to know the monthly). "I wouldn't appear when I'd been treated like that. But in a way the fault is ours. We should have showed how much we were fans of his by buying more of his records. How else do you think The Beatles appeared on it so quickly? Only because their fans aren't so lazy as to give their idols a big PUSH."

Billy had bought a new suit, sealskin, £105, specially for the occasion. "I am pretty choked about the whole thing," he said. "I have phoned my mother and father to tell them I won't be appearing. I am bitterly disappointed.

"I was going to sing three numbers, including my latest, 'Somebody Else's Girl'," he said, pleased at least to have got the plug in.

In some quarters the sympathy was not so forthcoming. Harsh words like "bighead" were bandied. "So, Billy Fury feels insulted at not having the top spot at the Palladium," wrote a disgusted R. Giffen of Surrey to the *Record Mirror*. "What a shame! It seems to me that someone should suggest to Master Fury or his manager that perhaps he doesn't deserve the star spot. [...] Any real star would not behave in such a manner."

There is a school of thought that suggests that Larry's bluster was a cover for Billy's bottling out. A year later, the *NME* journalist Derek Johnson wrote, "Remember the outcry last year, when Billy was withdrawn from a Palladium TV spot because he wasn't given star billing? I recall well him telling me afterwards that he was really rather pleased, because he would have been a bundle of nerves having to appear on the famous Palladium stage."

Perhaps an accurate insight into Billy's state of mind during the Parnes Panic comes from an account Andrew Loog Oldham gives in his book *Stoned* of a trip to Great Yarmouth in the summer of '63.

Andrew had been working in the music business in one capacity or another for a while and had just signed a promising band called The Rolling Stones, or rather he'd got a grown-up to sign for him, because he was only 19 and the age of majority back then was 21. The grown-up was Lionel Bart, composer of *Oliver!*, but that's another story.

Anyway, Andrew found himself in Great Yarmouth. He was a huge Billy fan, excited to be ushered into his presence backstage.

"Fury was not up to the fantasy," he writes. "He was not only stoned, he was bored. As David Bowie said later, sometimes it's better not to meet your idols, that way they stay intact. Parnes, on the other hand, lived up to my true pop Diaghilev image of him – a rare blend of art, money and sparkle on the job. Mr Parnes was a captain alert, while his artiste seemed to be floundering, without structure, a Nijinsky to the Maestro. I do not recommend piers in Great Yarmouth as a place to meet those who've shaped your life thus far."

Chapter Fifteen

"DON'T DIE, BILLY! DON'T DIE!"

Worries about Billy's health were never far away. Writer Mick Houghton went to see one of those summer concerts, too, or rather failed to see it. As he and his parents were walking down to the end of the pier...

"We passed droves of people walking back the other way," he remembered in the book *Love Is The Drug*. "I thought little of it until we arrived to find a young girl outside, sobbing her heart out. The show had been cancelled owing to Billy Fury's ill health. We trudged back to the B&B in silence... I went to my room and cried."

The fans had noticed how frequently their idol seemed to fall ill, cancel concerts, get carted off to hospital. They were worried and began to whisper that Billy was not long for this world.

"Many of you have mentioned that there is a rumour spreading around that Billy has only a year to live as he is suffering from a disease," said David Caldwell in the *BFM*. "Well, I for one certainly do not know how these rumours started, but I can assure you that Billy is in perfect health. The only health trouble he has had was when he went into hospital recently for an operation because of kidney trouble. So I hope this settles all your queries."

Frances Crook, the fan club secretary, wrote, 'Please, please, please don't write any more letters concerning Billy's health. I have been snowed under for the past two months with letters concerning a rumour that Billy has only a few months to live. THIS IS NOT TRUE. So please if you hear any more rumours just ignore them.'

But there is no smoke without fire. Why would they bother even mentioning the rumour if there wasn't some truth in it? And maybe a lot of truth.

Further evidence that Billy had one foot in the grave came in his latest EP, *Billy Fury And The Tornados*. This was produced not by Joe Meek (who was busily turning Heinz, now a solo act, into a big star), but by Billy's usual crew – Ivor Raymonde and Mike Smith.

Three of the four songs on the EP – two of Billy's own compositions, 'What Did I Do?' and 'Keep Away', and 'I Can't Help Loving You', by George Bellamy of The Tornados and Peter Pavey – are unremarkable.

The fourth, 'Nobody's Child', is a tear-jerker, a genre for which Billy had always had a predilection.

In his live act, he'd often do 'Old Shep', the Red Foley/Elvis Presley weepy about a dead dog that Elvis had recorded because his mother liked it. After a couple of verses that emphasise the closeness between man and his best friend, the tune lurches into pathos ramped up by the suggestion that Old Shep will have a secure place in doggie heaven.

"It's the sort of song that gives a dog a bad name," says Joe Brown, "to say it was sentimental would be too big a favour. So one night, when he was singing about poor old Shep, the boys and I took some stage mics off into the toilets, and when Billy came to the really weepy bit we pulled the chains."

'Nobody's Child' was a song Billy had known since he was a kid. Hank Snow, the country singer, had originally recorded it in 1949. Then Lonnie Donegan did it, Tony Sheridan recorded it in Hamburg, accompanied by The Beat Boys, aka The Beatles, then George Harrison did it again, years later, with the Traveling Wilburys.

Before releasing it on disc, Billy had been including it in his live act for a year or so to devastating effect.

The opening line tells you the general direction the song's going to take you: "As I was slowly passing by an orphan's home one day."

It gets worse. When the passer-by asks one of the orphans why he isn't playing with the other children, the boy "turned his eyes that could not see" and "began to cry".

Billy has the decency to omit the lines – included in the Hank Snow version – telling us that the child is invariably passed over for adoption because "when they see I'm blind,/They always pick some other child". All the same, the news that this child has "no mummy's kisses and no daddy's smile" has, down the years, done wonders for Kleenex sales.

It was when Billy performed the song live and got to the line, "Sometimes it gets so lonely here I wish that I could die", that the real drama happened. A thousand teenage girls, all too aware of the rumours, would chew their hankies, weep, then rise like Pentecostals, throw out their arms in supplication and shriek, "DON'T DIE, BILLY, DON'T DIE".

The song got on to the EP largely because the fans, wanting to shout, "DON'T DIE, BILLY" in the privacy of their own bedrooms, agitated to have it recorded and released.

"We've done it, chicks!" said the March 1963 edition of the *Billy Fury Monthly*. "Or rather, our Billy's done it! Remember that fabulous song, 'I'm Nobody's Child'? The one that had everyone in tears in Great Yarmouth when Billy was doing his summer season down there? That's the one! It's pretty well lined up for Billy's new LP [which subsequently turned into an EP]."

The record made number two in the EP charts.

Billy's first single of the year was 'Like I've Never Been Gone,' a song originally recorded and released the previous year by American rockabilly singer Chase Webster.

Ivor Raymonde's arrangement takes the song at a slower tempo than the US version, removes the flavourless twist beat and generally punches up the drama.

The dying fall of the opening phrase (coincidentally similar in rhythm and shape to the opening line of The Beatles' 'Please Please Me', which was around at the same time) demands to be whistled.

"Though not one of his best," the *Daily Express* ventured, "it's in the very top strata of late-night hot-chocolate records."

159

"'Like I've Never Been Gone' could easily be Billy fury's biggest ever hit," said *NME*. "His performance is first class."

"…should have you knocked all over the floor," said the *Billy Fury Monthly*. "Just to see what effect it had on some Fury fans, I played it to a couple of Billy chicks who really dig our boy – and they swooned."

The B-side is a Billy composition with a title straight from the back streets of Liverpool – 'What Do You Think You're Doing Of'. It's a minor key 'cheating with every guy in town' song with a hint, just a hint mind you but nonetheless noticeable, of that year's emerging sound, the blues: the overall feel isn't swampy enough, and the beat too formal for it to score any more than 1.5 on the Hoochie-Coochie scale, but all the same there are definite signs that somebody's trying to get the mojo working.

"Billy gives out with a touch of the Ray Charleses on this number," says the *BFM*, "with a strong rhythm and blues feeling all the way through. The intro is played by Billy's backing team, The Tornados, but I'm afraid I didn't like the organ sound on this occasion. Great for twisting, cats!"

In April, Billy confirmed that his next album would be steeped in "rhythm and blues".

The album was called simply *Billy*. It gave good value for your 32/6; 16 tracks, every one of them, apart from 'Like I've Never Been Gone', previously unreleased.

The sleeve notes are by Tony Barrow, pop correspondent for the *Liverpool Echo*, who'd also written the sleeve notes for The Beatles' first LP and who a month later would become full-time press officer for Brian Epstein's company NEMS.

He stresses Billy's credentials as "the most famous of all Liverpudlians", who "must be acknowledged as that city's golden pop monarch". He's keen to point out that though Billy's been called "Britain's Elvis Presley by many who intend this description as a mighty compliment" in fact he isn't anything else but "Britain's Billy Fury".

Barrow describes the album tracks as "material selected carefully to bring out the full measure of his style and the unusual characteristics of his voice", which is another way of saying "a bit of a ragbag".

There are even Latin American stylings.

On 'Our Day Will Come' everybody, even the backing vocalists, stresses the boss nova beat like a teacher for an arrhythmic dance class, and 'One Step From Heaven' does the samba like Carmen Miranda.

There are also more of the kind of epic ballads he'd been releasing as singles. 'I'll Show You' has a tune one could politely describe as minimalist, which takes nearly three minutes to rise to the kind of climax you get with a Roman candle.

There's an anodyne cover of Eddie Cochran's 'One Kiss' and 'Chapel On The Hill', written by Geoff Goddard (who wrote many of John Leyton's hits) which, according to *BFM*, "was sung so tenderly by Billy that I swear two of the recording engineers had tears in their eyes".

And yet, there are at least two tracks that provided real quality.

'Willow Weep For Me' is a jazz standard, previously recorded by Billie Holiday, Sarah Vaughan, Frank Sinatra, Ella Fitzgerald and Nina Simone. As a general rule, pop singers should steer clear of jazz standards, especially ones that have been previously recorded by Billie Holiday, Sarah Vaughan, Frank Sinatra, Ella Fitzgerald and Nina Simone. Billy proves he's an exception. He most likely took his inspiration, and certainly takes some of his phrasing, from the version Dakota Staton recorded on her 1960 *Time To Swing* album. He has the good sense, the good taste, to jettison his Elvis/Johnnie Ray mannerisms and give an uncluttered reading of the song. His low notes are robust, his high notes crystal. His phrasing's good. He stands revealed as what he's always been – a terrific singer. It makes you wonder whether, had his career been appropriately steered, he might even have joined the ranks of Billie Holiday, Sarah Vaughan, Frank Sinatra, Ella Fitzgerald and Nina Simone.

He also revisits his idol Ray Charles with a cover of 'Hard Times (No One Knows Better Than I)', a track that Charles had released as a single in 1961. Again, Billy takes the unadorned approach. The opening phrase "My mother told me" sung *a capella* before the drums, bass and guitar kick in, has a ring of absolute authority about it. It's not a Ray Charles impersonation. It's not a white kid trying to sound black. It's not a pop singer holidaying in the blues. It's a 23-year-old from Liverpool taking ownership of a song. And once again one thinks, if only... if only his management and advisors could properly have directed this talent we could have been left with a legacy of this stuff and perhaps spared the version of the 'Hippy Hippy Shake' backed by 'Glad All Over' that crops up in the next chapter.

The LP did well – 21 weeks in the Top 20, 10 of them in the Top 10. It also did much to confirm Billy's reputation as a specialist in misery.

You've heard the songs about potential suicides and blind orphans: now hear "how many nights must I be sad and blue?" and "here I am broken hearted".

Even his ostensibly happier songs come with a cloud of potential misery. 'Like I've Never Been Gone', though it's based on the assumption that when the protagonist returns from wherever he's been the relationship will continue just as before, nonetheless contains that seed of doubt. "Don't make me a fool for loving you" he sings, and you absolutely know she *will* make him a fool for loving her – otherwise why would he think it in the first place. The poor sap is cruising for a bruising.

His single release at around the same time as the album was 'When Will You Say I Love You?', written by Alan Fielding, who'd also provided Billy with 'Last Night Was Made For Love'. The record begins with an ominous piano cascade underscored with timpani, and you know straight away that what follows will not be 'Little White Bull' or 'Nellie The Elephant'. She smiles at him, winter turns to spring, all seems well, except – and here comes the kick in the teeth – she's not saying those three little words. Consequently, he has an emptiness that makes him feel so blue. "When Will You Say I Love You?" he asks. The sensible answer, of course, is "never, if you keep going on about it", but the ways of true love were never sensible. Heartstrings are there to be plucked.

"Though there is impact and commerciality in this song, it's the poorest I've heard from Billy," said *NME*. "In the past, he had hardly put a foot wrong in the choice and performance of songs, but this one is a mistake."

No, it wasn't. 'When Will You Say I Love You?', spent 12 weeks in the Top 40, five weeks in the Top 10 and two weeks at number three. It also gave him the triumph of simultaneously seeing his 45 high in the singles chart and his LP high in the album chart.

The B-side was 'All I Want To Do Is Cry'.

"Why don't you sing more cheerful songs," Maureen Cleave, the woman responsible for the 'youth page' in the *Evening Standard*, asked.

"I never feel cheerful enough," Billy replied.

"Like everybody else, I do have my gloomy moments," he said, years later, "and I kind of glorify mine."

The fans seemed to like it that way.

"In my teenage years, I fell in love and got my heart broken a couple of times," said Chris Eley, "and it seemed that Billy's records hit a chord in here. I mean Morrissey would have called it 'bedsit music', and I know where he was coming from exactly because, you know, your heart's broken and Billy's music and that voice was so emotionally charged, the way he used it. It was blues, actually. Even a ballad had a blues tinge to it with him."

"Billy is most popular in the north where they still like a bit of excitement," said Maureen Cleave. "His stage act used to be one of the most vigorous and inventive: there was a splendid moment when he eased himself artistically to the floor and rolled about. This moment alas has gone. He says he doesn't feel like it anymore. But there's enough subdued violence to keep people happy. 'My ambition in the singing bit is to be able to sing good. Now it sort of bugs me causing too much feeling around. I try to keep it to the singing. In the old days I would work myself up and work everybody else up too much. Before, I didn't care how far I went. Now… I let it go to a tingle at most.'"

To try and capture something of the tingle on record, in April he recorded a live album with The Tornados, called *We Want Billy!*, eventually released in October. It was semi-live, anyway: rather than taking the mikes out to a genuine concert and hoping for the best, they brought the audience into Decca's big orchestral studio, two or three hundred at a time, for two sessions, same setlist for each. Cliff's 'live' album had been recorded in much the same way at Abbey Road four years earlier.

Side one is a collection of rock'n'roll classics including Chuck Berry's 'Sweet Little Sixteen', Ray Charles' 'Sticks And Stones' and Arthur 'Big Boy' Crudup's/Elvis' 'That's All Right'.

It gives an accurate picture of late fifties/early sixties British live rock'n'roll. Overheated, overexcited, guitar drowned in echo, organ a little more Blackpool Tower than Booker T., singer pushing the tempo, drummer trying to hold it together, everybody intent on whipping up the tingle, the hysteria. They're good at it. Craftsmen. Play this record loud at home and, even if you've never heard rock'n'roll before, the urge (if you're a geezer) to smear Brylcreem in your hair and smoke, or (if you're a bird) to backcomb obsessively and scream until you're sick into a Woolworths handbag becomes irresistible.

Side two opens with Elvis' 'Just Because', then he moves on to the hits including 'Halfway To Paradise', 'I'll Never Find Another You', and closes with 'When Will You Say I Love You'.

The hits are de-orchestrated, no strings, no timpani, no gloss. It could be argued that his readings of the songs on *We Want Billy!* is better, less mannered, more affecting, than on the original recordings.

The screams are deafening. "You hear those screams, even when he's not singing," says Clem Cattini, providing a drummer's running commentary on the album for *Record Mirror*, "it's just a movement made by Bill. He can control an audience beautifully. He can't stop himself writhing like a snake.

"Fans who just hear him on his singles don't realise how good he is on the Chuck Berry and Ray Charles sort of stuff. He loses himself completely once he gets the rhythm going inside him."

Compare and contrast the audience reactions on Cliff's 1959 live album with this one. Billy's screams are more shrill, more determined. This wasn't only a difference between Cliff fans and Billy fans. It was indicative of a different stage in the gradual change in fan culture that happened between, say, 1955 and 1970. Wanting an autograph turned into wanting to touch. Wanting to touch turned into wanting to tear off a small piece first of clothing, then of flesh. And as the security grew tighter, the fans – some of them, anyway – became more persistent, more obsessive, more cunning.

In the innocent days of 1960, *Mirabelle*'s advice to a fan wanting to meet her idol went: "All you have to do is go round to the stage door at the theatre where they're appearing and tell the doorman you are a member of the star's fan club (don't forget to take your membership card to prove it or otherwise he might not believe you). Ask him to tell your favourite you are there and you should have no trouble at all! Oh! nearly forgot! There's one thing to remember, fans please: make sure you go round after the SECOND show of the evening, not the first."

By 1963, thing had started to get hairy.

In July of that year, Billy, on his way to enjoy a quiet lunch before driving to a gig, was spotted by fans. He escaped, but they scratched their names into the paintwork of his car doing £50 worth of damage.

Long-time fan Linda Shawley saw him in Blackpool around this time and, after the show, shrieked with the crowds around the back of the Winter Gardens, waiting for him to emerge. "There was a white car there and everybody adorned it with lipstick and kisses and everybody was waiting by that car, but he shot out of that door and he went down to Squires Gate Airport where he had a fast plane waiting for him."

Any pictures of his flat that appeared were studied with a magnifying glass and the mindset of Sherlock Holmes. Dedicated Furettes could extract enough clues from the pictures to figure out a general geographical area, then pin it down to a street.

"One day," said Lee Middleton, Billy's live-in lover, "I opened the door to two girls who yelled, 'It's his wallpaper', screamed and fainted in the hallway. It took me ages to get rid of them. They even went through our dustbins and we had to nail up our letter box. The final straw came when three lads beat up the hall porter – they were looking for Billy to do him over as their girls were always raving on about him. Luckily for us, but not for the poor porter, we were away."

"Billy has been having a hell of a time," Larry Parnes told the *Daily Mail* on November 11, 1963. "He'd come home at two in the morning after a show to find six girls sleeping outside his door and in the morning his car would be covered in lipstick."

"What's the secret of Billy's power?" asked the *Billy Fury Monthly*. "I've watched fans meeting Billy, and seen them looking as if they almost couldn't care less, and then, in less than five seconds, the tears start rolling down their faces. Not always happy tears but sad tears. The only audible answer you'll get is 'He makes me want to cry'."

The conclusion is that people who meet him "are definitely under some sort of 'spell'."

Billy told of one fan who had saved up for several months to come and see him. "Apparently, she got so excited when I came on she fainted and by the time she came to again my act was finished."

Billy and Lee had managed a holiday in Florida, from which they returned having spent a fortune on tacky souvenirs: "those plastic things you stir drinks with", "an old-fashioned pistol made into a lighter – now there's the sort of think I really like."

Larry organised a welcome-home party. Billy sang a few numbers and his fan club presented him with gifts; a live rabbit that he passed on to the fan club secretary and a travelling case complete with hairbrushes for Billy's one-nighters.

He was tanned, fit, loved and prosperous. Royalties from the hits, even after Mr Parnes had taken his cut, were rolling in.

"We like to see our Billy doing well," his mum told the *Daily Mirror*. "I'm trying to get him to invest some money in bricks and mortar.

Bricks and mortar is the thing. Which reminds me, I must get Billy made into a limited company next year. You can do that, can't you?"

Cliff had just bought himself a £31,000 mansion in Essex, Tommy Steele had a magnificent riverside place in Middlesex, Helen Shapiro had bought a £12,000 house in Hendon and Adam Faith had got himself a Tudor pile out in Esher.

Deep in the countryside, behind security gates, a pop star could find peace and privacy.

The more established representatives of the fixtures and furnishing trades looked on the tastes and peccadilloes of these "young gentlemen in the singing profession" and despaired.

"One of these young men wanted a carpet like the one in room number so-and-so in a hotel in Liverpool," an unnamed assistant furnishing manager told the *Evening Standard*. "Another wanted curtains like the one in room number something else in Coventry. A young man who makes a fortune quickly is not a discerning buyer."

Lee found a house in Kingston Hill, Surrey. "Larry helped us to design the interior of the new house," said Lee, "the first we'd ever owned. The dining room we did out in silks, Chinese style, and we even had a hand carved dining suite."

"The house has a hill at the back of it," Billy told the *Evening Standard* in September 1963, "with a sort of forest at the back. And then I've got fields and lots of sheds with all my old stuff in them I don't use – like old sun ray lamps and electric drills because I have a mania for woodwork and putting up fences. I like to be on my own. Sometimes when I am with my friends I think, 'I must get on my own fast.'"

The seclusion lasted until November.

"Billy began a national tour," said Lee, much later. "But one night he played a theatre in Kingston (this probably dates it to November 1, 1963) and was followed home by a few cars full of fans. Even though we had a six-foot wall, enormous solid electrified gates and a fool-proof double door entrance in the wall, his persistent fans came pouring over the walls.

"My mother [who was staying with them] had a breakdown and we had to send her home. When we had a three-foot extension built on the wall, our neighbours, whom we called the purple people-eaters as they all had blue rinses, complained to the council, so we had to take it down. The neighbours were very posh and really objected to having a pop person nearby. Now I'm older and more responsible I don't blame the purple people-eaters at all. I'd have hated to have us as neighbours."

Wondrous face.
CHRIS ELEY

"Have you heard about our draughts championship?" With Heinz and George Bellamy.
CHRIS ELEY

"I'm a terrible loner."
CHRIS ELEY

"…looking as if they'd just majored in Handsome at a top university."
ELVIS PRESLEY FAN CLUB

"…but Billy was the one Larry put all his attention into."
ALAMY

"We actually did get on really well from the very beginning." With Amanda.

Derby Day, 1964 (with Lee, hiding).

Under-rehearsing, with The John Barrry Orchestra.
MIRRORPIX

Working a fringe.
ALAMY

Aladdin and Princess Jasmine.
CHERYL KENNEDY

"I always think that I'm just about plodding along."

Judith, 1969.
MIRRORPIX

The animal lover.
PDSA

"I've been practising transcendental meditation for years through Mother Nature."
MIRRORPIX

"Billy's knowledge of birds and their eggs is unbelievable…"

"…in fact, he's working on a book about the subject."

Billy bought a house for his mum and dad, too. "It's in a garden area, if you know what I mean," he said, "with sort of fruit trees where the old man can have a place to tinker about."

"It's a very select district, isn't it?" said Jean. "It's six months since we had him home. I last saw him at a concert in London in April. He'll be in Liverpool on an autumn tour. We'll see him then, of course. But he telephones us once a week. If we don't hear from him, I begin to worry."

Jean and Albert called the house 'Wondrous Place'.

"They probably meant it as a compliment," Billy said. "But when I saw it, I sort of cringed."

The fans sometimes saw Billy and Lee around town in each other's company, provoking concerns that he was married, or at least spoken for.

The fears had been brewing for a couple of years at least. A fan, Barbara First from Huddersfield, had written of her distress to *Valentine* back in 1961. "I went to see Billy at a concert the other night and he was wearing a ring on the third finger of his left hand."

Valentine was able to reassure her. "Billy was given the ring by one of his relatives as a birthday present – the engagement finger is the only one the ring will fit."

"One thing I tell my boys – and I believe this is important," Larry said, "is that their girlfriends mustn't be allowed to interfere with their careers."

The soundness of Larry's advice had been confirmed when, in December 1959, Marty Wilde had married Vernons Girl Joyce Baker.

"They jived outside the church," said the *Daily Express*, "screamed 'I love that man' as the groom ambled in on his size 13 shoes. They stood on cars daubed in lipstick – 2,000 of them.

"Inside a woman wept ('Can I open my eyes now, is he really married?'). The vicar nervously urged anyone with a camera to resist taking pictures during the service, TV organist Cherry Wainer played an excerpt from 'The Merry Widow'. ('It was an awful *faux pas*.')

"And all this at the wedding yesterday of 20-year-old ex-butcher's boy Marty Wilde, rock'n'roll idol (born Reg Smith) to Joyce Baker, 18 ('I came out in heat bumps I was so nervous.')."

Three years later, the *Express* examined the consequences.

"His disc earnings fell from £10,000 a year to less than £1,000. He was no longer a top show business draw."

"When I married I knew what would happen to my disc sales," Marty told the reporter. "But marriage was the thing I wanted most from life. At present, I'm doing all right on ballroom dates. I could make £1,000 from them if I worked a full week, but I usually accept about three. Soon I start work on a film and I've got a new disc contract. If I get a hit disc now, I'll be in as good a position as I was three years ago."

Cliff, then 22, had never been linked with any serious girlfriend. Adam Faith realised, "It could be a danger to my career if I married." And "Billy Fury (21) claims that whenever he has taken up seriously with a girl she has jilted him."

"I don't think I'll ever get married," Billy told *Disc*. "Sure, I go out with girls, but not steady. I've never met the right one. I was in love once in Liverpool, before I came into this business, but it didn't work out. Every time I take a girl out now I compare her to the one back home. But you're only ever in love once... it's never the same again."

The *BFM* liked to give the impression that Billy was a serial dater, searching, searching, searching for Miss Right.

"Every so often I get ideas about one girl and think she's the greatest and think so for about a month, and then when I come out of a theatre and see another girl in the crowd I change my mind. It's all pretty difficult and I wouldn't like to be certain of marrying any girl until I'd got rid of my dream-girl complex.

"As for what my dream-girl looks like, I think that's impossible to say. After all, I've often thought of her as a blonde, but sometimes I think I'd prefer a brunette or even someone with red hair.

"If I'm forced to give a preference, then I go for simple full skirted dresses. Oh, yes, and nice clean neat shoes. Boys notice shoes far more than girls realise and it is ghastly to see a girl out in grubby shoes."

It was an ongoing tease for the fans, holding out the possibility that 'it could be you'.

"Any girl who wants the ingredients to be Billy's wife should follow the simple instructions herewith. Be kind, sincere, don't try to push yourself too much, don't get too plastered with make-up. Don't laugh at Billy when he says he's shy ('cause he means it), and above all, don't keep saying how wonderful he is, 'cause nothing makes a guy more embarrassed. OK chicks! Get in the line now for membership to the Fury Marriage bureau."

Jennifer of Burton-On-Trent wrote: "There are not many girls my age who are as potty on Billy as I am. I am 20 years old. If he got married it would break my heart. I would still be a great fan of his but us Fury fans would not like to think of him being married because it would ruin our dreams. I would cry forever more. So would all of his other fans. I don't want him to stop single all his life but on the other hand I don't want him to get married yet. Maybe in about 10 years' time."

"Dear Billy, We hear so many rumours that you don't want to get married. But I've got a problem. I'm in love with a pop singer, but he isn't in love with me, at least he couldn't be because I only met him once. And I haven't had the chance to get near him since. It's breaking my heart. What do I do? – Sally."

They were girls of their times – some of them were, anyway. Fans who could not allow themselves to entertain carnal thoughts about Billy without sanctifying the union with a ring, a cake and a vicar. In a sense they felt that they were already married to Billy – perhaps in the sense that nuns are 'brides of Christ'. A spiritual union, somehow more intense for its distance.

"Bill Fury, the guy we all love," wrote fan Sandra in *BFM*, "each in our own way, each thinking we love him more than the next girl. We hear so much, so very much about him, we just can't help loving him.

"I've met him twice, not that he'd remember, they were so brief, the meetings and so far between. I won't meet Bill again, I know that. I wouldn't have met him the first time if I hadn't known one of The Tornados who had taken me backstage to meet him."

The encounter is remembered in obsessive detail. "Billy was very nervous, I think. Maybe he was as nervous as me. It sounds silly I know, but he gave me that impression. When he did talk he never looked me in the eyes but when he thought I wasn't looking he'd watch me. Every move I made, everything I said, but as soon as I looked at him he'd look away. Please don't get me wrong. I don't mean he thought I was so wonderful he couldn't take his eyes off me. On the contrary, he was just weighing me up, wondering why anyone should want to meet him. He didn't say this, I saw it in his eyes.

"Billy's the type of boy who's [sic] eyes show his feelings, his thoughts, his moods."

Then she found her way to his parents' house.

"The second time I met him was at his Liverpool home. I never found anything different in his manner. He was just the same. He obviously didn't remember me but then I didn't expect him to, so I wasn't disappointed. We didn't talk long as he had to move on, but when he'd gone, I stayed and talked to his mum. We talked of when he was a child and how his hair used to be dead straight and his brother's just a mass of curls. She worries an awful lot over him, if he's getting enough food and sleep. The usual things a mother worries over. It wasn't just an act, she really felt what she was saying. I could have cried for her. It was her that gave us Billy and now she sees him as we do. What a price for fame? Granted she'd have to let him go if he got married, but it would have been to one person, not to a million as it is now."

The later breed of fans were more liberated in their desires.

For months, Mr Epstein and The Beatles kept John Lennon's marriage to Cynthia a secret. When, in November 1963, it finally hit the headlines, the fears that it would be the end of everything proved unfounded. Fans didn't necessarily want to marry a Beatle. They'd happily settle for something more fleeting.

Chapter Sixteen

"THE LIFE OF A POP STAR IS NOT ALWAYS AN EASY ONE."

Billy's 1963 summer season consisted of Sunday concerts only, in Great Yarmouth (which is where Andrew Loog Oldham tracked him down), Bournemouth and Blackpool.

"The rest of the time," said Maureen Cleave in the *Evening Standard*, "he will be keeping up with the hectic schedule of reading new film scripts between one nighters, TV, radio, opening various functions, songwriting, cutting new tracks for his LPs – and signing many hundreds of autographs."

He was also taking photographs and still planning that book about wildlife. And as well as reading film scripts, he was apparently writing one to be called *Sunday Kind Of Rebel*, set in Liverpool. "It's about a boy who doesn't mix much. He does a lot of thinking and in the end he gets killed very dramatically, stealing trucks. There's a lot of rebels about – I would like to be one myself."

And he was writing poetry. "They're in a kind of verse. They're about the truth in life. They're about the sort of things that people can't face up to, the nasty things they put in the back of their minds, fears and things. I write them down. I write about beautiful things too – one of the poems is about the countryside. Another is about suicide."

Every transistor radio on every beach that summer was playing records by the new groups, The Beatles' 'From Me To You', The Searchers' 'Sweets For My Sweet', Gerry & The Pacemakers' 'I Like It'. But Billy had the proper seasonal hit with 'In Summer'.

The song was written by Valerie and Elaine Murtagh and Ray Adams, who before turning to songwriting had sung the chirpy 1959 hit 'Seven Little Girls Sitting In The Back Seat' as The Avons.

'In Summer' was relentlessly (and, for Billy, uncharacteristically) chirpy. : "…tired and feeling blue/I think of all the things I can do in summer."

It was a good walking tune to have in your head as you scoured the prom for talent, twitching with the static from your nylon shirt.

It didn't please everybody. "When I listen to Billy, I want to hear a voice with sincerity and sadness in it," said fan K. Hartley of Crawley. "This is what has made him famous. I think if he makes another record like 'In Summer' he will be on the road to ruin and there must be thousands of his fans who feel the same way."

There weren't. It went to number three.

On Friday August 9, something new and wonderful came to the nation's TV screens. It began with the Surfari's 'Wipe Out' and a fast cut sequence of teens putting on crash helmets, getting on motorcycles and scooters and driving to the Rediffusion TV studios on Kingsway, London, where other teens were excitedly gathered. They stopped at traffic lights. The lights changed and the captions said, Red "READY", Amber "STEADY", Green "GO", and then "THE WEEKEND STARTS HERE". And that particular weekend started with, among others, Billy Fury.

Ready, Steady, Go! would be essential viewing for three years. The studio was stripped bare and filled with dancers, all of whom looked as they'd just blown their pay cheques at Kiki Byrne's on the King's Road, or John Stephen's on Carnaby Street. Sometimes the idols would arrive down a spiral staircase giving the studio the feel of a subterranean club. The hosts, Keith Fordyce and Dave Gel, were a bit too avuncular, but in later series the young, fashionably confused Cathy McGowan was delightfully inept.

The guests on that first show were – Billy included – not from the top drawer of cool. They included God-fearing Pat Boone, who made money bowdlerising Little Richard hits to make them 'suitable' for white American teens, and Chris Barber, who despite his association with Muddy Waters and Sister Rosetta Tharpe, was still a balding trombone player.

Billy showed up on time, did 'In Summer' and his new record 'Somebody Else's Girl' without getting banned for being, as Maureen Cleave put it, too "vigorous" or "inventive".

That new single, 'Somebody Else's Girl', is a standard 'I'm in love with the girl who's been leading me on because she's actually in love with some other man and has possibly even made some sort of commitment to him' song.

Freddie & The Dreamers also recorded the song as an album track with Freddie Garrity doing a pathetic little-boy-lost number. But Billy imbues the lyric with a nobility – manly strength in adversity.

The record made number 18, his first single not to go Top five since 'Because Of Love' the year before.

That autumn, Billy embarked on a three-month tour with Joe Brown, Karl Denver, Marty Wilde, Dickie Pride and The Tornados, opening in Croydon on October 4 and finishing on December 16 in Edmonton.

Dickie Pride and Billy had been close since the night in 1959, before a Sunday evening performance at the Grand Theatre, Wolverhampton, when they decided to cut their palms with a razor blade so they could mingle their blood to become blood brothers – alarming their tour manager and ruining their shirts.

Now, four years later, Dickie and his wife Trish had run into financial difficulties. Temporarily Billy and Lee took them in at the new house in Kingston. Dickie was often in trouble of one sort or another.

"He was very, very talented, but his head was gone," said Hal Carter. "It was just one of those things. He was a genius in my opinion, but with a couple of flakes missing... the trouble was, you never knew when you went into the room whether you were going to get the genius or a madman. Uncontrollable – he was like a wild stallion... there was no way you could do anything with him. If you tried to put a saddle on, he'd bite you!"

Billy liked to drive himself to gigs, either in his Ford Zodiac or in his new Jag. As we've already seen, he was not the most cautious of drivers. During the summer, after one of the Sunday night gigs, he was pulled over for doing 83 mph on the A33.

"The life of a pop star is not always an easy one," his solicitor told the court. "He was appearing at a Bournemouth show and was mobbed by fans. While driving back to London, he was followed by some girl fans and it took some time to shake them off."

It was Billy's sixth offence in two years. The solicitor begged the magistrates not to disqualify him. "This young fellow is starting a one-night stand tour in a few weeks and needs his car."

Endorsement and £55 fine.

Then on November 4, Billy and Dickie were driving back to Kingston from a gig in Wolverhampton with Billy at the wheel.

"Pop singer Billy Fury, 22, was in hospital last night suffering from concussion," said the *Daily Express*. "Billy was driving in thick fog along the M1 near Bedford when he stopped to avoid a 15-car pile-up."

Two cars behind then ploughed into the back of his Ford Zodiac.

As if to underline the dangers of touring, on the same night the coach carrying Julie Grant, who had a couple of minor hits that year, was involved in a crash as she travelled back from a gig at the Hammersmith Odeon. She survived, but the coach driver was killed.

For Christmas, Decca released a Billy Fury five-track EP and a single.

The EP gave full rein to Billy's love of Ray Charles with versions of 'That's Enough' and 'Tell Me How You Feel' from Charles' 1959 album *What'd I Say?*, together with a cover of the 1929 standard 'Am I Blue?', a song that Ray had released as a single in 1961. The other two tracks were a huge orchestral rearrangement of 'Wondrous Place' and a version of 'What Am I Living For?', a song released by Chuck Willis a few years earlier.

The single, 'Do You Really Love Me Too?', subtitled 'Fool's Errand', was the first to be released under a new regime. Taking their cue from Joe Meek, who produced his records independently and leased the masters to the record company which acted as distributor, Billy and Larry had formed their own independent production company, which they called Billtone.

The record provoked a direct confrontation between the old guard (Billy) and the new (The Beatles).

In the August 1963 issue of *Billy Fury Monthly*, a fan wrote...
"My idol is a guy named Fury
And if he was on *Juke Box Jury*
I'd vote for him all the way
'Cos he is here, and here to STAY"

Juke Box Jury was a BBC TV show on which a panel of four celebrities would discuss some of that week's new releases and rate them either as a HIT (ding) or a MISS (klaxon horn).

On December 7, 'Do You Really Love Me Too?' came up for consideration on the show. The panellists were the four Beatles.

The record was played on the *Juke Box Jury* juke box to the customary visuals of a) the record turning, b) close-ups of the audience's feet tapping and c) close-ups of the panellists listening intently. It faded (they never played the whole record) and David Jacobs said:

"Do you really love me too, Ringo?"

"Not you," said Ringo. "I didn't like it, you know. I've never bought one of his records, but he's very popular, so it's just uhh... no."

"Not bad," said George, "but I wouldn't buy it. And I thought the guitar is just exactly the same as Cliff's. In fact, it's only about a note difference." [Cliff's latest was 'Don't Talk To Me' and George was right.]

"The tune's not bad," said John. "It's quite pleasant. It's one of those you gotta hear again... uhh, tomorrow."

"I quite like it," said Paul, "and the same things John said jokingly. The only thing I thought, as well as the guitar bit being like the Cliff Richard bit, the tune is just a little bit like (sings) 'Well I feed the cows and I milks the sheep and I...'

"But I still think it'll be a hit."

The others agreed. It would be a HIT (ding).

They were right, too, but it took some time getting there. That Christmas, the Fab Four took the top spots, with 'I Want To Hold Your Hand' at number one and 'She Loves You' at number two.

'Do You Really Love Me Too' didn't make its first appearance until the beginning of January and took another month to climb to its highest position, at number 13.

It took a special kind of loyalty to stay true to Billy in 1963. Mick Houghton, the Billy fan who had cried when Billy had to cancel a concert in Great Yarmouth, finally saw his idol on Friday October 11, 1963 at a cinema in Bexley Heath. He wasn't too impressed with the rest of the bill.

"Karl Denver opened the show – I'd never liked his stuff or his 'famous' nasal whine. He ended, after a dreadful, interminable comedy routine, with 'Wimoweh', the audience, much to my embarrassment, singing along. [...] Joe Brown & The Bruvvers were next up and the girls went berserk. I slid further down my seat as he went into his cockney patter, telling them to 'Shut their cake holes'."

Even Marty Wilde disappointed him that night. But…

"…things picked up as The Tornados ran through 'Telstar', 'Globetrotter' and the like, but by now we were waiting for Billy Fury.'

"At last, a buzz of excitement. He was the star after all. He walked on and it reached fever pitch. The girls went wild – screaming wild. I just sat there, riveted, craning to see the stage amid a sea of waving arms and bobbing heads. His every gesture, every arm movement brought further hysteria.

"As to what he played, it's a blur of memory but it was rock'n'roll/ R&B stuff mostly. 'That's All Right Mama' and 'Sweet Little Sixteen' were in there somewhere along with some new songs, well new to me. Unlike everyone else that night he didn't just run through his hits, though he had every right to. He said little, and there was certainly no daft comedy stuff. He was cool. What a relief."

Two nights later Mick Houghton, along with 15 million others, saw The Beatles on TV on *Sunday Night At The London Palladium*. Cruelly, he switched his allegiances without a second thought.

Even the hardcore fans could be a little insensitive.

"Dear Billy," wrote one to the *Billy Fury Monthly*, "How can I meet The Beatles? – Jackie."

"Dear Jackie," replied Billy, "I don't know. I'm still trying."

In 1963, Billy had three Top five hits. He never had another.

CHAPTER SEVENTEEN

"THESE ODD BODS ARE THE NEW ARISTOCRACY OF GREAT BRITAIN."

In December 1963, Billy presented The Tornados with a gold disc for 'Telstar'. A month later he and the band parted company.

Marty Wilde had spotted a potential replacement and arranged for them to audition.

The Gamblers – Ken Brady (sax), Andy Mac (drums), 'Legs' George (keyboards), Tony Damond (trumpet and guitar), 'Blacks' Sanderson (bass) and Jim Crawford (lead guitar) – were a versatile six-piece from Newcastle with a resident gig at the Majestic Ballroom. Billed as "Tyneside's First Answer To Merseyside", they were already signed to Decca and had released one single, a cover of Smokey Robinson's 'You've Really Got A Hold On Me', which, in spite of a snappy advertising campaign ("You can put the North-East on the map by buying it NOW!"), didn't do much business.

At the beginning of February 1964 they were officially launched as Billy's backing band at a reception held amid a menagerie of crocodiles, monkeys and parrots at the Beachcomber Room in the Mayfair Hotel.

They'd already done a test session with Billy, recording, among other songs, a cover of Chan Romero's/The Swinging Blue Jeans' the 'Hippy Hippy Shake' and another of The Dave Clark Five's 'Glad All Over', both recent, massive hits.

On the Billy & The Gamblers versions, they're sung almost chorally, with Billy's voice – not sounding much like Billy's voice – one among many. Perhaps they were trying for a new sound. The sides were never released in the UK, not at the time, anyway, but did leak out into several European and Australasian territories and may, one hopes, have given teens in Paekakariki a momentary tingle.

A new producer was brought in for the January session. Mike Leander was a 22-year-old from Walthamstow in East London who, despite at the time being unable to properly read or write music (later he studied at Trinity College of Music), blagged his way into an arranger's job at Decca.

His subsequent credits are breathtaking. As well as working with The Rolling Stones, Van Morrison, Marc Bolan, Roy Orbison and a couple of hundred other major names, he scored the strings for 'She's Leaving Home' on *Sgt Pepper's Lonely Hearts Club Band* and executive produced the *Jesus Christ Superstar* concept album. And he managed Gary Glitter.

Billy and Mike recorded a range of material in a range of styles, including a never released cover of Elvis' 'Suspicion', the tapes of which have since disappeared and are regarded by collectors as 'the Holy Grail of missing Fury recordings'.

The single release that resulted from the sessions was 'I Will', a Vic Dana number from a couple of years earlier. Larry had heard it on the radio in the USA. Simultaneously, in London, Dick Rowe had come upon it while sorting through a pile of records at Decca. Both had earmarked it as right for Billy.

The Billy/Mike Leander version went back to the tried and tested Fury formula: beat ballad with lush orchestral arrangement.

Cilla Black, on *Juke Box Jury*, thought it was "too polished".

Mike Leander hit back, "Billy Fury is a singer who's really with it in every sense of the word," he said. "He walks into a recording studio for a new number… minutes later he's got it to perfection. Surely this is an advantage. I can't see Cilla's comment as a piece of criticism at all."

"I don't want to say I'm gonna cry my eyes out, baby, but I will," Billy sings, hoping to turn misery into gold, just like the old days.

He sang the song on *Ready, Steady, Go!*, peeking through the rails of the spiral staircase as he slowly ascends. Halfway up he sits down, not because he's tired or, God forbid, taken ill again, but because he still has 16 bars to go and it's only an eight-bar staircase.

The B-side is a version of 'Nothin' Shakin' (But The Leaves On The Trees)', an Eddie Fontaine song that had become a standard feature of everybody's live act – including The Beatles'.

Billy had two cracks at recording it. The first attempt was rejected as being too "loose". The second, recorded on March 9, featured, as session musicians, Jimmy Page and John Paul Jones – half of what would become Led Zeppelin. Even this version isn't quite as tight as it might be. The laxness of Jimmy's and John's customarily faultless timekeeping suggests they may have been sharing Billy's roll-ups.

'I Will' peaked at number 14.

At the beginning of 1964, The Beatles went to America. It's estimated that 73 million people watched them on the *Ed Sullivan Show*. Twelve of the entries in the April 4 *Billboard* Hot 100, including every one of the Top five singles, were Beatles records. Three-quarters of this group, let us not forget, were once rejected for the role of Billy's backing group.

Cliff's 'Move It' and Billy's *Sound Of Fury* were admired, in part, because of how close they came to the American product – the 'real thing'. Now the British product was the 'real thing' that the Americans tried to copy.

By the end of the year, The Rolling Stones, The Kinks, Dusty Springfield, The Animals, The Dave Clark Five, even The Bachelors and The Honeycombs, were making inroads on the US charts.

But while the British invasion moved unassailably onwards, Cliff Richard, Adam Faith, Marty Wilde and Billy Fury, the UK's biggest pre-Beatles stars, counted themselves among the gentlemen in England who thought themselves accursed they were not there.

Everybody had to adapt to new regime, or get another job.

Adam Faith became a guitar group, Adam Faith & The Roulettes, and started releasing Mersey-sounding songs written by Chris Andrews.

Cliff, who during the early months was convinced, as so many were, that the new lot were a passing phase, had initially dug his heels in: "I think The Beatles will ride high for maybe a year – then they will have to look to their laurels." Nevertheless, by 1964 he had abandoned his quiff and was combing his hair forwards, and The Shadows were doing the same.

There was concern from the fans about which way Billy would jump.

"Is it true? Is Billy coming to the point in his career where the wild one-nighters will finally disappear altogether? It certainly seems like it. Quite a few readers of *Fury Monthly* have also hinted that maybe Billy has given up the frantic stage movements and fast numbers to become an almost Mark Wynter singer, with scarcely any of the old fire in him. Yet at the same time the Big Beat is, if anything, getting worse. The records from not only the beat groups but solo singers get louder and more beatier as time goes by. Billy just carries on making slow or uptempo ballads mostly with strings."

In fact, Billy and Larry's response to the increasing beatiness of the beat was to diversify.

Billtone Records was their first venture, then, on August 25, 1964, *The Times* reported. "Popular singer Mr Billy Fury and his manager Mr Larry Parnes have linked up with the Bennett Cameras firm in a new venture to run record shops. First of the shops – to be known as *Billy Fury's Fab Record Shops* – opens at Peckham next month. A second is scheduled and others are likely to follow if they prove a success.

"'It would be our intention to expand into a nation-wide chain if this proves possible,' said Mr Michael Bennett, managing director of Bennett Cameras."

"Will the fans be able to buy a direct stake in the business?" asked the *Daily Mirror*. "'If profits keep up we might sell shares to the public in a year or so,' says manager Larry Parnes."

The shop did open, on Rye Lane, Peckham. Billy paid it a visit one Sunday in September. As it turned out, though, HMV had nothing to fear.

'Somebody Else's Girl' was made by Billy and Larry's new production company Billtone.

In April 1964, Billtone signed a band that Larry had discovered at Brad's club (a posh and groovy niterie on Duke of York Street, SW1) called The Trends. They had a couple of releases, a cover of The Beatles' 'All My Loving', released on Pye, and a follow-up, 'Wonderful One', produced by Tony Hatch, composer of Petula Clark's 'Downtown' and the themes from the long-running soap operas *Crossroads*, *Emmerdale* and *Neighbours*. Neither record bothered the charts.

Billtone also signed Billy's girlfriend, Lee Middleton, under her professional name 'Lady Lee'. Her first idea for a single was a cover of 'Anyone Who Had A Heart', the Burt Bacharach/Hal David song that Dionne Warwick had released the previous year. Then Cilla Black, bless her, beat her to the punch and took it to number one.

Next choice was 'I'm Into Something Good', a Gerry Goffin/Carole King song that had been a minor US hit for Earl Jean. With Mike Leander producing, a fine record was made with tough sax, soaring trumpet, handclaps and hints of ska. Then Lee made the mistake of telling her ex-boyfriend Alex Most all about it. Alex mentioned it to his former singing partner Micky Most, who had moved into songwriting and production and was looking for material for a new band called Herman's Hermits. Herman's Hermits took that song to number one.

Billy and Lee had moved again, to a mock Tudor five-bedroom house in Ockley, Surrey, which they bought fully furnished. Here they began to assemble a menagerie – a varying number of Chihuahuas, a Great Dane, an Alsatian, a Doberman, a monkey, sometimes a bird or two and a reckless carnival of other livestock that came and went

Then Billy acquired a racehorse.

He'd been a regular at Great Yarmouth Racecourse every summer season he'd been there. He'd often talked of becoming "the biggest dog breeder in Britain and it would be nice to have my own stables too", so this was not a whimsical purchase.

It made front-page news in the *Daily Express*: "Billy Fury makes £8,500 bid for 100-1 Derby hope.

"Pop singer Billy Fury was last night trying to buy a Derby racehorse for £8,500. The horse is outsider Anselmo, quoted yesterday at 100-1."

The plan was to enter the horse for the Derby. Despite the 100-1 odds, there was, it seemed, an outside chance of a miracle. Paddy Prendergast, Anselmo's trainer, had trained Ragusa, the outsider that had run in the previous year's Derby and, to everyone's astonishment, finished third.

The horse was flown over from Ireland on June 1, and Billy met him at Gatwick Airport.

"He is a magnificent looking horse," Billy said. "I'm not a betting man, but I've had a modest 10-shilling-each-way bet on him. After all this rain, he should do well, if he swims."

"Don't back Anselmo," Billy advised punters. "Buy my records instead."

He rented a pale grey morning suit with topper from Moss Bros and, on June 3, went along to Epsom.

The Queen was, of course, also in attendance, along with Prince Philip, the Queen Mother and the President of Sudan, who happened to be over on a state visit. Billy landed an invitation to meet them in Lord Derby's box. Lee put on her mink and went along as well but, to deter press speculation, they all had to pretend that she was Larry Parnes' date. Larry's accountant, a large bewigged lady called Vera, was Billy's.

Anselmo was ridden by Paul Cook, then just 18.

Santa Claus, the favourite, was at the back of the field for most of the race, with Oncidium and Baldric in the lead.

In the final furlongs, Oncidium fell behind. Scobie Breasley on Santa Claus put on a spurt and started challenging Baldric, Indiana and Dilettante.

But who's this, holding steady in fourth place? Why, it's the plucky 100-1 outsider Anselmo, right up there with the leaders.

On the final straight, Santa Claus came pounding up on the outside. He swept past Baldric, past Dilettante.

Indiana and Santa Claus battled it out and it seemed for a moment like a two-horse race, but then, as they swept past the finishing line... Anselmo came fourth.

All the same, fourth in a field of 17 is nothing to be ashamed of. Racing correspondent Clive Graham had said he'd eat his hat if Anselmo finished in the first six.

"I'd not ridden Anselmo before," Paul Cook said. "When you are having your first ride in the Derby at 18 years old you are dreaming. He wasn't a live prospect but he just gave me a great ride and ran terribly well. Billy was terribly excited and the Queen was in the paddock. You weren't to smoke in the paddock but he was doing circles of smoke in there."

"I'm sorry your horse didn't win," Her Majesty said to Billy, "he ran a fine race."

"Thank you, ma'am," Billy replied.

"I kept an eye on your horse, because of my association with him," said the Queen. Anselmo's dad was one of the Queen's own racehorses.

"You had bad luck," said the Queen Mother. "Better luck next time."

"The Royal Family were charming," Billy said later. "I was flabbergasted when I went into the box and saw them there. But they soon put me at ease."

William Connor, who wrote under the name Cassandra in the *Daily Mirror*, was sourly outraged by the presumption of a pop star hobnobbing with royalty: "Yesterday, we had the spectacle of Billy Fury, whose real name is Ronald Wycherley and who now owns a racehorse, being received by the old aristocracy at the Derby. These odd bods are the new aristocracy of Great Britain. Their musical talents are negligible, and their sorry secret is the capacity to exploit tribal sexual behaviour and to be young – a chore we all have to undergo in the raw part of our lives."

The workings of Larry Parnes' mind are impervious to speculation. Did he plan that Billy would make a film about a horse and acquire the horse to publicise the film? Or did the idea of making the film come afterwards, as a way, maybe, of tax-deducting the cost of the horse? Or did it all happen by coincidence, just like a showbiz movie...

INT. STABLES – DAY

PARNES: (MUSING TO HIMSELF AS HE FEEDS A SUGAR LUMP TO ANSELMO) If only we could find a really good subject for Billy's next movie.

STABLE BOY: Could you pass me those brushes, Mr Parnes. I've got a horse to groom.

PARNES: (EXCITED) What did you say, idiot boy?

STABLE BOY: I said, 'Could you pass me those...'"

PARNES: No, the second part.

STABLE BOY: I said, "I've gotta a horse to groom."

PARNES: No, just the first part of the second part.

In fact, the film's title, *I've Gotta Horse*, was most likely borrowed from Prince Monolulu, a tipster, who wandered around racecourses shouting – "I've gotta horse, I've gotta horse" – dressed either in impeccable morning suit with spats and topper or a kilt of sorts with embroidered weskit and tall feathered headdress. For a few shillings he'd give you a sealed envelope containing the name of a winner, whispering as he did so, "If you tell anybody the name of this horse, it will surely lose." His lamentable success record suggests that few of his punters could keep a secret.

Talk of a follow-up to *Play It Cool* had been bubbling for a couple of years. In 1963 plans were in the air for a film set in the Caribbean, shot in colour and CinemaScope. Then there was Billy's own script about the tearaway in Liverpool. Larry had frequently Parnesed on and on about other film deals with big-time Hollywood studios, but none of it came to anything.

This new one was a definite.

"I'm quite looking forward to it, now that the deal has been clinched," Billy said. "You see, in the past some of the atrocious scripts I read were enough to put anyone off."

Larry hired Ronald Chesney and Ronald Wolfe, who had had a huge hit with the BBC sitcom *The Rag Trade* and who would later score again with *On The Buses*, to come up with a script. The story, they were told, should involve a horse race and should be set, in part at least, in Great Yarmouth, so that Billy could complete the location shooting while simultaneously appearing twice-nightly at the Royal Aquarium theatre.

The story that Chesney and Wolfe came up with goes something like this:

Billy is an animal-mad singer appearing in a show on the coast (Great Yarmouth – got it in already). One day, he goes out to buy a dog and comes back to the theatre having bought a horse called Armitage.

He has a manager called Hymie (played by Michael Medwin), whose secretary Jo (Amanda Barrie) has a crush on Billy.

Hymie's worried that Billy's devotion to animals is getting in the way of his career, a suspicion confirmed when one day, during a rainstorm, Billy shelters Armitage in his dressing room, with, as they say, predictably hilarious consequences.

Then Armitage comes third in a race, contracts pneumonia and dies. Billy is sad.

To cheer him up, Hymie uses his record royalties to buy him a new horse called Anselmo, who Billy enters for the Epsom Derby.

As luck would have it, the race is on the same day as the opening of Billy's new show.

Nevertheless, Billy decides he can make both. He hires a vintage coach, and ferries the entire show's company, including The Gamblers, over to Epsom.

Meanwhile, the theatre manager (Bill Fraser), left with a full house sold and an AWOL cast, grows apoplectic with rage. Even more so when the outside broadcast TV cameras, live at Epsom, show them all, principals and chorus, in Derby day morning suits and fancy millinery cheering Anselmo on (intercut newsreel footage of real event doctored to make Anselmo win).

Luckily, everybody gets back in the nick of time and, still dressed in their finery, thrill the audience with a big finish.

Most of the songs were written by David Heneker and John Taylor. Heneker was the composer and lyricist of *Half A Sixpence*, which, starring Tommy Steele, was still running in the West End and about to transfer to Broadway. The following year, he'd collaborate with John Taylor again on the massively successful *Charlie Girl*, which ran at the Adelphi for six years, starred Joe Brown and was produced by Harold Fielding in association with Larry Parnes.

I've Gotta Horse, it has to be said, is not Heneker's best work.

In fact, though broadly enjoyable as a romp, and a must-see for Billy Fury fans, it's not anybody's best work. In some shots even Anselmo, even the dogs, Rusty, Speedy and Sheba, look embarrassed by the material they're having to deal with.

It is what it is. A prime example of cheapskate British movie-making with a chucked-together end-of-the-pier feel, made by a production team who, if they had any real feeling for or love of movies, music or dance, weren't given much chance to indulge it.

"People should just watch *I've Gotta Horse* for the mistakes," says Amanda Barrie, who played Jo, the love interest. "If anyone pointed out to [director] Kenneth Hume that we were behind in the schedule he would just tear up a few pages in the script. So if people found it difficult to follow, that's probably why."

Kenneth Hume was a TV arts-documentary director who hadn't done a full-length feature film since *Sail Into Danger* (1957).

More recently he'd caused a bit of a stir with a short dance film called *Mods And Rockers*, the score for which was made up of Lennon and McCartney songs.

He got on with Billy.

At the beginning of the shoot, Billy said, "There are two factors which are boosting my confidence enormously. The picture is going to co-star my horse Anselmo – and I shall enjoy working with him. And it's being directed by Kenneth Hume, someone in whom I have the greatest faith."

"He has an extraordinary presence," Hume told Judith Simons for the *Daily Express*. "Billy's only drawbacks in the past were his natural reticence and lack of confidence".

Judith Simons mentions that in the past, Billy had been "hindered by inarticulate speech". "Billy has a Liverpool accent," Hume said, "and the new aristocracy comes from Liverpool."

"I think my trouble was speaking so quickly that what I said came out as a mumble," Billy said. "I trained myself to talk more slowly by reading aloud. I'd get bored after a couple of minutes but it helped. Working with so many happy people and the animals helps me relax. My own animals are so good they'll get a lot of offers after this picture. They'll all have careers."

For a time, Kenneth Hume had managed Shirley Bassey and, in 1961, he'd married her, perhaps ill-advisedly: Hume was gay. Though to all intents and purposes Ken and Shirl were a happy couple, smiling for the cameras, they lived separately. When, in November 1963, Shirley gave birth to a daughter, Kenneth suspected the child was not his and relations soured. In 1964 they separated. They divorced in 1965. Two years after that, Hume took his own life. He was 41.

Everybody loved Kenneth Hume. During the filming, Billy would often take pity on him and his apparent distress about his failing marriage. After a hard day's shooting, he'd invite him back for a meal at Ockley. Kenneth would pour his heart out to Lee. It's understandable, then, given his personal problems, that perhaps he didn't do full justice to his talent in his work on *I've Gotta Horse*.

Lee is pretty sure that Billy enjoyed many one-night stands during their relationship, but *I've Gotta Horse* brought something a little more serious.

Amanda Barrie had been dancing, singing and acting professionally since she was a kid. She'd done more tellies than you've had hot dinners as well as movies, including *Carry On Cleo*, in which she simultaneously played Cleopatra and a major part in the nation's erotic fantasies.

"I met him when we first turned up to start doing the filming," says Amanda. "Larry asked me to look after him. We actually did get on really well from the very beginning. He was quite a sensitive soul. He was a bit of a little-boy-lost and incredibly good looking, I mean much better looking than his pictures. The Billy you met offstage was not the Billy of the silver suits at all. He really only got dressed up for the stage – he was a quite ordinary dresser usually – just T-shirts. He was not a vain man. I never saw him looking in the mirror. He wasn't a show-off. Definitely not all me, me, me. He was absorbed with walking round with a bag full of his dogs – his Chihuahuas."

Amanda was staying closer to Shepperton Studios than Billy. Billy's latest motoring conviction, at the beginning of August, had resulted in a six-month ban, so, when filming moved to Shepperton, it seemed to make sense, given the early starts, that Billy should stop over at her place.

"Although he was officially my lodger, it was not long before we became lovers. At first, Billy and I kept our relationship a secret. I knew vaguely that he had a girlfriend, although I think he must have stopped seeing her during the time we were together. We simply never talked about it. The crew knew we were together. I think the fans got a whiff of it but it wasn't like now. No one was tweeting about it. We made friends through the dogs really. He just moved in with his dogs, a 2.2 air gun and his shoe-box of marijuana.

"All the musicians smoked anything they could get their hands on. I had one try and was made ill enough for it to reverberate later. Must have been exceedingly strong stuff and I had a really bad time."

Billy, on the other hand, seemed to have a medical need for the stuff.

One day, while working at Shepperton, Billy collapsed. A doctor was sent for.

"The doctor said to me after examining Billy, 'Did you know that he smokes marijuana?' Well, you could have been locked up for smoking pot then. So when he said to me 'Do you know what he's doing?' I said quietly, 'Yes I did,' and he just said, 'Well it's keeping him alive.'"

Whether this conforms with modern medical thinking is a moot point, but this was 1964 and this was a Shepperton doctor who'd treated movie stars before.

"I was really shocked," says Amanda. "And I was even more shocked when he said, 'You must make sure he keeps on the marijuana.'

"So that was the reason that he smoked so much. He had the heart problem all along – a very frail heart and I suppose smoking stopped him ever getting nervous or over-excited. It was acting like a sort of heart drug. It was major. Well he started smoking first thing in the morning and he continued all day.

"Once he left his dope at my house and I had to ring my mother up to go and get it. I told her to look under the bed in this box – it was a Saxone shoe box he always kept it in. I said there'd be lots of stuff that looks like bird droppings. So she jumped into the car with it and came to the studio to deliver it. My mother was game for anything and she adored Billy.

"He had that adolescent quality about him. He was a sexy guy when he wasn't stoned."

Billy's sex appeal didn't get much chance to shine in 1964. Not publicly anyway.

His summer season at Great Yarmouth was another stab at a new direction.

"Larry Parnes has fulfilled his promise to establish Billy Fury as an all-round entertainer," said *NME*, ominously. "He clowns and dances in a well-blended production."

In other words, he was given little opportunity to demonstrate 101 ways to have fun with a microphone stand. Instead, he was dressed in top hat and tails and told to dance nicely for the ladies and gentlemen in neat routines arranged by choreographer Russ Taylor.

In Act 1 he had to sing a duet with Rolf Harris and, billed as Mr William Fury, take part in a section called *Let's All Go To The Music Hall* with Mr Rolf Harris, Mr Karl Denver, Mr Michael Yarwood and Mr Taylor's Dancing Darlings ("You know all the songs, so please join in and sing along").

In Act II he got a brief solo spot (closing with 'Nothin' Shakin' (But The Leaves On The Trees)', a truth sadly acknowledged as fans observed his motionless trousers, after which came *The Goodbye Time*, in which the entire company had to change into evening dress and do little dance routines.

"When I used to go to dance halls all I ever did was rock'n'roll. Now I've got just a few days to learn to dance up to professional standard," Billy told *Record Mirror*. "Russ Taylor's having a bash at teaching me three numbers for my summer season show at the Aquarium, Great Yarmouth. The learning part isn't too difficult. I can remember all the steps, I think. But I'm not confident that I'll look really good at it. It's the sort of show that has everyone in the show all the way through. I'm also doing a comedy spot with Rolf Harris. Fortunately, he's such an easy-going cat that this won't be hard for me. I expect I'll just feed the straight lines to him."

He put a good face on things when he spoke to the *Daily Express*, too.

"I've suddenly had the opportunity of expanding myself into more of an all-round entertainer – and I'm loving every minute of it."

"Billy wasn't that sort of a performer," Amanda says. "He was purely a music man and all the musicians really admired him. He wasn't a show business person. He was happier not being in the limelight."

In July, he released a cover of the power balladeer's power ballad, Conway Twitty's 'It's Only Make Believe'. He recorded it twice. The first time nobody seemed comfortable with the key. It's a song with a big range. Finding the key that suits your voice is crucial. You don't want to be grunting in the low bit or shrieking in the high bits. Conway's original version is in the key of Bb (although at various times in his career, he put it up, sometimes to B and sometimes C). Billy does it lower, in A, and makes it his own. He's husky and sexy on the low notes. He gives it the required welly on the high ones. He soars. The arrangement soars. He hopes and prays that the woman he loves will return his love. "The crashing, thumping backing builds to a shattering climax with the aid of a heavenly choir," (*NME*) but he knows "it's only make believe".

The B-side was a cover of Mississippi bluesman Jimmy Reed's 'Baby What Do You Want Me To Do', sung and played with a feeling for the form and utter conviction. It was the kind of record, and the kind of arrangement, that was bringing The Rolling Stones and The Animals big hits and great dollops of credibility. Prompted by them, promoters were bringing over the genuine article – package tours featuring Jimmy Reed, Little Walter, Muddy Waters, John Lee Hooker, Sonny Boy Williamson, Willie Dixon and the rest – and blues fans rushed to worship at their feet as if these middle-aged men had been newly discovered just for them. This was stuff that Billy had been listening to for years, itching, and now and then being given the chance to record, always as B-sides and album tracks, while the A-side was always power ballad or other. Under the circumstances he'd have been superhuman if now and then he didn't taste gall.

'Only Make Believe' went to number 10 and was a massive number one hit in Singapore.

As 1964 wore on there were increasing signs that the Billy Fury brand was on the wane.

Cliff had had his own TV series by this time. So had Adam. On November 4, 1964, ITV transmitted *The Billy Fury Show*, produced by Colin Clews and featuring the Ross Taylor Dancers (Ross Taylor was the choreographer from the Great Yarmouth show), Val Parnell's Orchestra and The Gamblers. Possibly it was the pilot for a series, but if it was, the series never happened.

Chris Eley, editor of the *Sound Of Fury* fan club magazine, is one of the very few people who have any memory of the show.

"Even back then I was acutely disappointed at the attempt to portray Billy without the Fury," he says. "It was terrible. Larry Parnes was trying to turn him into an all-round entertainer."

Among other delights, Chris remembers the show featured a James Bond spoof comedy sketch with the actor Tony Tanner, Billy reprising the saccharine 'I Like Animals' from *I've Gotta Horse* with a chorus of children, and a dance routine to 'Style', the Bing Crosby/Dean Martin/Frank Sinatra song from *Robin And The Seven Hoods*. The opening was a version of 'Hey, Look Me Over', the big hit from the Broadway musical *Wildcat*, which Billy had done in the Great Yarmouth show. It was given a slightly funkier arrangement than had been heard on Broadway, owing a lot to Damita Jo's cover of the song on her *Live At The Diplomat* album.

"It wasn't Billy Fury at all," says Chris, "until he got on with The Gamblers and did 'You Got Me Dizzy' [another Jimmy Reed blues, also covered by Damita Jo] and I thought, this is the real Billy Fury."

"I don't want to be just a pop singer for ever," says Billy, trying to convince everybody, including himself, that all-round entertainer was the way forward.

Unfortunately, it seemed that the world, or at least the UK charts, didn't want him to be a pop singer, either.

At the end of 1963, the *NME*'s chart analysis (a rough guide to overall sales figures) put Billy as the ninth best-selling artist in the UK. By July of 1964 he'd slipped to number 32.

Even *Billy Fury Monthly* was clutching at straws.

"Did you know that Billy has a large following in Mauritius?" it said in the September 1964 issue. "It is a small island in the Indian Ocean. I have had so many letters from there and they are all anxious to know more about Billy."

All the same, though, at the end of 1964, *NME* readers voted him Britain's second best male singer, one place below Cliff. Mick Jagger was number three, John Lennon five and Paul McCartney nine. The fans, though dwindling in numbers, were loyal enough to get down to the post office and vote.

His next single, 'I'm Lost Without You', was released at the start of 1965. It never rose higher than 16. The song bears a passing resemblance to Shirley Bassey's 'I Who Have Nothing', and it's what had by now become the standard issue Billy Fury heartbreak ballad, except in this case the misery shows signs of giving way to anger as the singer threatens the beloved who is leaving with overwhelming hatred: "I'll just hate you/…with every beat of my heart"

The affair with Amanda Barrie lasted for maybe six months.

Lee found out about it, moved out of the house they'd just bought in Ockley and got herself a flat in London. This left the coast clear for Billy and Amanda to move in together.

"I went to stay with him in that ridiculous mansion in somewhere like Surrey," says Amanda. "I stayed there a lot. There were just the two of us there in that huge mansion. Massive. Larry probably made him buy that."

Then Billy realised he'd left a healthy crop of cannabis plants back at the old house in Kingston.

"We went back to where he used to live and he booted me over the wall of the garden so I could pull up all the weed they'd been growing. And then I hopped back. I didn't weigh much in those days so I could climb over easily."

Most of the time, they lived in Amanda's place in town, on Endell Street in Covent Garden.

"We were living in a very small flat on the top floor. We didn't have a bathroom and we shared a toilet with the rest of the house. This wasn't much of a big deal. We had no bath so I bought one of those things – it was called a Blink. It was like a kitchen sink but the top tipped up and became a full-size bath. Luxury!

"Billy was never any good with money. He always screwed his fivers up and put them into his socks. Once when I washed his socks for him, I washed the money and I had to peg it up to dry on a clothes line. The only thing he really spent money on was his pot. Clothes wise, anything he needed was bought through Larry or got for gigs.

"I went down to Brixton to get his pot with him once. There were all these huge black guys sitting around the table with the pot in the middle. We met up with some wonderful West Indian musicians who were also drug dealers.

"The deals would be struck over endless cans of Coke. They all adored Billy."

Apart from the occasional trip to Brixton, it was a quiet life. Billy smoked his weed and popped out now and then for milk and papers. Amanda learned her lines for the next job.

"We used to go round Covent Garden wearing identical denim caps. We never got round to eating much food. Our principle sustenance was rum and Coke, so we both looked like skeletons. We never went out for a meal – don't forget I'd been a dancer. I only weighed six stone. A night out was the pub. He was very popular round here in the pubs. Otherwise we were either working or in bed. Let's be honest, that was the relationship. In many ways he was like a child. I couldn't have burdened him with my own anxieties and worries. He wouldn't have had a clue what to do about them.

"He was terribly sweet. He bought me really peculiar things. I remember he bought me a toy cannon. He took my mother out to buy her a present. He bought a little cat and you pulled its head and its tongue came out. I thought it was horrible.

"Then something very strange happened. One night as I was preparing a meal, Billy went out to buy cigarettes. He never came back.

"At first I was worried. Had he been in an accident? I called the police and the hospitals. Then I phoned his manager. He was not available, but someone in the office said, 'Just leave it, Amanda. He's had to go back.' From which I gleaned that Billy had returned to whoever he'd been with when we had got together. But there was something in the way that the message was related to me that made me do exactly as I was told. It felt like I was being warned off. I don't think he left me because he didn't like me. We never had a bad word. It had just been a normal day. It was his lifestyle I suppose.

"And I never saw, nor heard from Billy Fury again."

In fact, Billy had gone back to Lee. She was making another record at Decca with Ivor Raymonde. Billy turned up at the studio. They went for dinner and patched it up.

And Amanda shook herself off and went on with her acting career.

CHAPTER EIGHTEEN

"I'M STILL ON THE CAROUSEL, AND I WANT TO GET OFF BUT NO ONE'S STOPPING IT."

Early in 1965, the music journalist Nik Cohn interviewed Billy. He recalled the encounter 50 years later.

"I interviewed him in a Soho café. He mumbled his way through, avoiding eye contact. The only time he spoke out clearly was at the end, when he asked me for the five-quid taxi fare. A leering, hip-swivelling demon on stage, with a length of lead piping stuck down his silver lamé pants, he was crippled by shyness in everyday life, only at ease with horses and birds. He also had a prodigious love of pot, and pot cost."

Cohn had been one of Billy's biggest cheerleaders. In his book, *AWopBopaLooBopaLopBamBoom*, he describes him as "the closest that Britain ever got to producing a genuine rocker, someone almost in the class of Eddie Cochran".

He stood by his man even after The Beatles had arrived on the scene. For a bit, anyway.

"Nik was stamping around London kind of saying that Billy Fury pisses all over The Beatles," said Pete Townshend. "Then Billy brought out a song, 'I've Gotta Horse' from a movie of the same name. Nik never mentioned Billy Fury's name again."

Billy started 1965 off sick again. He was taken ill over Christmas and spent New Year in the London Clinic to undergo "a thorough examination" for a "mystery illness". All his January bookings were cancelled.

"I wasn't really ill," he later insisted, "just a little run down. I suppose it was being so busy towards the end of last year that finally caught up with me. I found that I kept falling asleep all day. So I decided to give myself a bit of rest, and I'm okay now."

The illness meant he couldn't be out promoting his New-Year release, 'I'm Lost Without You', a breathless confession of vulnerability with heavy tremolo guitar and too many modulations, which never made the Top 10.

In February 1965, he had made a trip over to New York, was reported to have appeared on a few TV shows, none of them memorable, and came home boasting that he had a movie contract in his pocket worth £180,000 (half a million dollars in 1965) for six films, three to be made in the UK and three in Hollywood.

Then it was back on the road for a 15-date tour with The Gamblers, The John Barry Seven, The Kestrels and Bobby Pattinson. Ominously, he didn't make the first gig of the tour at the Romford ABC. Excuses were made.

"The first night of Billy's tour caused some disappointment for fans when Billy didn't appear," said the *Billy Fury Monthly*. "I learnt the full story which was simply that Billy couldn't make the show as he was completely under-rehearsed with The John Barry Orchestra. This was no fault of anybody, but simply in order to have the stage show 100% perfect, he needed more rehearsal time."

Just a few days after the tour finished, he was back in the USA.

Jack Good, the genius behind *Oh Boy!* and *Boy Meets Girls*, had joined the British invasion. His US ABC TV show *Shindig!*, a loose variant of the *Oh Boy!* format, had been on air since September 1964 and had recently been extended from a half-hour to an hour.

Little Richard, The Everly Brothers, Sam Cooke, The Beatles, Sandie Shaw, Roy Orbison, The Miracles, Gerry & The Pacemakers, The Supremes, The Righteous Brothers, Aretha Franklin, Tina Turner – everybody except Elvis had done *Shindig!*

Jack had also tried to give his old friend Adam Faith a chance to break into the US market. Adam was on the show four times, gave stunning live performances but just managed the one US Hot 100 single – 'Talk About Love', which snuck in at number 97.

Now it was Billy's turn.

He seems originally to have been booked for two appearances, on February 24 and March 1, but somehow along the way these seem to have merged into a pre-recorded single appearance on March 31. Adam Faith was in the same show, featuring in the opening medley, singing two and a bit songs in his own spot, then taking part in the finale. Also appearing were Chuck Berry, the French *yé-yé* chanteuse Sylvie Vartan and the mighty Roosevelt 'Rosey' Grier, a pro-football player turned actor and singer who could have stood in for Hadrian's Wall.

Billy had just one song – his latest single, 'I'm Lost Without You' – sandwiched between Adam and Sylvie. His performance was underpowered. He seemed ill. Almost unable to stand. And very nervous.

"He looks a bit like early Gene Pitney," said Chris Eley. "But he wasn't performing live. Adam Faith was on the same show, live with [house band] The Shindogs, and you can understand why Adam had a hit over there. And then Billy comes on and of course he's just lip-syncing. It's such a waste."

Billy never had a record in the *Billboard* Hot 100. As ever, neither did any of the three films he was supposed to make in Hollywood come to anything, or even the three he was supposed to make in the UK.

I've Gotta Horse, the movie, was released in April 1965.

"Pop singer Billy Fury is a likeable lad," said the *Daily Mirror*, "but his personality on screen is hardly enough to raise the modest *I've Gotta Horse* above the general run of current British musicals."

"Billy has graduated," said Chris Hutchins in the *New Musical Express*. "He has moved up from the era of poor pop films (i.e. *Play It Cool*) to the kind of screen musical that Cliff Richard has been scoring success with for three years. And although *I've Gotta Horse* has none of the subtle wit and clever camera antics of The Beatles' *A Hard Day's Night*, I found it refreshing – nobody was corny, nobody was trying to be clever, and the result was good entertainment."

Tatler magazine called it "a harmless little British musical".

The Beatles' *A Hard Day's Night* had just been nominated for two Oscars. "Harmless little British musicals" were hopelessly out of time.

Even Chris Eley found *I've Gotta Horse* a bridge too far. "I didn't like it very much because it was so different from the Billy Fury that turned me on to popular music. After that, to my eyes, Billy Fury was a little bit diminished. I mean I still bought the records because they were fantastic."

After the film's opening, Billy was straight out on tour again – the *Get Ready Steady Go-Go-Go* tour, with The Gamblers, The Pretty Things, Dave Berry & The Cruisers, Brian Poole & The Tremeloes and The John Barry Seven.

That one finished up in Bristol on May 9. Back at home Lee and Billy went on a health kick. Sort of.

They cut back on their use of amphetamines and barbiturates (both, at the time, perfectly respectable prescription drugs highly recommended by doctors, although there was also a thriving black market in amphetamines for those who couldn't quite swing a quack), and spent their time together building aviaries for sick birds and looking after their many dogs.

Alan Smith, for *NME*, described a meeting with him in September 1965. He was obsessively flicking an oversized cigarette lighter and seemed edgy, so maybe cold turkey was kicking in.

"'I used to find myself shaking and sweating," he said, "and I hated going to bed. I went to a doctor about it. I think it was all due to overwork.'"

"You won't find him where the 'In-Crowd' goes, at the Pickwick or Scotch of St James clubs. He's more likely to be on a train for Scotland or the Lake District on a (feathered) birdwatching expedition."

"I don't like clubs," he told the *Record Mirror*. "I don't think I could go to the Ad Lib – that's one of those clubs, isn't it? I get a feeling of claustrophobia with all those people around me."

"He is writing, and illustrating with his camera, a book on birds," reported Patrick Doncaster in the *Daily Mirror*, as if it was a scoop, under the headline, "Fury Finds Calm Among The Birds".

"He had been out on a day's safari in the rain on the Sussex border when I talked to him this week.

"'I was after the great crested grebe,' he said with the enthusiasm of a Peter Scott. 'I got soaking wet but I did get some pictures of one.'

"'I go off for a whole day. Sometimes I get to the Romney marshes at six in the morning. Birds seem to be more on the move early in the day.'

"He has a new single due next week. Title: 'In Thoughts Of You'. The birds will love it. Fury Fan Birds, that is."

No journalist had been born, it seemed, who could resist the "bird" gag. "I couldn't help thinking of all the 'birds' I know who wouldn't mind watching HIM," said Peter Jones in the *Record Mirror*.

Fans could still be a problem.

One day, Billy found a young woman hiding in the bins. When he was less than welcoming, the young woman took an overdose, right there on the driveway. Lee stuck her fingers down the girl's throat to make her sick and they called an ambulance. In comparison, dealing with the dogs' anal cysts must have come as light relief.

"I tell you this, man. I've settled down a lot. When I first came into the money I used to go mad with it. In three and a half years I had about 10 cars, but for the past year I've only had one, a Zodiac. I don't even like to talk about my money these days. I've just got it invested and that's that. An' I'm happy."

'In Thoughts Of You', released on June 18, was his best in a long while. Specialists in heartbreak ballads are always at their finest when they're a little more delicate with the agony pedal. Billy remains delightfully restrained throughout. He sounds young.

Mike Leander's arrangement, with a Rachmaninov via Liberace angst–piano modified by a calming French horn, is extravagant, but at least sounds as if it belongs in 1965.

"THE WAY TRENDS ARE GOING AT THE MOMENT," said the *NME*, in all caps, "THIS COULD BE THE BIG ONE. CERTAINLY DESERVES TO BE."

In fact, the track went to number nine and was Billy's last Top 10 hit.

The follow-up, 'Run To My Loving Arms', is a fine example of the chaotic nature of Billy's recording career. Having produced a Top 10 hit with 'In Thoughts of You', rather than going with the same producer, maybe even the same songwriters for the follow up, he, or Larry, or Decca, chose an uninspired song and used Les Reed as musical director. Les had written songs for Tom Jones, Herman's Hermits and The Applejacks – all terrific sellers but a million miles from Billy's style.

"The song is typical of about four years ago," said the *Record Mirror*.

"From my experience," said Derek Johnson in the *NME*, "it needs to be heard a few times before it registers with full impact." It was 1965; getaway people didn't have that sort of staying power. It made number 25 for one week only, then quietly faded away.

Increasingly, and perhaps understandably, one gets the feeling that Billy was losing interest in show business and maybe even music, swapping both for ornithology.

"In the old days, I felt like I was on a carousel," he told Brian Gregg. "You know when you're a kid, life is like that. Now, I'm still on the carousel, and I want to get off but no one's stopping it."

In interviews, the actor Robert Mitchum was usually monosyllabic when asked about his films, his performances and his dramatic technique. But ask him a question like, "what's the strongest drink you've ever sampled?" and he would go on for hours about the strange powers of mescal and the strength of Polish Spiriytus Rektyfikowany.

Similarly, in an *NME* interview in which Billy was supposed be promoting 'Run To My Loving Arms', after a few standard exchanges about the record, the interviewer asks Billy whether he'd been doing much birdwatching lately. "I have had the most fantastic weekend," Billy replies. He'd been to the Norfolk Broads. "I had a special flat-bottomed boat that was made to go easily through the reeds and it meant you could get real close. It's migration time, you know, and this is the last opportunity to see many of them before they fly off to foreign countries. I saw a lot of reed warblers – very shy and retiring, they are – and lesser whitethroats and some garden warblers." He goes on to enthuse about marsh harriers, bearded tits and shovel bills, then becomes dangerously over-excited about a long-eared owl.

Billy Fury And The Gamblers was released in November. It was a perky EP that gave us a cover of Jackie Opel's ska classic 'Turn Your Lamp Down Low', a stonking version of La Vern Baker's 'Saved', a romp through

'You Got Me Dizzy', and a slightly under-powered swing through 'I Can Feel It', a song written by Tony King that Lee later had a crack at recording.

Billy was back in Great Yarmouth for the summer, doing another round of Sunday concerts, sometimes with Herman's Hermits and sometimes Dave Berry & The Cruisers.

In the autumn, there was another tour, with Herman's Hermits, Wayne Fontana & The Mindbenders and The Fortunes. Perhaps significantly, Herman and Wayne Fontana shared top billing, with Billy advertised as "special guest star". All the same, he owned the show.

"Billy Fury is one of the few solo singers who seem to completely fill the stage," said Norrie Drummond in *NME*. "He moves constantly and his technique with a mike is unique. He only had to raise his arm and the theatre filled with screams."

On his nights off, he did the usual round of one-nighters at ballrooms and clubs, including the California, Dunstable, the Domino, Manchester and the Imperial, Nelson.

"Last night I went to see Billy perform at the Wolverton Palace dance hall," Donna Chamber of Kempston, Bedfordshire, wrote to the *BFM*. "He was without a doubt tremendous. I have never seen such an act. He had everyone screaming and he sang with real sincerity and so well that everyone was so overwhelmed. It's nice to think that a great star like Billy will appear at ballrooms. It gives so many of his fans a chance to see him, whereas normally they wouldn't be able to."

A glutton for punishment, in September Billy had renewed his contract with Larry, signing on for another six years.

At Christmas – it had to come sooner or later – he went into panto, his first.

Amanda Barrie had pointed out that Billy was not a showbiz natural. Though, given a band, an audience, a spotlight and a mike stand he could put on a show like no other, he'd always been musician first and showman second. The smell of the greasepaint did not set his pulses racing – and anyway, given his health issues, a racing pulse was the last thing he needed.

He could manage lines, he could fix a few dance steps in his muscle memory and even sell a joke, but there's a world of difference between being able to do these things and wanting to do them.

Nevertheless, in December he started rehearsals to open as the lead in *Aladdin* – twice daily at 2.15 and 7 p.m. – at the New Theatre, Oxford, opening the day after Boxing Day. The Gamblers were booked to play six Chinese policemen, and he was flanked onstage by some of the finest showbiz pros in the business.

Sid 'The Atomic Xylophone Player' Plummer, cast as the wicked Uncle Abanazer, could provoke spontaneous hisses from the audience one minute, and the next thrill them with a rendition of 'The Sabre Dance' that turned his mallets into blurs. Sid was an old hand at this game. A few years earlier he'd given his Abanazer against Adam Faith's *Aladdin* at the Bournemouth Pavilion.

Ray Fell (Wishee-Washee) was a Liverpool-born comedian, billed as "The New Comedy Star", which would suggest that he was up and coming, except he'd already up and come to the extent that, unlike Billy Fury, he'd done a *Sunday Night At The London Palladium*, last act on before Shirley Bassey.

Lauri Lupino Lane (Widow Twankey) was a scion of Britain's number one showbiz family. His dad had introduced the world to the Lambeth Walk and his mum and most of his uncles were actors, singers, dancers and all-round entertainers.

The love interest was Princess Yasmin, played by Cheryl Kennedy, another artiste with showbiz in her genes. Her mum had been a band singer, as well as one of the original 1930s Ovaltineys on Radio Luxembourg ("We are the Ovaltineys, happy girls and boys"). Her dad, Rick, was a noted trombonist, who played in the Ted Heath Orchestra and on a thousand sessions. Cheryl was just 18, but she'd already starred in *Half A Sixpence* with Tommy Steele and singer/actress Marti Webb.

Billy had a couple of duets with Cheryl – 'Let's Make Believe' and 'Sweethearts And Lovers'. Her memories of him are unclouded by anything approaching a fluttering heart or fan-worship.

"He was just an ordinary guy. I liked him." Enough to buy him a present. "I knew he liked birds because he told me he had built an aviary at home, so I went to Petticoat Lane Market down on Commercial Road and bought him two budgerigars for Christmas. One blue one and one yellow. He took them home with him."

Angela Ryder, who played Scheherazade, remembers Billy running into problems with the songs. It was before the days of the radio mic. Billy found it difficult to make himself heard in that big barn of a theatre.

Angela gave him the basic tip of always facing front, but short of giving him a couple of years' lessons in voice projection and breath support, she couldn't do much else to help.

The show ended with Billy doing a regular three-song set with The Gamblers and a mike – which probably perplexed the kids expecting more in the way of "He's behind you!" and novelty xylophony, but made the wait worthwhile for the hardcore fans.

Judith Wills, a hardcore fan who became a journalist, later reproduced an entry from her diary in her book *Keith Moon Stole My Lipstick*.

"I've just had the best news anyone could ever give me. Billy Fury is appearing this Xmas in pantomime! He's going to be Aladdin. BUT guess where? Can you believe – he's coming here to our New Theatre in Oxford! This is amazing. I can't really believe it's true. Precisely one and a half miles from where I live in our caravan at Botley Road Estate. Billy Fury is going to come every day for weeks and weeks and weeks and be Aladdin. Right through to February. Of all the places his manager could have chosen he chose here. Thank you, God! Thank you Larry Parnes!"

Judith went to wait for Billy at the stage door.

"So I stand shaking with nerves as he is due to arrive for rehearsals. This I've discovered because his backing group The Gamblers, who are also in the show, have rented a houseboat on the Isis for the duration. The Vanden Plas car arrives and there he is – medium tall, very slim with a trilby with a feather in it – Billy Fury. I just manage to speak, 'Please Billy will you pose for a photo…'

"When the photo comes out my mother says he's got bird shit on his hat."

Don Chapman in the *Oxford Mail* was less easily impressed.

"I think I am right in saying that he is the first principal boy the New Theatre has ever seen who speaks with a broad Liverpool accent, ambles across the stage in a pair of Cuban heels, has a mop of unruly hair and says things like 'Get Lost!'"

Two shows a day were a slog for Billy. Cheryl Kennedy remembers that not long into the run he was struggling with a terrible cough. Eventually it grew so bad that he had to drop out. He was replaced by Jean Bayless, playing Aladdin as a britches part.

Jean was a big catch for the New Theatre. Four years earlier, she'd played Maria in the first UK production of *The Sound Of Music*. She had no trouble at all hitting the back of the stalls with her voice, mike or no mike. The reaction of Billy's fans when they heard the news is not recorded. The Gamblers, inured now to the stigma, remained in their Chinese policemen roles until the end of the run.

CHAPTER NINETEEN

"MR CONSISTENCY"

Billy's core fans remained true to him and desperately wanted Billy to stay true to himself, which meant more passion and less showbiz.

Pauline from Cambridge wrote to *BFM*. "I am one of Billy's most devoted fans. I am a member of his fan club, buy all his records on the day they are released and go to see him in shows whenever possible. With reference to the article written in one of the morning papers. I felt it my duty as a fan to write and beg for Billy's sake that you will do all possible so that he will not become a family entertainer (not for a long time yet)."

Others were drifting away. It's understandable. A lot of those original adopters, those who felt the first tingle in 1959, were by now married with children. In 1963, when Beatlemania happened, they were already in their late teens and early twenties, a bit long in the tooth for serious screaming and mobbing at stage doors. All that sixties stuff they talked about in the papers – the promiscuity and, later, the turning on, tuning in and dropping out – didn't seem particularly pertinent either, not when there's the electric to be paid and nursery schools to be sorted out.

"I still had all my old Billy records," says Penny from Manchester. "I used to put them on when my husband was out and dance around with the baby. I still do sometimes, if I'm honest. But I stopped buying records, really, I think when the kids came. And if I did buy a record it'd be something the kids would like. Christmas songs or something. I used to have the radio on, and I liked it when one of Billy's records came on the radio. But only the old ones. When did he stop making records? It must have been about that time, wasn't it?"

"I split up with my first husband not much more than a year after I married him," says Val from Leeds, "and I went back home to live with my mum and dad. And my old room still had all the Billy pictures in it. I had hundreds of them. And that felt weird. 'Cos there I was with a cot in the corner and Billy pictures all over the walls."

"I asked him whether he wanted to change his life at all at the moment," said David Caldwell, editor of *BFM*.

"'No, I don't think so. Everyone wants a lot of things to happen and everything to be exactly right, but it hardly ever happens to come out all the time.'

"Billy changed his mind later and told me that he would like to produce hit records."

Not long afterwards, *BFM* ceased publication.

"I never think of myself as being big," Billy told the *Record Mirror*. "I always think that I'm just about plodding along."

Billy's first single of 1966 was 'I'll Never Quite Get Over You'. Those involved in its making had all made hits happen for Billy before. It was produced by Mike Leander and written by Geoff Morrow, David Martin and Chris Arnold. Morrow and Arnold's 'In Thoughts Of You' had gone Top 10 in the previous year.

"The timbre of Billy's voice is ideally suited to putting over a wistful lyric like this, and he makes his usual faultless job of it," said *NME*. "Middle of the charts, I estimate."

Not even the middle. 'I'll Never Quite Get Over You' was Billy's first record not to make the Top 30 since 1962. Perhaps the title put people off; there's something mealy mouthed about that 'quite'. Would Witney Houston's 'I Will Occasionally Love You' have done so well, one wonders, or Gloria Gaynor's 'I Will Just About Manage'?

The tune's a problem, too. It rambles. Even a specially trained butcher's boy would never have been able whistle it accurately.

And if it wasn't the title or the tune it was almost certainly the B-side: 'I Belong To The Wind'. It's asking for trouble.

The next, 'Don't Let A Little Pride (Stand In Your Way)', released in May, had a good hook and a worryingly assertive guitar riff, but didn't even make the Top 100.

There was a minor bounce back with 'Give Me Your Word,' released in July. The song had been a favourite of Billy's for years. His grandmother – the one with the radiogram – had the Tennessee Ernie Ford 1955 version on a 78. It was, the ad said, "the most powerful and exciting ballad that Billy has ever recorded". Mike Leander did a lovely job on the production and the arrangement was fine. In most people's books it's up there with 'Halfway To Paradise' as one of Billy's best. It had plenty of airplay, yet still stalled at number 27.

However, it would be another 16 years before Billy's name was seen again in the Top 100.

"We keep him in demand by not over-exposing him as an artist," said Larry. "Too much publicity can be bad for you."

On April 10, Billy played the Marimba Club in Middlesbrough, then a week at La Dolce Vita, Newcastle, and on to the Garrick Club, Leigh, the Tower Club, Warrington, the Domino Club in Manchester and a one-nighter in Birmingham at the Smethwick Baths. He'd gone from pulling out of the Palladium because he wasn't top of the bill to wowing them at Smethwick Baths. Pop is a fickle business.

The Sunday concerts at Great Yarmouth were rather more subdued that year than they'd been in the past. The programme describes him not as "Mr Sex on Legs", not "The Country's Most Exciting Performer" but as "Mr Consistency".

It goes on to say, "Billy has been appearing at clubs and ballrooms for many months all over England. All these new venues have proved a great success and in fact Billy has already been asked to make return appearances in these places," as if a repeat booking at the Smethwick Baths is the stuff rock dreams are made of.

Larry was still talking the talk. "We've sent a black and white and a colour film of Billy to America," he told the *Record Mirror*, "it'll be shown on all the big television shows, so that should be big over there."

And don't forget, he was still huge in Mauritius.

When Billy's contract with Decca came to an end in December, they were in no hurry to renew. So Larry did a deal with Parlophone.

In return for a minimum of nine recordings a year, plus others as the company would "reasonably require" for a period of five years, Billy was to receive a retainer of £5,500 a year and a royalty of 3d (about 1½p) per album and a halfpenny (¼p) per single sold.

As it turned out, Parlophone didn't even "reasonably require" the nine records a year. Over the entire duration of the contract, only 11 singles were released. None of them charted.

Lee wrote to Larry, suggesting that Larry had lost interest in Billy's career and that Billy's comparative lack of success could be blamed on the manager's failure to publicise his singles.

Larry countered that he hadn't lost interest and implied that any lack of success was Billy's fault because Billy had insisted he wanted more control over his career when he had renegotiated his contract. Larry also hinted that his own personal problems were taking up his time.

He also mentioned Billy's ill-health and his recent refusal to pose with the lions at Longleat (life-threatening photo-ops being the surefire way to ensure chart success).

At the beginning of 1967, Peter Jones, editor of *Record Mirror*, interviewed Mr Parnes. "I told Larry we often got letters from fans complaining that Bill seemed to be living the life of a recluse and they didn't have much opportunity to see him. Said Larry, 'I'll answer those letters personally. One can understand some of those criticisms, but I can show you a pile of mail from fans saying, 'Dear Larry, thank you for the way you manage Billy…'

"'Billy has just signed this massive new contract with EMI. It's for five straight years. No options after the first years, just five straight years. So any hints that Billy isn't going to be very busy can be forgotten.

"'I feel the ideal set-up for Billy is that he should work on personal appearances for 20 weeks a year. You can kill an artiste by over-exposing him and I don't want Bill to be like that.

"'Recently he's been working the clubs up North. I could rave on and on about how good he is, how he is received by these more adult audiences. Best way of proving it would be for me to take you up to one of his shows… judge for yourself."

It's not recorded whether Peter took him up on the offer or whether he was invited to view the pile of letters saying, "Dear Larry, thank you for the way you manage Billy."

1967 saw the release of The Beatle's *Sgt Pepper's* album and the Summer of Love. It was the year in which the BBC ever so slightly loosened its corset and debuted an entire new station devoted to pop. Wonderful Radio 1 kicked off on September 30.

It was also the year that Keith Richards' house was raided by a task force of 19 police officers who found, when they had battled their way through the "loud strains of pop music", Mick Jagger – "and I was of the opinion," said the police report, "that he was wearing make-up."

Sitting next to him was "a person I now know to be male but at the time I had thought he was a woman. He had long fairish hair and was dressed in what would be best described as a pair of red and green silk 'pyjamas'. I searched him and this was all he was wearing. I formed the opinion he too was wearing make-up. All the time I was in the house there was a strong, sweet, unusual smell in all rooms."

Mick and Keith were both arrested and later sentenced to three months and 12 months respectively. Both sentences were later quashed.

1967 was also the year in which Brian Epstein took his own life.

The first of the Parlophone singles was released in January.

'Hurtin' Is Loving' (with 'Things Are Changing' on the B-side) was written by Peter Asher and Gordon Waller, who as Peter & Gordon had had a couple of hits. The B-side, 'Things Are Changing', was written by Gordon Waller and Sharon Sheeley, who once allegedly had an affair with Billy while she was engaged to Eddie Cochran, was in the car when Eddie was killed and was now an item with Gordon.

And, of course, Peter Asher was the brother of Jane Asher, who was Paul McCartney's girlfriend.

Pop in 1967 was a small and enclosed world, perhaps best compared to the Mormons of 19th-century Utah, who dressed alike and had unconventional sexual mores.

'Hurtin' Is Loving' is a minor-key sado-masochist's lament. The protagonist cannot hurt his beloved because it's against his – better nature? sexual preference? religion? – no, 'pride'. "Too proud to hurt" is a condition so rare it never cropped up on either Jerry Springer or Jeremy Kyle.

The final lines sound like a Google translation of a Japanese blog about neurosurgery: "I'm feeling the agony of feeling the agony of love. My memory does me wrong. It does me wrong. I wish you were gone."

"Absorbing material," said *NME* – which could be a coded euphemism for "toilet paper". "Doesn't strike me as a logical hit, but deserves success."

Peter, Gordon and Sharon were part of a small circle of friends –
songwriters, producers, record execs, pop radio people – who spent their
weekends at Ockley going for nice country walks and taking top-quality
drugs.

Among their number was another Liverpudlian (near as dammit).
Kenny Everett was an elf of a thousand voices, simultaneously manic and
shy, very funny, very rude (in every sense of the word) and terrifyingly
insecure. He was one of the many DJs who'd made the transfer from
pirate radio to Radio 1, and was now an up-and-coming national
celebrity. He was introduced to the Ockley set by Don Paul, a former
singer with The Viscounts who'd co-written 'Don't Let A Little Thing
(Stand In Your Way)' for Billy.

Kenny wrote of his first trip to Ockley in his delightfully inaccurate
autobiography, *The Custard Stops At Hatfield*. "He [Don Paul] lived in a
flat in Fulham which was filled with a strange mixture of arty weirdos
like a sex-change frock designer and a man who tattooed goldfish, and
one day we were all lying around this flat smoking pot when in walked
Billy Fury with his almost-wife, who was Lee!

"They invited us all to their mansion in Sussex which Billy had
bought with the money he'd made from 'Halfway To Paradise' and all his
other hits.

"Most people about to take a car journey to Sussex might take the
precaution of going to the loo and packing a sandwich. We threw LSD
down ourselves and squanged into Lee's little car all believing we were
pineapples."

Kenny enjoyed the experience and frequently came back for more.

Richard Kerr, another songwriter, who eventually would write major
hits for Barry Manilow and Dionne Warwick as well as less favoured
songs for Billy, has occasional flashbacks of a weekend spent with Billy,
Lee, Kenny and Bernie Andrews, a BBC producer.

"I remember it so clearly – the word was going round this [the LSD]
was JL's stuff [John Lennon]. It was on blotting paper. And we were at
Billy Fury's one summer afternoon. And I only ever took the stuff twice
because it had a very bad effect on me. But I remember Kenny was there
and Bernie was there and it was a very warm afternoon and Bernie was
lying on a blanket in the corner of one room. It was a very strange time.
Kenny really liked it. He seemed to have a lot of fears and taking acid
meant it could go one way or the other."

During one of these trips Kenny became paranoid and decided that suicide was the only logical course of action. Lee didn't indulge him.

"Look if you are going to kill yourself," she said, "could you do it outside? We've just bought this new carpet, you see..."

Another, sadder, visitor was Billy's blood brother, Dickie Pride. Dickie was now separated from his wife Trish, and addicted to heroin. Desperate for money, he came to Ockley and tried to blackmail Billy, threatening to go to the press with various stories (drugs, living in sin – there was no shortage of infractions that could, in the right journalistic hands, have been turned into major scandals and maybe even put Billy behind bars). Luckily, Lee was on hand. Showing as little sympathy for Dickie's nonsense as she had for Kenny Everett's, she chucked him out on his ear. No more was heard.

When the guests had packed up their blotting paper, their suicide attempts and the blackmail fantasies and gone home, Billy and Lee would relax back into quiet domesticity.

They'd thought about getting married, but never did. They thought about adopting children, but never did. "I decided a long, long time ago that I wouldn't go in for children," Billy said in a TV interview years later. "I had the idea that I was going to cough off a lot earlier in my life. And I didn't want to leave kids around without a father. I like to live every day like it's the last.

"The first time I was badly ill was around 1967. One of the valves in my heart had closed up. The blood wasn't getting through. The only way for the blood to come out was through my mouth, so I had to quit. They hadn't done a great deal of heart surgery by then, so I was trying to hold off for as long as I could."

"He couldn't cope with anything to do with the heart," Lee said. "I remember there was a song – it was a big hit but I can't remember what it was called and it had a heartbeat on the backing track [possibly 'A l'Ombre de Nous' from the film Un Homme Et Une Femme, or maybe Sophia Loren's and Peter Sellers' 'Goodness Gracious Me']. He would just turn it off. Always inside him – he knew he wouldn't live long."

There are those for whom "living every day like it's the last" would mean hi-jacking a Lear jet, filling it with cocaine and sexual partners, flying it to a lawless part of Colombia and dancing in a lake of blood while an orchestra of defrocked priests plays hot-cha devil music on marimbas with their private parts. To Billy it meant photographing wildlife.

He turned the swimming pool at Ockley into an oversized bird bath planted with bullrushes. "I'd rather see it like this than just a pool for people to splash in once or twice a year," he told the *Daily Mirror*. "It's taken a lot of people a lot of time to find truth and honesty through transcendental meditation. I've been practising it for years through Mother Nature."

In the woods surrounding the estate, he'd set up various birdwatching hides, each with its own neat stash of dope – an escape for those difficult times when his parents, or anybody else who might be shocked to witness the nifty manufacture of a three-skin spliff, came to visit.

Tony Hall, producer, publicist, record exec and another regular weekender wrote an article in the *Record Mirror* praising Billy for being one of the most genuine, sincere and honest men in the music business: "To be happy, Billy doesn't need a big house or a luxury flat, a fast car, flashy birds and discotheques. Just give him the simple life.

"Billy's knowledge of birds and their eggs is unbelievable. In fact [here we go again] he's working on a book about the subject. Which could well turn out to be one of the most comprehensive of its kind ever published.

"Bill is… a person who doesn't make many friends. Because he's been kicked too often. But when he gives, he really gives… To hear Bill sitting by the fire in the early hours of the morning, playing guitar and singing songs to himself and other people was a revelation. At heart he's basically a contemporary folk singer. With a sad warmth in his voice that, in all seriousness, reminded me of Tim Hardin."

In March 1967, the supertanker *The Torrey Canyon* ran aground on Pollard's Rock between Land's End and the Isles of Scilly, spilling nearly 120,000 tons of oil into the Atlantic. Birds that landed on the oil were often unable to take-off again and died.

A rescue effort brought volunteers from all over the country, including Billy and Lee, who bought a camper van and drove down to Cornwall. They were on the beach when the planes of the RNAS and RAF came to drop explosives, napalm and kerosene to burn off the oil. Afterwards, detergent was released into the sea to neutralise more of the oil. This killed more wildlife. In all, it's reckoned that something like 30,000 birds perished. The rescue effort was a messy, hopeless, heartbreaking experience.

Meanwhile the career continued, just, to rumble along.

Patrick Newman, the BBC's long-suffering Booking Manager (Variety), had perhaps noticed Billy's absence from the charts and wondered, with a sigh of relief, whether he could at last send his Artist's Index Card, with its pencilled warnings, to the archive.

It was not to be.

Things had been going reasonably well. At the start of June, Billy appeared on *Saturday Club* with his new backing band The Plainsmen (The Gamblers had decided to call it a day and soon went their separate ways).

Everybody showed up on time, sober and ready for work. Nobody was rude to the Blessed Brian Matthew, the show's host. Strings and sticks remained unbroken and nobody dropped a plectrum. Years later, tracks from this show turned up on a Billy Fury, *Live At The BBC* album. They're good.

Billy's next BBC booking was for the *Joe Loss Show* on June 9, 1967.

Having accepted the booking, Billy realised he had a gig in Wales the night before, and figured that leaving Cardiff in the early hours to get to London for a 1 p.m. call wasn't worth it for a couple of songs, so he phoned the BBC to say he wasn't coming.

All hell never breaks loose at the BBC, but strength of feeling was such that the telegrams that were sent to Billy, Larry and anybody else vaguely involved barely minced words.

Poor Patrick Newman dictated a letter, reminding Billy that this was not his first no-show and adding, "With this in mind it would seem that an element of risk surrounds any attempt to engage you. Accordingly, we are also withdrawing the offer made recently to your agent (and verbally accepted) in connection with the programme *Monday, Monday* for 26th June."

When the *Joe Loss Show* was broadcast, an announcement was made: "From your *Radio Times* you will have expected to hear Billy Fury. Billy Fury has failed to put in an appearance and the Corporation regrets any disappointment to his fans."

Larry wasn't going to take this lying down and neither were the fans. A Mrs Peggy Nuttall of Rugby fired off a strongly worded letter complaining about the wording of the announcement in which she felt "a slur was cast on Billy's integrity".

On June 15, the BBC received a letter from Mr Parnes' solicitors: "According to my instructions, the announcement was that Mr Fury had failed to appear and the Corporation apologised to listeners who might be disappointed. I have advised Mr Parnes that this statement was clearly defamatory and likely to cause the artiste considerable damage to his professional reputation. I further understand that at no time did Mr Fury or his manager or agent sign a contract with the BBC to appear.

"My client's artiste has been in show business for some nine years and enjoys a high reputation as a talented and reliable performer. He recently won a Radio Luxembourg competition in which, among other competitors, were Elvis Presley, The Beatles, The Rolling Stones etc."

This was true. On the Luxembourg 'Battle of the Giants' contest, 5,000 listeners voted for Billy and just 1,300 for The Beatles.

Larry's letter contained a request for a further announcement to be made apologising for the first announcement, and insisting that damages should be paid.

Letters, threats, denials, demands and counter-demands followed.

Not until September did Larry admit that, actually, he might have been mistaken about the contract not being signed. He popped round to see Patrick Newman at his office, suggested the whole incident be dismissed as a silly mistake and hoped that it wouldn't be held against Billy. Patrick expressed "certain views about the difficulty of booking this artist."

Drink was taken.

Larry told Patrick "of the simple country boy Billy Fury was and how he was really only interested in bird-watching (in the purest sense of the word) and goldfish and animals in general."

The following day a large box was delivered to Patrick's office with a note attached.

"Dear Pat [!],

I thoroughly enjoyed our little meeting, and as I ran you dry on champagne, I thought the least I could do was to get you a little re-fill, and I hope you enjoy it.

Kindest regards.

Yours sincerely,

Larry"

Bookings soon followed on the all-new Wonderful Radio 1.

Vintage champagne, it must be added, was seldom used as diplomatic currency at the BBC once Radio 1 got properly underway, and barely figured at all in, for instance, dealings between John Peel and The Undertones.

That summer involved the usual round of Sunday concerts in Great Yarmouth and the release of another single, an odd choice again.

'Loving You' was an Elvis song from the 1957 film of the same name. Billy's version is an exercise in bland, with an easy-listening bum-chick-bu-bum-chick floaty-string arrangement that successfully irons out any creases where traces of passion or hope could lurk.

The B-side, 'I'll Go Along With It', is a relentlessly chirpy, tambourine-heavy anthem to apathy, enlivened by a manic flute solo. Billy's vocal is magnificent and, with its very English pronunciation – the sort of thing Syd Barrett was doing on Pink Floyd's 'See Emily Play', and young David Bowie on 'The Laughing Gnome' – bang on trend. But a Bowie-Barrett supergroup backed by George Formby on banjolele, Billy Butlin on spoons, Princess Anne on sousaphone and real angels on backing vocals couldn't have turned 'I'll Go Along With It' into a hit.

The next one was even banger on trend.

Richard Kerr, the man who'd had a bad time with John Lennon's special LSD at Ockley co-wrote, with Jonathan Peel (not to be confused with John Peel) a fine piece of psychedelia called 'Suzanne In The Mirror'. It was produced by Don Paul, another of the Ockley set, and blessed with an arrangement by the young Tony Visconti, recently arrived from the US and soon to be the maker of magic for among others Marc Bolan and, most notably, David Bowie.

Don multi-tracked Billy's voice and Tony added Mellotronish flutes, a trombone bass line and a four-to-the-bar snare, all of which were very, very 1967, and ought to have been recorded by a band with a name like Leonard's Lilac Lawnmower or The Daisychain Pharmaceutical Company. "Resurrected in willow time," it begins before a series of quatrains in which the invitation of his lover's eyes fades into the gloom, and the cry for help fades into a roomful of supposed misery.

Songs like this don't get written on any old acid. It has to be JL's stuff.

"They were strange words," Billy said, "and I never knew what they meant. I just sang them."

Though it's definitely from the same psychic location as Traffic's 'Paper Sun' and Keith West's 'Excerpt From A Teenage Opera', both of which were massive hits, 'Suzanne In The Mirror' wasn't.

Even now Richard Kerr isn't sure why, and wonders whether it was just that Billy "was past his prime, I guess."

CHAPTER TWENTY

"DON'T WRITE BILLY FURY OFF. ONE GOOD SINGLE AND HE'LL BE RIGHT BACK."

Billy's relationship with Lee was coming to an end.

Inertia's the most likely explanation. To paraphrase Alvy Singer, Woody Allen's character in *Annie Hall* – "a relationship is like a shark. It has to move forward constantly or it dies."

What Billy and Lee had on their hands was a dead shark.

Fidelity had never been a notable feature of the relationship.

"I never had a wild time with women," Billy told the *Sunday Mirror*, years later. "Almost everybody who was involved with me – my road managers, lighting guys and the band – all had a wonderful time. I was so shy I'd lock myself in the bathroom. Later on when I used to do the club circuit, the women who screamed after me were much older. But I still locked myself in the bathroom."

But there's little doubt that from time to time a kind heart would break through the shyness, the bathroom door would open just a crack, and discussions about the meaning of life would ensue.

Towards the end of 1967, Lee sneaked off for a holiday in Tunisia with a man she'd met, asking her friend Judith Hall to cover for her.

Judith didn't. She spilled the beans. The details of who declared what feelings to whom, when the feelings were declared and how they were shown are inevitably hazy, but the upshot was that Lee and Billy split up, Judith moved in with Billy and Lee eventually married the disc jockey Kenny Everett, who, in the fullness of time, turned out to have been gay all along – which is another story.*

'Beyond The Shadow Of Doubt', released right at the end of 1967, sounded like a real contender. It was a convincing song, written by Canadian singer/songwriter Ralph Murphy, properly produced by Vic Smith (aka Vic Coppersmith-Heaven), who later produced most of The Jam's finest hits, and intelligently arranged by Alan Tew.

It copped some decent reviews.

"It has been a while since we last had a Billy Fury single and this one has certainly been well worth waiting for," said *NME*. "It opens rather moodily with Billy singing reflectively in low register – but it soon erupts into a gripping rhythmic ballad with an enveloping all-happening orchestration. From the performance point of view, it's one of the best tracks Bill has waxed."

Larry did his best to talk it up, telling the *Record Mirror* that Billy had been in that "lull that every dynamic artist gets at some stage of his recording career" but now he "has a flurry of bookings going right through February, March and April, has five major television appearances and is right now out of the temporary doldrums.

"I honestly believe this new record will be a smash."

To which Billy added that although he'd been ashamed of some of his records, "I don't cringe when I hear the new one", a line which, as advertising slogans go, could be improved.

He put his "doldrums" down to a lack of perspective. "I felt the business was getting on top of me. But that was the rushing around on one-nighters."

He felt the fans had got things out of proportion, too, "there was this feeling once that people were looking up to me too much. People shouldn't waste their lives in that way." But now, he'd mellowed. "On cabaret dates I wake up early in the morning, eat at country pubs and meet great people. Then an afternoon studying wildlife and then my own

---

*   Told in *Cupid Stunts: The Life And Radio Times Of Kenny Everett*, by David and Caroline Stafford.

life begins on the stage in the evening. I get that excited feeling in my stomach. I try to time my arrival in the club or hall so there's no waiting around. I get there just in time to go on. A good drink and all is well.

"In the old days a newspaper article attacking me could make me cry, literally cry. Now I simply put up a deliberate mental block just so these things don't upset me. I feel different in a lot of ways – in a way it's like finding myself after a time when I didn't know what was going to happen next. Of course I want a hit record. But whatever happens I've developed a different feeling inside myself. And this cabaret scene suits me very well."

The live shows never stopped exciting the punters. "Billy Fury may qualify as a pop veteran, but he's lost none of his stage excitement over the years," said *NME*. "His voice is a lot stronger these days, and his patter, although not perfect by any means, is a lot less nervous. Don't write Billy Fury off. One good single and he'll be right back."

By this time Billy had acquired another race horse. First Rate Pirate, like Anselmo, was entered for the Derby with Paul Cook riding again – a 500-1 outsider. It's an indication of the fall in Billy's fortunes that the Pathé News coverage of the race mentions the horse and its rider, but not the owner.

But Giles, the *Daily Express* cartoonist, still seemed to think Billy's name was big enough to work into a convoluted joke. In Paris, workers were striking, and rioting students were tearing the cobbles from the streets and using them as weapons against the police. Giles' cartoon shows some French students, with their English supporters, saying to one of their number, "Drucilla, the committee has decided that you shall have the honour of being thrown in front of Billy Fury's horse at Tattenham Corner."

"First Rate Pirate," said *The Times* in its account of the race, "jumped off last and, predictably, finished last."

Billy and Larry, having worked now with Tony Visconti and Vic Smith, seemed to be adept at spotting the starmakers of the future, but never quite able to become part of that future themselves.

They did it again when Kenneth Pitt, manager of Manfred Mann, recommended a first album by a new up-and-comer. Larry gave it a listen and thought it was just the sort of thing that might "get Billy out of his rock'n'roll phase" and "bring him up to date". The album was a collection of 14 strange and wonderful songs, all ever so slightly touched by whimsy, written and sung with impeccable English vowels by a 20-year-old David Bowie.

Billy covered track two side two – 'Silly Boy Blue', a song about the Dalai Lama in which rain is falling on the Lhasa Mountains and "People are walking the Potala lanes" (the lyric is usually transcribed as "Botella lanes", which doesn't mean anything. The Potala Palace was the Dalai Lama's home until the 1959 Tibetan uprising.)

Billy, clearly inspired by the new boy, gives an impressive performance, sounding healthier than he had for years, hitting and holding the high notes with precision and power. Vic Smith and Alan Tew take the song slightly faster than the Bowie version, and give it a Spectorish sound, with a bigger orchestra, a huge snare drum and swimming pool reverb.

But still it failed to chart. Perhaps there was just too much good stuff around. In April 1968, The Beatles' 'Lady Madonna', Otis Redding's '(Sittin' On) The Dock Of The Bay', Tom Jones' 'Delilah', Louis Armstrong's 'What A Wonderful World' and Julie Driscoll's 'This Wheel's On Fire' were all elbowing each other for chart space. And, as if to add insult somehow to injury, just as Larry had decided once and for all to "get Billy out of his rock'n'roll phase", re-releases of both Billy Haley's 'Rock Around The Clock' and Buddy Holly's 'Peggy Sue' had made the Top 40.

In August 1968, the *Daily Mirror* announced that "Billy Fury, the pop singer who once called marriage a 'hang up' went out shopping yesterday... for an engagement ring. He bought a £250 diamond antique ring and presented it to blonde Judith Hall, a former fashion model. And then they celebrated their engagement at a champagne party at the penthouse of Billy's manager, Larry Parnes, in Kensington, London."

Judith told Chris Eley that they almost forgot that the press would want to see a ring and so they picked one up at a jeweller in Guildford on the way to the celebration. Then, having got back in the car and driven off, they decided the first choice was too gaudy, so drove back for something a little more discreet.

"Judith, the daughter of a retired printer, is 29," the *Mirror* continued. "Billy, who became one of the most eligible bachelors on the pop scene, is 28. He said: 'I've had second thoughts about marriage.' Judith, who wore a silver crochet dress, said: 'I had the same feelings about marriage as Billy. We were both against it. That is until we met...'"

They hadn't fixed a date for the wedding.

"'We hope it will be some time in the winter on a day when snow is falling,' Judith said. Billy explained: 'One of our first dates was on a snowy day and it was a great moment. But we'll probably get impatient and marry before the snow comes.'"

Larry used the engagement to talk up Billy's career a bit more in *Record Mirror*, telling them that though Billy's working life was mostly spent in cabaret clubs on the chicken-in-a-basket circuit, he "hasn't dropped a penny in earnings".

"An artiste must develop in different fields [Larry was possibly the only man in the music business who still used the word 'artiste']. Right now Billy's writing some wonderful material – there's an LP on the way on which he wrote all the tracks. Now he's really concentrating on that side of things. I believe he can be up there in The Beatles class for writing modern standards.

"And Billy has changed. He used to hate going out of the hotel he was that shy. But now he fixes all his own arrangements, copes with everything. He has new confidence and it's wonderful to see."

His little boy was fleeing the nest.

The LP never materialised, but Billy did write both sides of his next single.

'Phone Box (The Monkey's In The Jam Jar)' nicks a couple of tricks from Bowie, opening, like Bowie's 'We Are Hungry Men', with sound effects and chat, and spreading the whimsy on thick with a nod to The Beatles' then current interest in playground rhymes ("Oompah, Oompah, stick it up you're jumpah", "A, B, C, D, can I bring my friend to tea?").

"Come in wherever you are, the monkey's in the jam jar." With a Coke bottle prominent in the percussion and a novelty tuba solo, once again it had all the hallmarks of a winner in the manner, perhaps of The Scaffold's 'Lily The Pink'.

And the B-side, 'Any Morning Now', brought a mystical union between The Mamas & The Papas and The Dambusters that alone is worth the price of the single.

And yet.

There would never have been a hope of the paying punters accepting the new hippy-dippy Billy anyway. For a very short time he worked with a backing band called Dr Marigold's Prescription and tried the new material live, but the cabaret clubs didn't want songs about the Dalai

Lama and Monkeys in bloody Jam Jars. They'd paid nearly £3.00 for the egg mayonnaise, the plaice and chips, the black forest gateau, the schooner of sherry and the bottle of Hirondelle, and now they wanted 'Halfway To Paradise' and 'In Summer' and 'Like I've Never Been Gone' and some dirty stuff with the microphone stand. And next time, have the decency to wear a shiny suit or we'll have a word with the social secretary and you'll never work in Accrington again.

On November 27, 1968, Billy and Judith were married at Haringey Register Office in North London. Judith's parents were the witnesses. The marriage reveals Judith's real age to be 33, five years older than Billy.

It was the quietest of quiet weddings. The press was not invited. No mention of it appeared until six months later, when it proved a useful nugget of news to help publicise the release of Billy's latest single.

Billy's family weren't there, either. Indeed, they weren't even told about the wedding until sometime later, when bride and groom showed up at Wondrous Place and made the happy announcement. Even Judith was never quite sure why. Relations between Billy and his family were up and down throughout his life and one can only assume that this was one of the down times.

There'd always been a degree of rivalry between Billy and his little brother, Albie. For a time, Albie had tried to carve himself a career in the music business, but it didn't pan out.

"He was great," says Chris Eley. "He looked pretty good and he sang really well."

Billy was never exactly encouraging. When Hal Carter produced one of Albie's records, Billy wouldn't speak to him for six months. They were close as brothers, and they fought like brothers, but they were brothers.

Judith Wills, the Fury superfan who recorded her Billy dreams in her diary and later saved them for posterity in her book *Keith Moon Stole My Lipstick*, had a brief fling with Albie.

"What attracted me to Albie was his GSOH [Good Sense Of Humour] and the fact that his brother was the person I had dreamed of day and night from the age of 13, whose face had adorned my bedroom walls since I first saw a photo of him on the front cover of a magazine, whose records I'd nearly worn out playing them on my Dansette and who still had the power to turn me into a dumbstruck fan every time I met him."

Judith (W) and Albie visited Judith (H) and Billy. Judith (W) remembers Billy getting cross with Albie for constantly asking him for money. Eventually, Billy wrote a letter to Albie telling him he couldn't help him anymore as he "wasn't that flush" and advising him to go back to Liverpool to get a job.

Albie did this. At which point Judith (W) learned that he had a wife back there and finished the relationship.

Billy's Christmas record was 'Lady', with a tune written by the German maestro Bert Kaempfert, who'd composed 'Strangers In The Night' for Mr Sinatra and 'Wooden Heart' for Mr Presley. 'Lady' is essentially 'Strangers In The Night' Mk II, with strings, harps, timpani, and muted bass doing eccentric slides. It's the sort of record that was tailor-made for the first dance at a wedding reception, that moment when the bride whispers in the groom's ear, "I gave you specific instructions to stay sober."

"...the sort of record that, three or four years ago, would have provided Billy Fury with a massive hit," said *NME*. "Parlophone should have waited until after the Christmas rush before releasing it – because then it would have stood a distinct chance."

The releases began to tail off. In 1963 there had been five singles, two EPs and an LP. In 1969 there were just two singles, 'I Call For My Rose', another fairly straight ballad, and 'All The Way To The USA', a Status Quo-style rocker, both written by Liverpool songwriter Jimmy Campbell.

NME wasn't impressed. "Can't remember the last time Billy Fury had a hit, so, even if he came up with a magnificent record I couldn't be too optimistic about its chances. And I'm afraid this disc isn't particularly sensational."

Chapter Twenty-One

"OUR NAMES WERE WRITTEN IN BIRO ON THE WINDOW – BILLY FURY AND MARTY WILDE."

Between 1969 and 1971, a mini-Armageddon, largely drugs related, came to the world of rock'n'roll and showbiz.

Brian Jones drowned in his swimming pool. Jimi Hendrix choked on his vomit. Janis Joplin overdosed. Judy Garland overdosed. Frankie Lymon (of Frankie Lymon & The Teenagers) overdosed. Tony Hancock (British comedian) overdosed. Alan 'Blind Owl' Wilson (of Canned Heat) overdosed. Mary Ann Ganser (of The Shangri-Las) possibly overdosed. Brian Epstein had already overdosed and The Beatles split up and sued the arses off each other.

Gene Vincent went, too, in October 1971, of a ruptured stomach ulcer, exacerbated no doubt, by the years of heavy drinking.

The generalised optimism that had been around in the sixties, the feeling that a corner had been turned, that this might – regardless of your scepticism towards astrology – be the actual Dawning of the Age of Aquarius, had crashed and burned. And all those trippy notions – that drugs were pretty good, that if you asked "War, what is it good for?" Lyndon Johnson might think "good point" and stop the bombing, that there was nowhere you can be that isn't where you're meant to be – were now greeted with howls of derisive laughter.

The seventies started badly for Billy.

"In your career you have lows when things change," Marty Wilde said.

Once, when he and Billy were on tour together, "I can remember vividly that a promoter had booked us for a gig and when we came to the venue it was more like a civic hall than a proper theatre. Our names were written in biro on the window – Billy Fury and Marty Wilde. That was a low."

Unlike so many others, Billy (and Marty) resisted the temptation to dismiss the works of those who had superseded them as rubbish. They kept up.

"He moved on a hell of a lot with music," says Marty. "I remember one time when he was over in my house and he was talking about Marvin Gaye's new album *What's Going On* – which was quite a revolutionary album in a way. Billy loved that album. He also pointed me in the direction of the Eagles when they first appeared on the scene. He said, 'You have to listen to them – they are fantastic.'"

At this time, Billy's health was also seriously deteriorating. Early in 1970, he was admitted to hospital in Carlisle, suffering abdominal pains – presumably his kidneys again – and kept in for observation for a couple of days.

And his contract with Parlophone was coming to its end. The nine singles a year had never materialised, and neither had the album. He'd tried a range of styles, from surreal psychedelia to soppy ballads via Status Quo head-banging, and nothing had clicked.

It's possible that tracks were recorded for an LP. No master tapes have ever been found, but Chris Eley painstakingly assembled a 'might have been' version from acetates and second-generation rough mixes and released it in 2011 as *The Lost Album*, on the Peaksoft label.

The last two Parlophone singles were released in 1970 – 'Why are You Leaving?' in May and 'Paradise Alley' in November, both Carole King songs, neither particularly distinguished, although in the career of a man not known for the cheeriness of his output, a man who recorded 'Billy, Don't Jump' and 'Nobody's Child', 'Paradise Alley' takes the biscuit for utter, doomy despair as the singer pleads to be shown "pastures of plenty", to be saved from the "rivers of none", begging to be told when his time is come".

Both records were produced by Mike Hurst, former band mate of Dusty Springfield in The Springfields and producer of Cat Stevens' 'Matthew And Son', Manfred Mann's 'Mighty Quinn and P. P. Arnold's magnificent 'The First Cut Is The Deepest'.

"The publicity was absolutely bugger all," says Mike. "Nothing. The singles died a death. But then it was Billy Fury. And it was 1970."

There wasn't another single release for two years, and that was on Fury Records, a label Billy had set up with Hal Carter and Lisa Rosen – more of whom in a moment.

'Will The Real Man Please Stand Up' is a clumsy song, possibly about Jesus, generally advocating, as so many songs of the time did, brotherhood and understanding. It had airplay. Tony Blackburn made it his record of the week on Radio 1. All the same, extant copies of the single are these days classed as 'very rare' and change hands for £20 or £30 – which tells you all you need to know about how many were sold at the time.

"It was a very short stage of my career," Billy said, years later. "I got on to Fury Records and it didn't go too ace so I thought I'd get off again as fast as I can. It probably lasted for a year or 18 months. That label wasn't good for anybody at all."

One of the other people it wasn't good for was Jo-Jo Ellis, a persona briefly adopted by Bernard Jewry between his first materialisation as Shane Fenton (who duetted with Billy in *Play It Cool*) and his second as Alvin Stardust.* His sole Fury release, 'The Fly', didn't.

The Fury Records label folded not long after it was founded.

---

* One of the authors once found himself in a café in Essex. All around were framed photographs of Shane and Alvin. I asked the café's owner about them. "He's my nephew," she said, taking an early one from the wall and giving it a wipe with her sleeve. "First I had to call him Bernard, then it was Shane and now it's Alvin." There was a wistful pause. "He's always called me 'Auntie Eileen'," she said. One can only be glad she never found out about Jo-Jo.

In December 1971, Billy's heart, dicky since his childhood rheumatic fever and further damaged by the years of heavy smoking and junk-eating on the road, showed signs of giving up. The trouble he'd had in 1967 returned – or rather it had never gone away. One of the valves was closing up.

"I felt very tired and exhausted and had a bit of trouble breathing," he said. "Then I became very ill."

He was booked into the National Heart Hospital in London for surgery.

"I put the operation off as long as possible because they were working on different and newer techniques. I had to have a valve opened because the blood couldn't get through there and it was going back into the heart. They decided that they would widen this valve for me."

Billy hadn't been able to get private health insurance because of his long-standing medical problems, so was admitted to a public ward.

Hal Carter told Spencer Leigh: "I remember the night before he had bypass surgery. He was so white, so frightened, he wanted me to get his clothes and get him out of hospital."

Billy had always reckoned he'd be lucky to see 30. In April, he celebrated his 31st birthday, so, according to his reckoning, he was already living on borrowed time.

He asked Larry to send for Lee.

Understandably, Lee, now married to Kenny Everett, found the request a little odd, but, "I finally decided to go because if he'd didn't pull through I'd never forgive myself. When I reached his bed he just hugged and hugged me and burst into tears. Next day he had the operation and pulled through."

Lee reports that Billy told her he was at least half conscious throughout the surgery.

"He was aware of all that happened – maybe because of his amazing drug tolerance the anaesthetic hadn't put him completely out; he even remembered them sawing through his ribs. For the rest of his life he lived in fear of another operation."

On the day after his discharge from hospital, he showed up with Judith at Lee and Kenny's farm in Cowfold, West Sussex. Understandably, this caused a certain amount of friction. Relations between Lee and Judith were inevitably frosty. Kenny, according to Lee, had never got on with

Judith anyway. Billy needed a lot of looking after and Judith wasn't feeling too well either.

To further add to the tension, it quickly became apparent that, even before Billy had started calling for his ex from his hospital bed and depending on her for post-operative nursing, his marriage was not going swimmingly. There were outbursts and incidents. Eventually, according to Lee's account, Kenny grew exasperated by Judith and asked her to leave.

She did. Billy stayed, and Kenny and Lee nursed him back to health.

The convalescence lasted a long time.

Larry Parnes' management contract had expired and not been renewed. Hal Carter, Billy's friend and former road manager, had taken on the duties and it was up to him to deal with the flak resulting from the illness. A January tour was cancelled. That was supposed to have been followed, in late February and March, by a rock'n'roll revival tour featuring Billy, Vince Eager, Little Shelton and The New Gamblers. That, too, had to be cancelled at short notice.

"The decision landed the 31-year-old singer in the middle of a showbiz rumpus," said the *Daily Mirror*. "Upset tour organiser David Stones said: 'Theatres have been booked all over the country. Now I must cancel the whole show.'"

Hal Carter claimed that Billy had pulled out on doctor's orders.

David Stones would not let it lie. "I went to see Billy last Wednesday and offered to cancel the first week of the tour if he didn't feel up to it. I suggested that he just play the second week when all the dates were in the Home Counties and I offered to cut his spot to 20 minutes. For some reason he wouldn't even speak to me. And I am convinced that, while his health may have been a contributory factor, another reason is that he simply didn't want to do the tour."

Billy's marriage was effectively over. And he'd found a new love.

Lisa Rosen was the only daughter of Cecil Rosen, property magnate and philanthropist. She barely knew who Billy was.

"I was a Cliff fan and Billy was older than me so I didn't really know much about him to be perfectly honest. When we met I was only 18 and I was living at home with my parents. There was a club down the road and I knew the owner, so I used to trot down there on my own in the evening. On this particular night, the friend I was with yanked me into the dressing room, said 'Come with me,' and there was Billy. Initially we were both so shy we didn't say anything to each other, but when he came back to the dressing room after his set, we got talking.

"The club where we met, Gulliver's, was in Down Street in Mayfair, just opposite the Hilton Hotel, and on the corner facing the Hilton was a coffee shop. Everybody always ended up there for breakfast – so that's how it happened. We were talking all night – my friend David and me and Billy. We just clicked.

"He had an aura about him like no other pop star around at that time." Lisa started driving Billy to his gigs.

"I was impressed straight away – you couldn't not be. He was very sexual in front of an audience – he moved and grooved. He was a sex symbol and the audience used to go wild for him wherever he played.

"Mind you, he could be a bugger. When I went to the first gig, I was standing on the side in the wings. I was amazed that he only did 17 minutes and walked off. I said, 'You can't walk off after 17 minutes. All these people have waited all night to see you and they've paid good money to be here and you can't walk off after 17 minutes, get back on stage.' He said, 'Well, I've done about 12 numbers!' And that was that. Songs were shorter in those days."

The occasional brisk run-through of 12 songs in 17 minutes at out-of-the-way supper clubs could very easily have constituted the rest of Billy's career, were it not for a strange rumbling in the zeitgeist.

In 1969, a surprise hit at the Woodstock Music & Arts Fair – apotheosis of all things hippie – was Sha Na Na, a small army of singers, dancers and musicians who wore distinctly un-hippie gold lamé, cutoff T-shirts, white socks and brothel creepers, greased and combed their hair into DAs and sang Danny & The Juniors' 'At The Hop', Gene Chandlers' 'Duke Of Earl' and Elvis' 'Jailhouse Rock' with fierce commitment. Jimi Hendrix, who followed them, had trouble winning back the crowd.

A month later, in Toronto, Canada, 20,000 people turned up to see a rock'n'roll revival show, featuring Chuck Berry, Little Richard, Jerry Lee Lewis, Bo Diddley and Gene Vincent, together with new boy John Lennon, whose band featured Eric Clapton, and, as a last-minute addition, the British attention-seeker, political contender and founder of the Monster Raving Loony Party, Screaming Lord Sutch.

In 1971 a new musical, *Grease*, set in a fifties high school amid love, cars, bad boys and good girls with a clutch of freshly minted rock'n'roll, doo-wop and cheesy ballads, was nominated for seven Tony awards and didn't close on Broadway until 1980.

It wasn't hard to see what was happening. The War Children and the first wave of Baby Boomers, the Billy fans who had drifted away when the kids came along, the people who'd bought the records of Buddy and Eddie and Gene, who'd seen them live at their local Odeon or Hippodrome, who'd mourned when Buddy died, when Eddie died, when Elvis shaved off his sidies, were now in their thirties with mortgages and salad spinners from Habitat. As the sixties came to an end and the seventies got into gear, they found they couldn't summon much enthusiasm for Marc Bolan, Gary Glitter, The Osmonds or the Bay City Rollers. Neither did King Crimson's bitonal escapades in a dance-defying 11/4 time signature or Pink Floyd's 23 minutes of strophic noise, have quite the same effect on their joy bits as, say, 'Good Golly, Miss Molly'.

At the beginning of 1972, massive numbers of the Fury generation bought Don McLean's 'American Pie' because it had the same effect on them that the *petit madeleine* dipped in tea had had on Marcel Proust. Lost times were remembered.

Few of the Baby Boomeres – the British ones, at least – had ever owned a pick-up truck, and even fewer had driven a Chevvy to the levee, but all of them had in spirit. They did believe in rock'n'roll, fervently: music had indeed saved their mortal souls and they were willing to teach anybody who cared to ask how to dance real slow.

And, as they remembered, they began to mourn their lost youths. They wanted to have their nerves shaken and their brains rattled. They pined for rip-swoggling, hog-hounding, help-me-Jesus-I-got-Satan-in-my-Levis rock'n'roll.

In the back pages of *New Musical Express*, nestling among the ads for loon pants and tank-tops, there appeared offers of "drape jackets, finger length, two button, velvet collar, half-moon cuffs, £25", "drainpipe jeans, £3.00", "brothel creepers, £8.25". Teds, it seemed, were on the move again.

What had begun in Woodstock and in Toronto came to London in earnest on August 5, 1972, when Wembley Stadium hosted The Rock'n'Roll Show, an extravaganza that brought together Little Richard, Jerry Lee Lewis, Bill Haley, Chuck Berry, Bo Diddley, Screaming Lord

Sutch, Gary Glitter & The Glitter Band, Roy Wood (with his new band Wizzard), Joe Brown, Emile Ford & The Checkmates, Heinz and Billy Fury. A young Malcolm McLaren was also on hand, selling T-shirts.

Publicity for the event was huge. Lord Sutch went into overdrive, promising that his act would be enhanced by the inclusion of a couple of strippers. To make sure he was being noticed, he then upped the stakes.

Later, at Bow Street magistrates court, Police Constable Christopher Thomas reported that he was "on duty at 10 Downing Street when Mr Sutch leapt from a double-decker bus shouting, 'Come on girls.'" Upon which, "four naked girls proceeded up Downing Street to Number 10."

All were arrested and summoned to appear at court where Sutch tried to make up for the models' more decorous appearance by wearing football shorts with boots and ball, top hat and bright green hair.

The strippers were fined £50 each. Sutch claimed that "he had not organised the bus nor the naked girls. They were on a tour of London to advertise the show and his sole intention in going to Downing Street was to invite Mr Heath [the then Prime Minister] to the concert as there would be lots of young people there." Implausibly, the case against him was dismissed.

On the big day, specially chartered planes flew from France "loaded to the portholes with Gallic Teds" and British Rail laid on extra train services.

No promoter could expect Little Richard, Chuck Berry and Jerry Lee Lewis to share a stage without trouble. Chuck Berry was put on last, effectively topping the bill. Fair enough, one might assume, because he'd had the most recent hit with 'My Ding-A-Ling', an exercise in single-entendre that had as much to do with rock'n'roll as Gracie Fields' 'The Biggest Aspidistra In The World'.

"No one, and I mean no one should have the nerve to be over me," Little Richard complained to the press. "I'm gonna play Chuck's 'Ding-A-Ling'. Oo-ee, if he is being paid more than me, then I'm gonna scream and scream like a black lady!"

To no avail. Chuck did go on last. Little Richard did not sing 'My Ding-A-Ling'. And he screamed, to the audience's delight, like Little Richard.

To be honest, by the time Chuck hit the stage, the show had been going on for 11 hours. When it was good it was very good, but people grew tired. The event was not slickly organised. There were longueurs.

Booing and slow hand claps were heard. Original Teddy Boys and Retro Teddy Boys in half-moon cuffs and £8.95 brothel creepers were itching to rip the place apart or at least find a municipal garden where havoc could be wrought. Beer cans were thrown. A lot of beer cans.

Billy came on reasonably early in the running order and sang five numbers. It was, according to the press, "one of the better performances of the day." When he launched into 'That's All Right', the Wembley crowd was uplifted like it was 1966 all over again and Geoff Hurst had just deflected that last-minute shot off the crossbar and over the line.

The same zeitgeist that had given birth to Sha-Na-Na, the Toronto rock'n'roll show, the London rock'n'roll show and *Grease*, also birthed *That'll Be The Day*, a British film produced by David Puttnam, directed by Claude Whatham and written by Ray Connolly.

Ray Connolly knew his subject. He was about the same age as Billy, born in the same neck of the woods, went to school in Ormskirk and worked on the *Liverpool Daily Post*. He'd interviewed The Beatles in their prime and Elvis too. His book, *Stardust Memories – Talking About My Generation*, a collection of pieces about and interviews with the great and the good of the sixties, remains a go-to source.

The screenplay, set in the very early sixties, is about a lower-middle-class teenager, Jim MacLaine, who turns down a university place to escape from stifling provincialism and enter a world of sex, fun and rock'n'roll: in other words, a boilerplate rites-of-passage movie made original by observations so cruelly accurate that sometimes it could be a documentary.

At the end of the film, MacLaine, played by David Essex, leaves his wife, mother and young son, buys a guitar and decides to run away with a band.

It was intended, according to Lord Puttnam, to symbolise "the moment when the fifties ended and the sixties started. Which wasn't 1960. It was more like late 1961."

"*That'll Be The Day*'s about reality" says Ray Connolly. "It's about me, that film: me in the universality of being adolescent. We're all Jim MacLaine. For a bit." Ringo Starr was cast opposite David Essex, playing Jim's savvy friend, Mike. Billy was offered a cameo, playing Stormy Tempest, a singer left over from the gold-lamé and Brylcreem fifties, now reduced to doing his act for a holiday camp dance contest. In other words, he was being asked to send himself up.

Lisa remembers Billy's initial reaction. "'I'm not bloody doing it. I don't want to do it.' But I was adamant. I said, 'Oh yes you will.' I forced him into it."

In order to raise extra publicity for the project, Puttnam had struck a deal with Ronco, a company that had recently applied its expertise for selling innovative gadgets (the Chop-O-Matic was one of theirs, as were the Inside-The-Shell Egg Scrambler and GLH-9 Hair-In-A-Can) to the record business, packaging compilations into budget LPs (*Duane Eddy's 20 Twangy Tracks*, *Foster & Allen Sing The Country Hits*) and ensuring sales with garish TV ads. The *That'll Be The Day* soundtrack, featuring hits of the late fifties and early sixties in their original versions, together with some new material, was right up their street.

Keith Moon was also signed up for the project early in its development.

Peter 'Dougal' Butler, Moon's chauffeur, minder and friend, remembers an early meeting with David Puttnam. "He mentioned that they had signed up Billy Fury to play the singer. But they needed to record some music. A lot of the stuff they wanted to use was old stuff, but they also wanted about four or five tracks of new stuff. Keith and me were good friends with Neil Aspinall so we went to see him, and Keith and him sort of produced the soundtrack album."

Neil Aspinall was The Beatles' former roadie, then head of Apple (The Beatles' company, not the computer firm).

On October 13, a supergroup assembled at Olympic Studios in West London: Keith Moon on drums, Jack Bruce on bass, Ronnie Wood on guitar, Graham Bond on sax and John Hawken of The Nashville Teens, Spooky Tooth and Vinegar Joe on piano.

The new material included a wonderfully cheesy re-recording of 'A Thousand Stars', covers of 'That's All Right, Mama' and 'What'd I Say?' and two brand new ones – 'Get Yourself Together', a swampy slide-guitar blues written by Billy, and 'Long Live Rock', a song by Pete Townshend.

The Who had already recorded 'Long Live Rock', but their version wasn't made public until their album *Odds And Sods* was released in 1974. In the sleeve notes for *Odds And Sods*, Townshend remarked: "Well, there are dozens of these self-conscious hymns to the last 15 years appearing now and here's another one. This was featured briefly in the film for which Keith made his acting debut, *That'll Be The Day*. Billy Fury sang it. This is most definitely the definitive version."

Viv Stanshall, of The Bonzo Dog Doo Dah Band, also contributed a couple of tracks: an ineptly played harmonica solo with extensive backing vocals called 'What In The World', and a three-and-a-half-minute summary of the film's plot in 'Real Leather Jacket' in which Jimmy spends a "packet" on the titular real leather jacket, "with a lot of zips."

Peter 'Dougal' Butler remembers that at least some of Viv Stanshall's recording was done not at Olympic but at Morgan Studios in Willesden, North-West London, where he'd recorded with the Bonzos. Pete drove Billy there from Puttnam's production office.

"He was always quite shy," says Pete, "and he was on the old wacky-baccy. He told us it was to keep his nerves down. He did tell us he had heart problems and this, that and the other. Viv Stanshall was there, and they'd put these screens up around him, as was usual when they were doing the vocals. Anyway, Viv has got this whacking great long joint and obviously Billy had a puff so he's laughing. And the next thing that happened was Viv fell off his stool and all the screens collapsed on top of him. So we sort of dug Viv out to make sure he was all right, and he looked up and said, in his best posh voice, 'Well... this never happens at the Olympic Studios'. Billy thought it was very funny."

Viv Stanshall, Keith Moon, Graham Bond and Ronnie Wood were all fond of a drink, chased, more often than not, with a few assorted pills and a smoke and then another drink. Ronnie's the only one to have survived past 60.

Some of the tracks from the album appear in the film only fleetingly: others don't appear at all. But they didn't half have a good time recording them.

"A lot of boozing went on and in the end it got too much for Billy," Pete said. "He decided to not come in anymore and just laid his vocals on afterwards. He couldn't take the pace."

Nevertheless, Billy and Keith, introvert and extravert, yin and yang, bonded.

Lisa first met Keith and Peter Butler one night when Billy had arranged a dinner at a fancy restaurant. Peter and Keith offered to pick her up on the way over. She was still living with her parents. Peter and Keith were both wearing full-length mink coats.

"The sight of them at our door was enough to give my father a heart attack. When I told him we were off to meet Billy at the Inn On The Park Hotel, in Mayfair, he predicted we'd never be allowed in. He was mortified – he stood outside the door going, 'Come back here – you're not going to embarrass me or humiliate me!' And I said, 'You're not going to intimidate me! I'm going.' And he said, 'No you're not.' And I said, 'Yes I am.' And we ran out the door. Off we sped in Keith Moon's Rolls-Royce. And at the Inn On The Park everyone seemed to be lining up for us as we climbed the staircase to the bar – or perhaps it was because Keith was handing out £20 notes to everybody he met."

Billy's location filming for *That'll Be The Day* was at Warner's Holiday Camp, Puckpool, and the Lakeside Inn, Wootton Bridge, both on the Isle of Wight. Lisa went with him.

"It was parties every night. Fortunately, we had the whole hotel to ourselves."

"Keith used to take poppers 10 at a time between two slices of bread," says Lisa. "That was his lunch. He had a sound system in his room and he made the whole hotel vibrate and rock with the sound. He was very good to Billy – he really loved him.

"I remember one night, when I went downstairs to the hotel club, I saw two policemen waiting. Ringo and Keith were always playing tricks, so I thought it was them in fancy dress. In fact, the owner had called the police and they raided the place, although miraculously nobody got arrested. The police seemed to enjoy meeting the rock stars. They collected some autographs for their kids, and left."

"We were at the Shanklin Hotel," Peter Butler says, "boozing every night and every day. Billy took part, but not so much as Keith and Ringo Starr. Booze was frowned on on the set, so what we used to do was we used to have brandy and ginger and I would hide it in Lucozade bottles. I'd have a box of Lucozade bottles, maybe eight bottles a day, and they would be wrapped up in that orange cellophane. I'd pour it down the drain and pour the Courvoisier brandy in halfway up the bottle, and then top it with ginger ale and put the cap back on. And we would be onstage, and I'd take one to Ringo and we'd pass it round. Everyone thought we were drinking Lucozade. And by about four o'clock everyone was… We had some great times.

"I mean, I think Bill thought, 'Well, this is proper rock'n'roll.' Back at the hotel every door was open all night and all you saw was legs in the air. Billy didn't participate in all that but Keith did – well, he'd participate in anything. There were lots of local girls. I mean, nothing had really happened in Shanklin for 30 years until Billy Fury and Ringo Starr and Keith Moon showed up. The beauty queen of the Isle of

Wight was there once. A great night that was. But Billy wasn't really promiscuous then. Not like Keith."

Anyway, Billy had his girlfriend with him.

Much of Billy's onstage performance in the film is obscured by David Essex and Ringo talking to each other and doing stuff, the way people do in films, but all the same, you can't take your eyes off Billy. He is the main man; whippet thin, with black leather trousers, gold medallion, silver jacket and frosted pompadour.

"He was a striking guy," says Peter. "So good looking, but thin as a bird."

There is a poignant moment in the film when Jim MacLaine (David Essex) asks the drummer in Stormy Tempest's band (Keith Moon) whether the songs are their own. "You have to be American to write rock'n'roll," the drummer replies.

Unless, of course, you're Billy Fury.

The film was released in April 1973 to mostly good reviews. It filled cinemas for weeks. The backers made a decent profit.

The Guardian said it was "consistently enjoyable", the *Daily Express* "unusually entertaining", the *Evening Standard* said it was "excellent".

Billy, even sending himself up, was a magnetic presence. It's the thing about stars: no matter how dated and absurd their act seems – and in 1973, the preening sexuality of the *Oh Boy!* idols seemed very dated indeed – the magic still happens. Buster Keaton, in a mildewed print of *The General*, still mesmerises. Fried banana Elvis at Vegas, doing his karate moves in his jumpsuit, has still got it. A bit of it, anyway.

"Billy had a break with *That'll Be The Day*," says Marty. "It showed everyone what he was capable of and it reminded people of his quality. People take you for granted – they think you are finished, that you're over as an artist or things have moved on and you're no longer relevant to the scene. Billy was successful in that film and it sort of brought him back. I think they acknowledged that although they'd moved on in some areas musically and they were slightly more advanced in some things, Billy was where it all started."

"I remember after the film Keith and me had a meeting up at Apple with Neil Aspinall," says Peter Butler. "Apple had moved up to St James just round the corner from where it had been. We came out of there and were just walking up Piccadilly, and we just turned left into Barclay Street when we bumped into Charlie Watts. We got talking and we told him we'd just done a film called *That'll Be The Day* with Billy Fury. And he said, 'Blimey! That's amazing 'cos we are thinking of taking him on tour with us to America. If he can get a backing band together, we'd love him to support us on the American tour.'

"Sadly it didn't happen. If Bill had had someone like Dave Edmunds or Jeff Lynne to produce him at the time, it would have really been something. The film could have propelled him somewhere else, but he wasn't a well bunny so he couldn't have done the Stones tour."

For the same reason, when Ken Russell offered Billy the part of the Doctor in his film of The Who's *Tommy*, he had to decline. Anyway, Moon would have been around. There's only so much a dicky heart can take.

The *That'll Be The Day* soundtrack album – 40 tracks of non-stop classics plus Viv Stanshall's harmonica noodlings, packaged in some of the ugliest artwork ever to disgrace a record rack – was advertised on TV more than Hovis bread. It sold 600,000 units, hit number one in the UK album chart and stayed there for seven consecutive weeks.

It was the only time Billy was at number one.

The sun was shining again on rock'n'roll and the old timers (some of them approaching 40) were making hay. In the early seventies, Chuck Berry, Carl 'Blue Suede Shoes' Perkins, Fats Domino, Jerry Lee Lewis and many lesser luminaries, all toured the UK.

Bill Haley played 50 UK dates at the beginning of 1974, encouraging singalongs to 'See You Later Alligator' at the Stevenage Locarno, Blighty's in Farnworth and the Bedworth Civic Hall.

Nobody, it seemed, was ready to hang up their rock'n'roll shoes.

Marty got together an old-time package tour, *The '74 Rock & Roll Road Show*, featuring himself, Billy, The New Tornados, Heinz and Tommy Bruce: just 15 dates, opening at the Usher Hall in Edinburgh at the end of May and winding up at the Hemel Hempstead Pavilion in mid-June. It sold out. More dates were added.

Then, in January 1974, Hal Carter got an advance from Warner Bros Records for Billy to make a new single, his first in more than two years. He brought Marty in to produce.

The chosen song seems an odd choice in the midst of a rock'n'roll revival. 'I'll Be Your Sweetheart' is an old music-hall waltz, written by

Harry Dacre, who also wrote 'Daisy Bell (Bicycle Built For Two)', with the well-known lyric "Daisy, Daisy, give me your answer do".

Billy's version starts in traditional style with solo piano accompaniment, then develops into a raucous Memphis barroom singalong with grimy guitar and ragged backing vocals.

The B-side's one of Billy's own songs, 'Fascinating Candle Flame', a rumba with a dying fall, produced by Tony Meehan, The Shadow's first drummer. Rare existing copies change hands for £35.

Keith Moon knew everybody and was everywhere.

Having become a part of Billy's life, he remained a presence.

"We were always in some bar or restaurant," says Peter Butler. "One night, Billy's estranged wife, Judith, rang him and asked him to come and pick up his barn owls."

Billy had nowhere to put them.

"Bill said to Keith, 'You know you said you had an aviary,' which, as it happens Keith did – at Tara House, his house at Chertsey."

Keith was only too pleased to help.

"'My dear boy, my dear man, we will go together'.

"We drove over that night. It took us ages to find this place. It was down near Dorking. Anyway we got there and the wife – she wasn't happy."

Lisa takes up the story. "When we arrived outside the house the drive was all covered with shingle, so when Billy and Moony get out of the car you could hear them walking up to the house. Suddenly there's this bang. And there's another bang. And they both start running back to the car – I could hear them on the shingle. And I said 'What's happened? What's going on?' And Moony said, 'She's sitting in bed with the gun aimed out the window waiting for Billy!'"

To be fair, Peter Butler remembers nothing about the gun – and it is something you'd remember – and another account suggests that it was Moony who'd taken the gun. Who knows? We mention it here merely in appreciation of the extra frisson of drama it adds to the story.

"We got the owls back," says Peter, "and put them in Keith's aviary but unfortunately they only lasted about a week. The foxes got them. We were devastated of course – and then we had to tell Bill. The aviary had all been wired up properly but the foxes dug underground and got in. Bill was devastated. I mean, we apologised but... what can you do?"

Lisa and Billy moved around London for a while – St John's Wood, Mill Hill, and eventually back to St John's Wood and a house in Cavendish Avenue.

"It is a lovely, old fashioned romance," Billy told the *Daily Express*. "She makes me happy. She looks after me."

"Anyone who thought Billy Fury a typically dumb product of the fifties rock era should see his life-style today," said the *Daily Express* article. "His home is a beautifully appointed £100,000 mansion in London's St John's Wood, close by the residence of that other talented Liverpudlian, Paul McCartney."

They had just the two dogs with them in London. King, the Great Dane, and Tiger, the terrier.

Along the way, they also decided to buy, for another reported £100,000, a 100-acre farm near Llanwrda in the Brecon Beacons, where Billy planned to breed horses and sheep and spend time birdwatching.

"I don't have pop idols any more," he said. "My idols now are people like Peter Scott and Graham Dangerfield. Yes, I am very concerned about animals and the preservation of wildlife. I have my own nature reserve in Brecon, Wales.

"I'd begun to dislike the environment in the English counties – everything was so tidy; all the hedgerows were being ripped out," Billy said. "I decided to move somewhere really wild where there were still birds.

"Also I'm in touch with a few RSPCA centres – I always have been. They take care of household pets, but I look after any wild animals that come their way – foxes, badgers, stoats, weasels, any birds at all. I've always enjoyed looking after them and bringing them up.

"You know when I was a kid all the hedgerows and waste lands were filled with wild flowers. Now you don't get them because everything is sprayed with DDT – especially in the more accessible places like the Home Counties, where the councils have more money and have been merrily spraying away.

"Suddenly the buzzard, the sparrow hawk, the peregrine falcon were all gone. Small animals and insects feed on the plants. They pick up the poison and then a bird eats them and it goes down with it. And then a fox or a badger eats the dead bird and it goes down with it. And there you go – the never-ending chain."

"Billy wanted his nature reserve," Lisa said. "God, we had all sorts of animals there. And we also got all sorts of complaints. It could be a nightmare. He'd already built the aviaries in the garden here in London. But when we got to the farm it was different. It was his dream. But the farmhouse had no heating. Just bare floor boards. The only thing that was a fixture was a sink in a square room that they called a kitchen. We used to freeze there. We had to wear two coats 24 hours a day. We just had one fire in the living room. We had Scottish wildcats that escaped. And we had snowy owls. But we received a petition from the neighbours because all night you'd hear them. And we had herons. We had some white doves flying free in the garden and they multiplied and multiplied until there was about 60 of them. Shit everywhere! They would nest in the pipes and all sorts.

"So, one night we were on our way from seeing Diana Ross at the NEC in Birmingham when I noticed this big barn in the middle of nowhere while we were driving and I said to Billy, 'Our doves would be so happy in there'. So Billy stopped and had a look. When we got back home we packed them all in boxes and drove back towards Birmingham the next day and released them in the barn. We were so happy they had a good home. And then we drove back.

"They were home before we were!"

At the time, Billy was drinking too much.

"And that caused a lot of other problems. It wasn't always easy. Once, under the influence of drink, he decided to take an RSPCA van parked outside our house for a drive. It ended up in a ditch, completely wrecked. I'll never forget Billy's poor face. After those heavy drinking sessions, he would cry and be terribly upset over what he had done."

Hanging around with Moon can't have helped. Keith went into rehab in the mid-seventies and described his daily regime to a stunned doctor:

"I always get up about six in the morning. I have my bangers and eggs. And I drink a bottle of Dom Perignon and half a bottle of brandy. Then I take a couple of downers. Then it's about 10 and I'll have a nice nap until five. I get up, have a couple of black beauties [a combination of amphetamine and dextroamphetamine], some brandy, a little champagne and go out on the town. Then we boogie. We'll wrap it up about four."

Keith was to die in September 1978.

In 1976, Billy was admitted for a second heart operation to replace two of his valves.

"I had to decide what kind of valve I wanted. It could have been a plastic valve, which is an American invention, or a human valve, which I chose. I don't know who it belonged to before.

"I know that big strides have been made in the improvement of heart surgery and I had confidence," he told the *Daily Express*. "When I went into hospital this time, I did expect to come out again. All the same I wrote a goodbye letter to Lisa and made my will...

"After my operation I felt I had been reborn. Everyone was so beautiful and kind. I felt very warm to the human race. I loved everybody."

"If I never worked again I'd be all right financially. But I am too young to retire!"

He was wrong about his financial security.

"Pop star Billy Fury is sick, out of work – and on the verge of bankruptcy," said the *Daily Express* in March 1978. "The Inland Revenue yesterday issued a bankruptcy receiving order against him. They claim he owes £16,000 in back taxes. A close friend of the 37-year-old fallen idol whose hit records like 'Halfway To Paradise' once earned him £1,000 a week said: 'For the past few months, Billy has been living from hand to mouth with friends. He is still very unwell. He has undergone two major heart operations and he does not know if he will ever be able to work again'."

The taxes – closer to £17,000 – dated back to 1962. Billy had left all that sort of thing to Larry and, clearly, Larry had left all that sort of thing to chance.

Billy went to Lisa's dad for advice. He told him he didn't have much alternative but to declare himself bankrupt.

Because of his health, Billy was allowed to sit down in court. He was described as "of no occupation, lately a singer", which must have hurt.

The fans – and their mothers – wept for him. One wrote to the *Daily Mirror*: "The news that former pop star Billy Fury, 38, is now broke and in ill-health is very sad. He gave so much pleasure to my children in the sixties and I enjoyed watching them dance to his music in our front room. I hope Billy's troubles are soon over and that his health improves and he moves on to happier times – Mrs M. Williams, Tunbridge Wells, Kent."

Larry, meanwhile, was still doing well. In 1972 he'd bought the lease on the Cambridge Theatre, in London's West End, and taken to managing John Curry, the Olympic figure skating champion. In 1976, he "presented the world premiere season of a new and unique theatre form" with *The John Curry Theatre Of Skating*. The show broke all box office records for the Cambridge.

Nevertheless, perhaps because of misplaced loyalty, perhaps because he felt that without Larry he'd still be working at a Liverpool department store, perhaps because he was still feeling that post-operative buzz, very warm towards the human race and loving everybody, Billy never spoke a word against his former mentor.

"He still saw Larry," Lisa says. "We all went out together. My father kept saying he should sue Larry but he wouldn't do it. I think Gilbert O'Sullivan was the first to win a case against his manager. But Billy wouldn't do it."

Billy would have had a tough time getting anything out of Larry anyway.

A few years later, in 1982, Paul McCartney, appearing on BBC Radio 4's *Desert Island Discs*, told Roy Plomley that The Silver Beetles had never been paid for the Scottish tour they did with Johnny Gentle back in 1960. Parnes subsequently sued both McCartney and the BBC for defamation. Both parties eventually settled out of court and Roy had to read out a formal apology on air, adding that McCartney's remark had only been a joke.

You don't mess with the Parnes.

CHAPTER TWENTY-TWO

"I SAID TO HIM 'DO YOU FANCY A LITTLE GO BEFORE YOU GET TOO OLD?'"

In the same way as Ronco had been in the Inside-The-Shell Egg Scrambler and Hair-In-A-Can business long before it started selling records, K-Tel had been doing the Miracle Brush and Teflon-coated pans.

K-Tel's boss, Philip Kives, had practically invented the compilation album. In 1966, he put out *25 Country Hits*, followed by *25 Polka Classics*. Both did nearly as well as the Teflon, and probably provided better non-stick properties.

In 1972, K-Tel's *20 Dynamic Greats*, featuring tracks by Deep Purple, Cilla Black, Argent and Blue Mink, held the number one spot for eight weeks, despite fierce competition from the Stones' *Exile On Main Street*, Elton John's *Honky Château*, Simon & Garfunkel's *Bridge Over Troubled Water* and David Bowie's *The Rise And Fall Of Ziggy Stardust And The Spiders From Mars*, finally relinquishing it, not to Rod Stewart's *Never A Dull Moment*, but to *20 Fantastic Hits* (Slade, The Osmonds, the Bee Gees, the Chelsea Football Team) on the Arcade label.

Billy was said to have just £152 to his name at the time of his bankruptcy.

Not long after the proceedings were over, K-Tel (did they hang around outside the bankruptcy courts on the off-chance?) approached him and offered to pay off his debts if he would re-record his old hits for release on their label. The advantage to them was clear. For the price of a couple of studio sessions they'd own masters – not *the* masters but masters all the same – of Billy's biggest hits to exploit as they wished without reference to Decca, Parlophone or Larry Parnes.

It is, of course, heresy even to suggest that the K-Tel versions are better than the originals, but they do have their moments. Seventies technology, even if it's, as purists will claim, inherently inferior to that of the fifties and sixties, was easier to control and produces a cleaner mix, and Billy's vocals are less mannered, more Billy, than they'd been 10 or 15 years earlier.

Billy was discharged from bankruptcy in 1978. The K-Tel record, *The Golden Years*, 20 tracks of compromised classics, was released a year later. It didn't chart.

There was, however, a late flowering.

Hal Carter, his manager, and Tony Read, sometimes styled his "personal manager", took it upon themselves to engineer the comeback of Billy Fury.

"Tony kept saying to me, 'He's dying. He's just like a cabbage living down there. He's fading away.'" Hal suspected he was relying too much on Lisa for emotional and maybe financial support. "He wanted to earn his own money again. He felt trapped."

So Tony Read approached him. "I said to him, 'Do you fancy a little go before you get too old?' And he said yes."

Hal and Tony secured a deal with Polydor Records for one album and four singles.

Then Billy had second thoughts.

So, Hal and Tony booked a studio, hired musicians and recorded backing tracks for 'Be Mine Tonight', a song by Carl Simmons. They played it to Billy and asked him once again if he'd come in to do the vocal.

"I couldn't turn them down. They'd spent four or five grand on this track. So I kind of had to do it."

"He agreed to make another record, but not to go touring," said Hal. "He said, 'I don't mind doing the odd week, but then I want to leave it out for a month.'"

'Be Mine Tonight' is an old school Billy Fury ballad with strings, double-tracked main vocal, 'You've Lost That Lovin' Feelin'' backing vocals, a screaming alto sax and hints of a Rachmaninov piano.

They recorded a B-side, too, one of Billy's own compositions, a vaguely psychedelic piece called 'No Trespassers'.

The single was released in October 1981 and was treated to a proper press launch with celebs like Kenny Everett (who was still just about Lee's husband), Buster Bloodvessel from Bad Manners and long-time Billy fan Ian Dury.

Billy gave Ian some sound advice.

"'Buy yourself a farm, and dig a few holes,' he said. 'It's very good for you.' He told me he couldn't do a lot of digging because of his heart." But, Dury continued, naffly, "there are plenty of us out there who will dig Billy Fury forever." Indeed, Ian's song 'England's Glory' namechecks Billy as one of the "jewels in the crown". "With Billy Bunter, Jane Austen, Reg Hampton, George Formby, Billy Fury, Little Titch, Uncle Mac, Mr Pastry and all."

"There's only ever been two English rock'n'roll singers," Ian said, "Johnny Rotten and Billy Fury."

That December, Billy gave an interview to an *NME* journalist in the Polydor Records office. The journalist describes Billy: "His Scouse accent lends a laconic air to everything he says. His current fringe and the forward fall of his blond hair and his high angled cheek bones give Billy an uncanny resemblance to Anthony Booth in his days in *Till Death Us Do Part*.

"Forty years old last April, Billy wears a row of tight gold chains round his neck, which like his face and hands is leathery from a permanent sun tan. 'One thing about me,' he offers in a speaking voice that is so ghostly soft it sometimes sinks into a near whisper, 'is that I'm a terrible loner. I think I was born with three brick walls around me. No – four brick walls. I knocked the back one out. It's only in the past few years that I've been able to break the rest of those walls down at all.

"'This has all to do with shyness and paranoia and being vague. And being super critical of myself.

"But all the shyness I had, I could throw away when I was on stage with 30 minutes of exhibitionism. It was a way of letting the cap off. People sometimes would think I was a moody sod. But I was just shy."

"I couldn't come back to the business the way I did before," he told the *Sunday Mirror*. "In many ways the pop business helped to wipe me out and to go back in at the same level would just be asking for trouble. This, for me, is like putting my toe in the water to feel the temperature. If things go well I can see myself dividing my time between the farm and recording now and then.

"I don't see myself performing on stage. I don't think I'm fit enough for that. And appearing on TV? I think the only way you could get me in front of a TV camera and millions of viewers would be to break an arm and a leg."

The single didn't chart but Billy was content. Over the years he had learned to lower his expectations and never thought it would go "as high as a flea would jump."

Besides, he was busy with his farm, looking after the wildlife and turning acres of marshland into managed wetlands for birds.

He also bought another racehorse. "I'm going to take my time over breaking him in," he said. "Take as long as is necessary. You can do it more quickly if you are prepared to be a bit brutal. But then you run the risk of breaking his spirit as well. And that's the last thing you want to do."

"In Wales there was bugger all to do," said Lisa. "I was usually up before him – although he wasn't up late unless he was on the rampage. We both did the watch for the red kite for the RSPB, because the kites used to fly over the farm. So we did the watch at nesting time."

Billy often saw his old friend Marty. Marty's business, now a family concern, was going well. Earlier that year 'Kids In America', a song recorded by his daughter Kim, written by Marty and his son, Ricky, who also produced the track, had brought delight to the world and sold by the truckload.

"We used to meet up a lot at weekends," Marty said. "He would come over here to my home in Hertfordshire and we would spend weekends together. Billy used to go into the forest opposite with his binoculars, wellie boots, an old raincoat and old waterproof hat. He'd just disappear for three or four hours at a time. He loved animals all his life."

There were, however, drawbacks to living in the countryside, particularly in the middle of Wales. The winter of 1981/82 was bad, the coldest since 1890 and the snowiest since 1878; December, temperatures of -20 centigrade were recorded.

"The winter had made it very tough for Billy there," Tony Read told the *Daily Mirror*. "They were snowed in for weeks and had to dig their way out to the road over a mile away. With that and all the animals to feed and take care of it had obviously been too much."

"Just recently I've been told that if I want I can go on till I'm 60 or so," Billy said, "but I'm not sure about that. These days they tell me there's nothing wrong with me and that I've just got a plumbing fault." He laughs at the medical euphemism. "I don't feel so bad"

On March 7, he collapsed with critical kidney and heart failure.

Lisa thought the best thing to do would be to take Billy to hospital in London. So, she drove him 210 miles through the night for treatment. (Tony Read maintained that it was he, not Lisa, who drove the 210 miles but Tony, as Chris Eley puts it, "romanced a lot".)

"The doctors found he was bleeding from the kidneys because his blood was so thin," said Lisa. "He was paralysed down one side and couldn't see."

He was given a blood transfusion. The doctors didn't think he would make it through the night, but he was made of tougher stuff than they'd imagined.

"I was on a 12-hour ticket," Billy said. "It was that close. It was a very emotional time. I received thousands of cards and flowers and many were from Merseyside."

Incredibly, and perhaps unwisely, a month or so after coming out of hospital he was back at work, recording new tracks at Eden Studios in Chiswick with Stuart Colman producing.

Stuart was a perfect choice: a musician (he'd joined Pinkerton's Assorted Colours, played piano and bass and could give you, at the drop of a hat, a tune on the concertina) and a rock'n'roll fan of unquestionable credentials. In 1976, he'd organised a protest march of nearly 5,000 Teds in drapes and drainies, Capri pants and pony tails, who marched from Hyde Park to Broadcasting House where they presented a petition demanding more rock'n'roll on the BBC. The outcome was that Stuart was given his own Saturday morning show.

The musicians assembled for the Eden sessions included Terry Williams on drums, Pete Wingfield on piano and Billy Bremner (not to be confused with the footballer of the same name), a guitarist who could do rockabilly in his sleep.

The recordings, far from being the work of a man whose health and talent are fading, are among Billy's best. It wasn't just the equipment that had improved over the years. Whereas 25 years earlier British musicians were trying hard to get the feel and licks of their American role models and – with a few notable exceptions – not making a very good fist of it, by 1982 they were world class. If you recorded in Nashville or LA, you couldn't find better than the likes of Williams, Wingfield and Bremner. They do Billy proud and, for his part, Billy rises to the occasion.

Four tracks from the session were released. 'Love Or Money' is a fairly straight rendering of The Blackwells' 1961 hit, which Billy tarts up with playful growls and Buddy Holly hiccups.

'Love Sweet Love', written by Billy, is a spinally affecting shuffle with a piano solo that makes you smile and say "Yessss" before you notice that the other people on the bus are looking at you funny.

'Let Me Go, Lover!' was a huge hit for Hank Snow, Dean Martin and Ruby Murray (who was rhyming slang for a curry – "Fancy a ruby?" – before Andy came along and stole her thunder). The Billy version holds back from the overheated passion usually invested in the song and does it almost as a cha-cha with synths and mariachi trumpets.

'Devil Or Angel' was a doo-wop, originally done by The Clovers and later covered by Bobby Vee with The Crickets. It is much enlivened when the impeccable vocal performances are interrupted by an unhinged alto sax solo.

Even Billy was surprised by his performance.

"I didn't think I could sing like that anymore," he told Stuart Colman.

"If you listen to the first middle eight," said Stuart, "he sounds exactly as he did when he was 18 and he was amazed that he could do that."

Live performances, however, became trials of strength and will. "I reckon I could just about stand on the boards," Billy said. "But I'm too old to rock'n'roll."

That July, he played *The Blue Boar Rock'n'Roll Festival* in Hucknall, just north of Nottingham. Marty was there, along with The Stargazers, and second-age rock'n'rollers like Shakin' Stevens' band, The Sunsets, Crazy Cavan & The Rhythm Rockers and Johnny & The Roccos.

Brian Shuttlewood, an unreconstructed Teddy Boy and founder of the Isle Of Wight Rock'n'Roll Society who'd got to know Billy during the filming of *That'll Be The Day*, was DJing. "Billy arrived to be ready for his 10.15 appearance," says Brian in his blog. "Then I got the news. Billy was not going on."

Backstage with Fury's Tornados, 1974.

've Gotta Horse.

"In Wales, there was bugger all to do."
CHRIS ELEY

Fury and Moon, enjoying the effects of Lucozade in *That'll Be The Day*.
STUDIO CANAL

Discussing the transient nature of fame with David Essex.

After his discharge from bankruptcy, 1979.

"We plan to get married as soon as possible." Billy and Lisa.
MIRRORPIX

Back in hospital, 1982.
MIRRORPIX

Burton upon Trent, Staffs.
CHRIS ELEY

Hucknall, Notts.
CHRIS ELEY

Sunnyside Inn, Northants.
CHRIS ELEY

With mum.
MIRRORPIX

Embracing tech: Billy with Walkman.
MIRRORPIX

"...do you fancy a little go before you get too old?" Recording with Stuart Coleman.
MIRRORPIX

'All the force comes from the twist of his foot..."

..going right through his arms like lightning or something."

Billy Fury Way, West Hampstead.
ALAMY

Mill Hill Cemetery.
CAROLINE STAFFORD

Chris Eley was in the audience. "I waited all day, sat through all the rockabilly bands. Marty Wilde came on and he was pretty good, but then it seemed as though Billy wasn't coming on. The Stargazers ran over. I remember getting the word that there were buses of people there from Holland waiting to see Billy."

"He was not able to do it," says Brian Shuttlewood. "He was sweating profusely and was worried about singing to a specialist audience, an audience of serious fifties music-lovers. I was asked to go to talk to him. I found him walking about, very nervous."

"I said: 'Hello Billy, remember me?' He looked at me and said: 'That'll be the day.' We both laughed because it sounded silly. 'Billy,' I said, 'I've got to get back – I'm the DJ. Can I tell them that you're OK and raring to go?'

"'I'm thinking about it', he said.

"'Don't disappoint them,' I replied and left. I hoped that the others in there would not try to force him.

"When the time came to go on, he was opposite me in the wings. He looked across and made a sign to me as if to say: 'Here goes.' He came on to rapturous applause and launched into his first number, stumbling with words, not hitting the right key. He was hopelessly lost."

"I think he opened with 'Wondrous Place' or something," says Chris. "But I can't remember. He forgot the words. He was singing the wrong words for the wrong song."

"He turned to the band and gave a signal to start again," says Brian. "He looked into the audience. What I can only describe as the epitome of a Teddy Boy, with large quiff, drape coat and beetle crusher suede shoes, looking for all the world a mean hombre, looked at him and said: 'We love you Billy,' and the song began again, this time perfectly."

"We were all with him," says Chris. "He might have been singing the wrong words, but we were with him. He laughed sheepishly, and when Billy did that, everybody goes to bits, don't they? And he was brilliant. It was a great summer night. He was in his brown bomber suit, and he rocked. He did 'Halfway To Paradise' and a couple of rock'n'roll numbers and I was 14 again. I was absolutely mesmerised."

In the August of 1982, 'Love Or Money', one of the songs from the Eden sessions, was released as a single with 'Love Sweet Love' on the

B-side. For a moment, tantalisingly, it snuck into the Top 60, his first single to make it into the Top 100 since 1966. The flea was jumping higher.

He began to talk of a "comeback". Getting back in the charts had once seemed impossible, but now, he told the *News Of The World*, he was determined to do it, even if it killed him.

"I can't resist having a go. It sounds like I'm putting my head back in the lion's mouth. But I won't let this health thing dictate to me. I keep battling on, even though the odds are stacked very high against me."

At the beginning of September he was on hand for Radio 1's 15th anniversary concert at the Hammersmith Odeon, hosted by John Peel and Tony Blackburn.

He brought the house down at one of the Buddy Holly-week concerts, organised by Paul McCartney at the Lyceum ballroom in London.

And he was back in at Eden Studios recording more tracks with Stuart Colman.

"The final sessions were a sad state of affairs because Billy wasn't a well man," said Stuart. "He was frail and he had so many health problems over the years. He was getting erratic towards the end. I was booking studio time and he wouldn't turn up, partly because his confidence in his own ability was ebbing."

"Two things I personally remember about Billy," says Frankie Neilson, A&R Manager at Polydor, "is one time being in the studio with him to record a vocal track and we had to turn down the lights in the studio very low because of his shyness, but, when he started singing, out came this perfect voice, which even after 20 years he had not lost."

Among the songs they recorded was a version of Ray Charles' 'This Little Girl Of Mine'. It's a storming rocker, and Billy's trying, but he sounds tired.

In September, the BBC news and features show *Nationwide* sent a film crew down to the farm in Wales.

Billy showed off. "He decided to ride my big stallion on the day," says Lisa, "and he bought a motorbike specially for that show so he could round the sheep up. Usually I used to run around the fields rounding up and go to the markets and things like that."

Farm life on *Nationwide* looked fun but Lisa was less impressed. "He could be a bugger. He was very reclusive. I mean, we'd go down the pub together, but that's about all we could do in the countryside. That was it."

The *Nationwide* feature also showed Billy in the recording studio with Stuart, listening to a recording of himself singing 'Halfway To Paradise', rolling his eyes and saying how much he hated it. How much he hated listening to his old recordings in general.

By the end of September, he was back in hospital again, but downplayed it in an interview. "Oh, it wasn't much, this last one. I call them my 3,000 mile services. I usually go into hospital about nine times a year.

"My wife Lisa is a beautiful girl and it seems terrible that she should have had to go through so much because of me. That's why now I'm looking forward to perhaps making it to 50, when I'll celebrate with a party. But when it comes down to it, when you really think, when you are on your way out of this life, that's when you find out that really you're frightened of dying."

'Devil Or Angel', another of the tracks from the Eden sessions, was released as a single in October with 'Don't Tell Me Lies', one of Billy's songs remixed from a version recorded at Pye 16 years earlier on the B-side. It made the Top 60 again.

Gigs were booked to promote the single and Hal Carter found a backing band, The Haleys, who learned the complete works before starting rehearsals with Billy.

"The first time we all met was at the first rehearsal, which took place in my living room," said Mark Haley, the keyboard player. "It was clear that Billy was not a well man, yet his charisma filled the room like a charge of electricity when he walked in. To this day I've never met anybody with such a powerful natural presence."

They opened in Slough. Judith Simons of the *Daily Express* visited him backstage before the show. "Though I need all this emotionally, I'm almost risking my life for it," he told her. "I'm actually terrified about being back in the theatre."

He wore black leather. The screams that greeted the opening line of 'Only Make Believe' "would have deafened The Beatles." During 'Johnny B. Goode' the stage exploded with fireworks.

He was worried about doing the new single, 'Devil Or Angel'. "The record meant a lot to Billy," says Mark Haley, "but I think he was a little concerned about doing new material that might be unfamiliar to his fans. Not after we finished. The song went over really big and from then on you couldn't stop him singing it.

"That night the audience would not let him leave the stage. In the end he said he'd have to stop or he might pass out. He literally gave everything. It remains the most charismatic performance I've seen during my career and I've worked with the best. He needed 30 minutes after the show to get his strength back, during which time a long line of people queued to meet him. Billy was absolutely thrilled by the response during and after the show. We all were."

Chris Eley caught up with him again at the beginning of October in Burton-on-Trent. "Billy comes on with [guitar player] Mick Green and it's loud, it's blisteringly loud. And he's doing stuff like 'Unchain My Heart'. And there's this frail guy on stage – I mean there's nothing to him. And the power coming from him is immense.

"Actually, the outfit he was wearing could have been better – pinky red trousers and a pink T-shirt with love hearts on."

Afterwards, "he was made to stand there in this room, no table, and people were queuing, all the way through this night club and all the way out the door, to see him and get his autograph and a picture. This is a guy who'd been desperately ill, who was really worn out. I could tell he was worn out. He was absolutely drained and he shouldn't have been standing there. He should have been at least sitting down."

In Norwich on October 19 Billy could only manage 45 minutes of his set.

"I was drained, finished," he told James Rudy of the *Eastern Evening News*. "It took me fully five minutes to recover. There are a lot of songs I would have loved to have done. But I guess 'Johnny B. Goode' really finished me. It was always a toughie.

"When I was asked by Polydor if I would lay down some tracks for them, I thought it would be really on a part-time basis and they promised me that it would be, without the pressures. But as things carried on, I seemed to get all the pressures again. And then they wanted me to do some live shows. I have done a few, which I actually enjoyed very much, but I just can't go night after night…"

At the end of October, he appeared on *The Russell Harty Show*, the top-rated talk show of the time (Parkinson was off air). Billy looked nervous and laughed occasionally. He didn't seem to like Harty much. Harty's speciality was to pry with disingenuous charm.

"Have you looked at death at all in any of your illnesses?" he asked.

Billy manages to answer with a thin smile: "Sure. I think I've looked at death twice... oh no, three times... no sorry, four times."

"Keep it going..." Harty continued, "...five... six? And have you learned anything through it?"

"I've learned... I've been shy all my life and I've missed out on meeting a lot of great people and I missed out on a lot of musical experiences because of my shyness. In the last 12 months, I decided to get on with my life and do the things I enjoy, and just forget about tomorrow."

And then Billy, painfully thin but still achingly beautiful, finished the show with a gut-wrenching version of 'Halfway To Paradise'.

He began to pop up on TV. Once singing 'Maybe Tomorrow' on a show called *Greatest Hits*, and again, in December, on Marty Wilde's *This Is Your Life*. Billy looks frail in a white skin-tight T-shirt, his guitar slung over his shoulder. He and Marty hugged. Marty, 6'4" in his socks, looked as if he might crush him.

"I nearly fell through the floor when he walked through the door, he was so very thin," says Marty. "I had my arms round him on the show, so I could feel how thin he was. There was something terribly wrong."

Maggie Stredder of The Vernons Girls was shocked by Billy's appearance, too. "He was very thin. Very thin. And I found that quite frightening. And he was down, very sad – it was more pronounced than ever before. He was just bones."

"That was the last time I ever saw him," says Marty.

"He was running out of time," said Hal Carter.

Billy and Lisa spent New Year at a friend's house in Regent's Park. The DJ Tony Prince was there with his wife, Christine. "As we got nearer to midnight and the champagne started to kick in, I stood up and sang 'Halfway To Paradise' to Billy. You'd have to be pretty drunk to do that, wouldn't you?"

Later Billy told him, "I don't think I've too many days left. Every day is so very important to me now."

"He was a very sick person," says Lisa. "We had become very good friends with his cardiologist and they used to come over for dinner with us. He told us that Billy would have to undergo a third open heart operation. Billy looked at me and said, 'Lisa, I just can't face it. I just can't.'"

His last live performance was a conference gig he agreed to do for Polydor employees at the Holiday Inn, Leicester. Not with a bang, then, but a whimper.

On Friday January 21, 1983, he was booked to do a pre-record for a Channel 4 music show called *Unforgettable*, presented by Alan Freeman and aimed at "recreating the mood and the hits of an unforgettable era – the show will juxtapose established acts performing today with early film clips of how they used to look."

The show was to be filmed at a nightclub called Cinatras in Croydon.

"Billy had a bad chest on the Friday," said Hal Carter. "We rearranged it for the Monday and he whacked through six songs in a three-hour session and we went for a meal. On Tuesday, he was involved in the TV show itself. After the show, everyone was applauding and asking for autographs and he felt good."

Billy taped six numbers although only four were aired: 'Only Make Believe', 'Halfway To Paradise', a particularly good rendition of 'When Will You Say I Love You' and 'Jealousy'. Weighed down with gold jewellery, he wears a black leather suit and transparent shirt. At his feet, young women in sequinned dresses and black stockings writhe and paw at Billy, clutching at his legs as he makes his way rather unsteadily down the steps. He doesn't look comfortable.

He seemed tired on the Thursday, so the next morning Lisa left him to sleep late. When Tony Read came round to take him to the studio, he couldn't wake Billy – he was unconscious. Tony phoned an ambulance that took him to St. Mary's Hospital.

"On Friday morning," said Hal Carter, "I got the bloody phone call…"

CHAPTER TWENTY-THREE

"...THE GREATEST ROCK AND ROLLER IN THE WORLD. IN THE WORLD!"

The funeral was held on Friday 4th February 1983, at St John's Wood Church next to Lord's Cricket Ground.

Larry, Marty and Kim Wilde, Eden Kane and Jess Conrad were all there. Joe Brown, still dealing with another loss, was too upset to join them. "I'm stunned," he said. "I saw him only two weeks ago when he came to my mum's funeral."

Jean Wycherley had to be helped into the church by Billy's brother, Albie.

His dad was too ill to attend and would die soon after his son.

For all sorts of reasons, an enmity had developed between Billy's family and Lisa. They sat apart from each other, at opposite sides of the church.

Billy is buried at Mill Hill East Cemetery in North London. The grave is beautifully tended by fans, and kept supplied with fresh flowers.

"I couldn't understand why the funeral was in the South when it should have been in Liverpool," said Marty.

Reading between the lines, Jean probably agreed. She would have preferred her son to have been buried in Liverpool (although there is a lectern in Liverpool Cathedral dedicated to him).

In 1987, Dame Shirley Porter, the Conservative leader of Westminster City Council, ordered the sale of three cemeteries for five pence each. This was done to save the council the annual maintenance costs of £422,000, the upkeep of the cemeteries passing on to the new owner after the sale.

However, the maintenance agreement applied only to the immediate purchaser of the cemeteries and not to any subsequent owners. The purchaser re-sold the cemeteries for £1.25 million on the day of purchase.

Because the new owner wasn't required to maintain it, the cemetery in which Billy was buried became overgrown, headstones were vandalised and the place was frequented by drug addicts. Following a public outcry (good old Screaming Lord Sutch started a campaign), the council bought the graves back in June 1992 for something in the region of £4.25 million. Somebody made an awful lot of money.

As always, the obits prompted a flurry of interest in the man and his works.

Channel 4's *Unforgettable* programme, recorded a few days before Billy's death, went out as scheduled, as did the *Greatest Hits* programme he'd recorded for ITV the previous November. It showed Billy tanned, coiffed, leather clad and beautiful, singing 'Maybe Tomorrow'.

In February, a Decca compilation album, *The Billy Fury Hit Parade*, released the previous year, rose to number 49 in the album chart.

A month later, the long-planned Polydor album, *Billy Fury – The One And Only*, a collection of the two last singles and their B-sides, together with other tracks recorded over the previous couple of years, was released and made a showing at number 56.

A couple of months after that, another single from the album, 'Let Me Go Lover', with a cover of Bobby Rydell's 'Forget Him' on the B-side, made number 59 in the singles chart.

There have been countless other compilations – greatest hits, best ofs, rarities and so on – most remarkable among which is *His Wondrous Story*, released in 2008 on the 25th anniversary of Billy's death. It became the surprise hit of the year, rising to number 10 in the album charts and outselling Kanye West, Foo Fighters, Mark Ronson, Take That, Amy Winehouse, Michael Bublé and Britney Spears.

The will wasn't settled until 1986. Billy's mum, Jean, and brother, Albie, contested it, exacerbating the animosity that had already sprung up between them and Lisa.

In 2004, Jean became Honorary President of Billy's fan club, *The Sound Of Fury*, but resigned when she learned that Lisa would be a patron, switching her allegiance to a rival club, *In Thoughts of You*. The row has continued unabated ever since.

"My solution," says Chris Hewitt, Furologist and founder with Albie of Billy Fury Ltd, "is that it's about time the two sides sat down in a room to plot a way forward. Billy came from a working-class background and was a gentle sort of person, not a businessman. He relied on people around him. Those people should sort this out for his sake. It's pathetic, really."

Jean died on May 17, 2017 in a nursing home (outliving Billy by 34 years) and was cremated at Springwood Crematorium in Liverpool. As well as being Billy's mother she'd always been his number one fan. As Chris Eley said, "Jean would sit in the front and be one of the girls, which must have been rather disturbing for Billy. She would even scream. She didn't want to be quiet and be the guest of honour, she wanted to be working. And when we were doing the bronze statue she went around with the bucket, and woe betide anybody who didn't stick some money into the bucket. She was lovely. She was tough."

The 'bronze statue' stands on Albert Dock, Liverpool, outside the Piermaster's House. Enthusiastic fans (including Jean) had spent the past five years raising £44,000 to fund the piece. It depicts Billy in performance mode, shoulders characteristically hunched, arms outstretched.

"All the force comes from the twist of his foot," said the statue's sculptor, Murphy, "going right through his arms like lightning or something. Just going through his foot to his hands."

The statue was originally unveiled at the Museum of Liverpool Life in 2003, and moved to its present spot four years later. Jean and Albie were at the unveiling, an honour given to one of his earliest fans and mentors, the producer of some of his best TV appearances and finest album. Jack Good was well into his seventies and sporting a bushy white beard.

"I used to be Jack Good," he said. "Now I'm Father Christmas. I don't have much to say to you, except what a fantastic event this is and what great taste you all have in supporting Billy Fury. I reckon that he was, at his peak, the greatest rock and roller in the world. In the world! I know there were others around. Elvis went into the army and started taking a few pills. Cliff had got religion and started being a bit soft. Billy rocked on. He was a great rock and roller. I'm thrilled about this event. He was the first one of that stature, magnificent stature, to write his own songs. Now people say: 'Oh that all started with The Beatles.' It was Billy Fury who did it first and he did it marvellously well and he wrote his songs with all his heart.

"We used to get together to try to find ways to get Decca to make his favourite songs, which we finally achieved with *The Sound Of Fury*, which was a record that Decca really didn't want to make and I don't know why. They only gave us six hours, two three-hour sessions to do it, and the whole thing was done there and then. There was no editing, there was no changing of channels or anything, and the thing was done in six hours, the whole album.

"It's a tremendous tribute to him and the guys who were playing with him. I think it's a major achievement. Well, I've said all I have to say about Billy.

"He was great."

Jack Good himself died in September 2017.

A stranger tribute to Billy came in 2011.

In West Hampstead, North-West London, there is a walled pathway that runs beside a railway line for half a mile or so all the way from West End Lane to the Finchley Road. It was dingy, grubby and much used for drug deals and other nefarious goings on, and it had never had a name.

In an attempt to improve the general area, the Safer Neighbourhoods Team, the Office of Public Management and members of the local community decided to give it one. Apart from psychological benefits, this would also help the police when pursuing criminals by preventing radio messages like – "The suspect's just run up that... you know, that alleyway thing that runs up the..."

Because of its proximity to the old Decca studios in Broadhurst Gardens, they decided it would be called "Billy Fury Way", and to further spruce the place up, commissioned a mural from a company called Graffiti Life.

An official opening was arranged, during which the alley was blessed by a local vicar.

"God the Father Almighty," she said. "We thank you for this place and for the inspiration of Billy Fury in this community. May this place be filled with Your love. May Heaven and Earth be ours Because Of Love and may we know the sun in the palm of our hand and the sweetness of life. Bless this place oh Lord, and may it remind us of the journey to 'Paradise'."

Later that evening they all had a knees-up at the Castle on the Finchley Road.

Wondrous place.

ACKNOWLEDGEMENTS

We are grateful for the many absorbing hours we spent at the British Library and the BBC Written Archives Centre and to the many people without whose help we'd still be stuck on page one...

They include (in alphabetical order): David Barraclough, Amanda Barrie, Laura Beaumont, Hilary Bonner, Joe Brown, Billy Butler, Pete Butler, Clem Cattini, Chris Charlesworth, Tom Climpson, Terry Dene, Charlie Dore, Caroline Dunlop, Vince Eager, Chris Eley, Brenda Evans, Lee Everett-Alkin, Simon Flavin, Roberta Green, Adam Hicks, Harry Jackson, Cheryl Kennedy, Richard Kerr, Massimo Moretti, Bill Oddie, Harry Parker, David Prest, Carol Reyes, Alexei Sayle, Linda Sayle, Linda Shawley, Warren Sherman, Trevor Simpson, Todd Slaughter, Sue Thompson, Lisa Voice, Jeff Walden, Muriel Walker, Bruce Welch, Joyce Wilde, Marty Wilde, Kipper Williams, Trisha Wilson.

Every effort has been made to trace the copyright owners of the photographs used.

We apologise to anyone we've missed.

SELECTED BIBLIOGRAPHY

Adams, Roy. *Hard Nights: My Life in Liverpool's Clubland*. Cavernman Publications 2004

Aizlewood, John. *Love is the Drug*. Penguin 1994

Babiuk, Andy. *Beatles Gear: All the Fab Four's Instruments from Stage to Studio*. Backbeat Books 2002

Baldia, Peter. *Billy Fury Worldwide Discography*. 2016

Balls, Richard. *Sex & Drugs & Rock'n'Roll: The Life of Ian Dury*. Omnibus Press 1988

Barreca, Regina (Ed.). *Sex and Death in Victorian England*. Macmillan 1990

Barrie, Amanda. *It's Not a Rehearsal: The Autobiography*. Headline Book Publishing 2002

Bragg, Billy. *Roots, Radicals and Rockers: How Skiffle Changed the World*. Faber & Faber 2017

Breese, Charlotte. *Hutch*. Bloomsbury 2002

Brett, David. *Hurricane in Mink*. Aurum Press 2014

Brocken, Michael. *Other Voices: Hidden Histories of Liverpool's Popular Music Scenes 1930s–70s*. Ashgate Publishing 2010

Brown, Joe. *Brown Sauce*. Joe Brown Productions Ltd 1986

Chesser, Dr Eustace. *The Sexual, Marital and Family Relationships of the English Woman*. Hutchinson 1956

Cohn, Nik. *AWopBopaLooBopALopBamBoom*. Paladin 1969

Crowther, Geoffrey. *The Crowther Report*. HMSO 1959

Davies, Hunter. *The Beatles: The Authorised Biography*. Heinemann 1968

Eager, Vince. *Rock n' Roll Files*. Magna Books 2007

Everett-Alkin, Lee. *Kinds of Loving*. Columbus 1987

Everett, Kenny. *The Custard Stops at Hatfield*. Willow 1982

Fletcher, Joseph. *Situation Ethics: The New Morality*. Westminster Press 1966

Fletcher, Tony. *Dear Boy: The Life of Keith Moon*. Omnibus Press 1998

Frame, Pete. *The Restless Generation*. Rogan House 2007

Harding, Bill. *The Films of Michael Winner*. Muller 1978

Hepworth, David. *Uncommon People: The Rise and Fall of the Rock Star*. Bantam 2017

Kinsey, Alfred. *Sexual Behaviour in the Human Male*. W. B. Saunders Co 1948

Kinsey, Alfred. *Sexual Behaviour in the Human Female*. W. B. Saunders Co 1953

Kureishi, Hanif and Savage, Jon. *The Faber Book of Pop*. Faber & Faber 1995

Kynaston, David. *Austerity Britain*. Bloomsbury 2007

Kynaston, David. *Family Britain*. Bloomsbury 2009

Kynaston, David. *Modernity Britain – Opening the Box*. Bloomsbury 2013

Kynaston, David. *Modernity Britain – A Shake of the Dice*. Bloomsbury 2014

Leigh, Spencer. *Wondrous Face*. Finbarr International 2005

Leonard, Geoff, Walker, Peter and Bramley, Gareth. *John Barry: The Man with the Midas Touch*. Redcliffe 2008

Levin, Bernard. *The Pendulum Years: Britain and the Sixties*. Jonathan Cape 1970

Lewisohn, Mark. *All These Years*. Little, Brown Book Group 2013

Loog Oldham, Andrew. *Stoned*. Secker & Warburg 2000

Lulu. *I Don't Want to Fight*. Time Warner 2002

McLeod, Hugh. *The Religious Crisis of the 1960s*. Oxford University Press 2010

Miles, Barry. *Paul McCartney: Many Years from Now*. Harvill Secker 1997

Monkhouse, Bob. *Crying with Laughter*. Century 1993

Mort, Frank. *Capital Affairs: London and the Making of the Permissive Society*. Yale University Press 2010

Nash, Graham. *Wild Tales: A Life in Rock and Roll*. Viking 2013

Norman, Philip. *Shout!: The Beatles in their Generation*. MJF Books 1997

Noyer, Paul. *Liverpool – Wondrous Place: From the Cavern to the Capital of Culture*. Virgin Books 2007

Peel, John and Ravenscroft, Sheila. *Margrave of the Marshes*. Bantam Press 2005

Repsch, John. *The Legendry Joe Meek*. London Woodford House 1989

Robinson, John A. T. *Honest to God*. SCM Press 1963

Sage, Lorna. *Bad Blood*. Fourth Estate 2000

Sayle, Alexei. *Stalin Ate My Homework*. Sceptre 2010

Schofield, Michael. *The Sexual Behaviour of Young People*. Longmans 1965

Seebohm Rowntree, Benjamin. *English Life and Leisure, A Social Study*. Longmans, Green & Co 1951

Simpson, Trevor. *Small Town Saturday Night*. Milltown Memories Publications 2007

Spencer, Stephanie. *Gender, Work and Education in Britain in the 1950s*. Palgrave Macmillan 2005

Stafford, David and Caroline. *Fings Aint Wot They Used T'be: The Life of Lionel Bart*. Omnibus Press 2011

Stafford, David and Caroline. *Cupid Stunts: The Life and Radio Times of Kenny Everett*. Omnibus Press 2013

Stafford, David and Caroline. *Big Time: The Life of Adam Faith*. Omnibus Press 2015

Tomlinson, Ricky. *Ricky*. Time Warner 2003

Wallis, Ian. *American Rock'n'Roll the UK Tours 1956–72*. Music Mentor Books 2003

Whitehorn, Katharine. *Selective Memory*. Virago 2007

Wills, Judith. *Keith Moon Stole My Lipstick*. The History Press 2016

Winner, Michael. *Winner Takes All*. Robson 2004

Yates, Nigel. *Love Now Pay Later – Sex and Religion in the Fifties and Sixties*. Society for Promoting Christian Knowledge 2010

NEWSPAPERS AND MAGAZINES

Billy Fury (The Sound Of Fury Official Fan Club Magazine), *Billy Fury Monthly, Birmingham Mail, Creem, Daily Express, Daily Mail, Daily Mirror, Daily Sketch, Daily Telegraph, Evening News, The Glasgow Herald, The Guardian, History Today, Hit Parade Magazine, Honey, Jackie, Liverpool Echo, Liverpool Evening Express, London Evening Standard, Manchester Evening News, Marty, Melody Maker, Mirabelle, Mojo, New Musical Express, The News Of The World, The People, Photoplay, Picturegoer, Record Mirror, Rolling Stone, Sunday Mirror, The Times, Valentine, The Word*

TELEVISION PROGRAMMES

The Carroll Levis Show. In various forms, Radio Luxembourg, BBC
Radio and TV 1935–59
All Your Own. BBC 1952–61
The Jack Jackson Show. ATV 1955–59
Six-Five Special. BBC 1957–58
Cool For Cats. Associated-Rediffusion 1958–61
Oh Boy! ABC TV 1958–59
Boy Meets Girls. ABC TV 1959–60
Drumbeat. BBC 1959
Juke Box Jury. BBC 1959–67
Panorama. BBC 1959
Wham! ABC TV 1960
The Mersey Sound. BBC 1963
Ready, Steady, Go. Associated-Rediffusion 1963–66
Shindig! US ABC 1964–66
Top Of The Pops. BBC 1964–2006
Nationwide. BBC 1969–83
The Russell Harty Show. LWT & BBC (with different titles) 1972–84
Whatever Happened To The Likely Lads? BBC 1973–74
Unforgettable. Channel 4 1982–83
Mr Parnes, Shillings And Pence. Channel 4 1986
The Billy Fury Story. BBC Omnibus documentary 2012
The Sound of Fury. BBC4 2016

SELECTED WEBSITES

45cat.com
americanrocknrolluktours.co.uk
beatlesbible.com
bigbopper.talktalk.net/boppersite_003.htm
billboard.com
billyfury.com
bradfordtimeline.co.uk
britishbeatmerchant.wordpress.com
discogs.com
eddiecochran.info

eddiecochran.info
en.wikipedia.org
genome.ch.bbc.co.uk
hofner.com
icedjamb.com/some-days-in-the-beatles-lives
imdb.com
infobeatlesjpgr.blogspot.co.uk
nowdigthismagazine.co.uk
officialcharts.com
ohboy.org
phillipsacetates.com
reverbnation.com/markjhaley
rockabillyhall.com
sites.dwrl.utexas.edu/countrymusic/the-history
tcm.com
theanfieldiron.blogspot.co.uk
thebillyfuryfanclub.org
triumphpc.com/mersey-beat/a-z/bridgetoofar5.shtml
tv.com/shows/ready-steady-go/episodes/
tv.com/shows/shindig/episodes/

PLAYS

Bower, Alan. *Like I've Never Been Gone.*

DISCOGRAPHY

This is not in any sense definitive or complete – just the main UK releases, as well as some compilations and re-issues that may be of interest.

SINGLES

Decca

Maybe Tomorrow/Gonna Type A Letter	1959
Margo/Don't Knock Upon My Door	1959
Angel Face/Time Has Come	1959
My Christmas Prayer/Last Kiss	1959
Colette/Baby How I Cried	1960
That's Love/You Don't Know	1960
Wondrous Place/Alright Goodbye	1960
A Thousand Stars/Push Push	1961
Don't Worry/Talkin' in My Sleep	1961
Halfway To Paradise/Cross My Heart	1961
Jealousy/Open Your Arms	1961
I'd Never Find Another You/Sleepless Nights	1961
Letter Full Of Tears/Magic Eyes	1962
Last Night Was Made For Love/A King For Tonight	1962
Once Upon A Dream/If I Lose You	1962
Because Of Love/Running Around	1962

Like I've Never Been Gone/What Do You Think You're Doing
Of? 1963
When Will You Say I Love You?/All I Wanna Do Is Cry 1963
In Summer/I'll Never Fall In Love Again 1963
Somebody Else's Girl/Go Ahead And Ask Her 1963
Do You Really Love Me Too? (Fool's Errand)/What Am I
Gonna Do? 1964
I Will/Nothin' Shakin' (But The Leaves On The Trees) 1964
It's Only Make Believe/Baby, What You Want Me To Do? 1964
I'm Lost Without You/You Better Believe It, Baby 1965
In Thoughts Of You/Away From You 1965
Run To My Lovin' Arms/Where Do You Run? 1965
I'll Never Quite Get Over You/I Belong To The Wind 1966
Don't Let A Little Pride (Stand In Your Way)/Didn't See The
Real Thing Come Along 1966
Give Me Your Word/She's So Far Out, She's In 1966

Parlophone

Hurtin' Is Loving/Things Are Changing 1967
Loving You/I'll Go Along With It 1967
Suzanne In The Mirror/It Just Don't Matter Now 1967
Beyond The Shadow Of A Doubt/Baby Do You Love Me? 1968
Silly Boy Blue/One Minute Woman 1968
Phone Box (The Monkey's In The Jam Jar)/Any Morning Now 1968
Lady/Certain Things 1968
I Call For My Rose/Bye Bye 1969
All The Way To The USA/Do My Best For You 1969
Why Are You Leaving?/That Old Sweet Roll (Hi-De-Ho) 1970
Paradise Alley/Well... Alright 1970

Fury

Will The Real Man Please Stand Up?/At This Stage 1972

Warner Bros

I'll Be Your Sweetheart/Fascinating Candle Flame 1974

Polydor

Be Mine Tonight/No Trespassers	1981
Love Or Money/Love Sweet Love	1982
Devil Or Angel/Don't Tell Me Lies	1982
Forget Him/Your Words	1983
Let Me Go, Lover/Your Words	1983

EPS

Decca

Billy Fury – Maybe Tomorrow	1959
Billy Fury	1961
Billy Fury (No. 2)	1962
Play It Cool	1962
Billy Fury Hits	1962
Billy Fury And The Tornados	1963
Am I Blue?	1963
Billy Fury And The Gamblers	1965

Magnum Force

Suzanne In The Mirror	1985

ALBUMS

The Sound Of Fury. Decca	1960
Billy Fury. Decca, Ace of Clubs	1960
Halfway To Paradise. Decca, Ace of Clubs	1961
Billy. Decca	1963
We Want Billy! Decca	1963
I've Gotta Horse (Soundtrack Album). Decca	1965
The Best Of Billy Fury. Decca, Ace of Clubs	1967
The World Of Billy Fury. Decca	1972
That'll Be The Day (Soundtrack Album). Ronco	1973
The Billy Fury Story. Decca	1977
Billy Fury: The Golden Years. K-Tel	1979

The World of Billy Fury Vol.2. Decca	1980
The Billy Fury Hit Parade. Decca	1982
The One And Only Billy Fury. Polydor	1983
The Fortieth Anniversary Anthology. Deram	1998
Billy Fury – Love Songs. Decca	2002
Billy Fury Live At The BBC. Decca	2006
Classics And Collectibles. Decca	2008
The Sound Of Fury – Billy Fury And The Tornados –	
The Radio Luxembourg Sessions. Castle Communications	2008
The Complete Parlophone Singles. Peaksoft	2010
The Lost Album. Peaksoft	2011
The Sound Of Fury. Decca	2014
Billy Fury – The Missing Years. Peaksoft	2016
The Unforgettable Billy Fury – The Five Classic Albums. Peaksoft	2016

DVDS

Billy Fury – His Wondrous Story	2007
Play It Cool	2014
I've Gotta Horse	2015
The Sound Of Fury	2015
That'll Be The Day	2017

INDEX